Hindsights

the autobiography of an unknown artist

Stan Erisman

Hindsights

Published by Stan Erisman
Publishing partner: Paragon Publishing, Rothersthorpe
First published 2020

© Stan Erisman 2020

The rights of Stan Erisman to be identified as the author of this work have been asserted by him in accordance with the Copyright, Designs and Patents Act of 1988.

All rights reserved; no part of this publication may be reproduced, stored in a retrieval system, or transmitted in any form or by any means, electronic, mechanical, photocopying, recording or otherwise without the prior written consent of the publisher or a licence permitting copying in the UK issued by the Copyright Licensing Agency Ltd.
www.cla.co.uk

ISBN 978-1-78222-807-3

Book design, layout and production management by Into Print
www.intoprint.net
+44 (0)1604 832149

Cover illustration: *Introduction to Music*, oil painting, by Stan Erisman, 1972

The Foreword to the *Hindsights* series can be found in Book 1, *Natural Shocks*.

Hindsights

To be, or not to be, that is the question:
Whether 'tis nobler in the mind to suffer
The ***slings and arrows*** of outrageous fortune,
Or to take Arms against ***a Sea of troubles***,
And by opposing end them: to die, to sleep
No more; and by a sleep, to say we end
The heart-ache, and the thousand ***natural shocks***
That Flesh is heir to? 'Tis a consummation
Devoutly to be wished. To die, to sleep,
To sleep, ***perchance to Dream***; aye, there's the rub,
For in that sleep of death, what dreams may come,
When we have shuffled off this mortal coil,
Must give us pause. There's the respect
That makes Calamity of so long life:
For who would bear the Whips and Scorns of time,
The Oppressor's wrong, the proud man's Contumely,
The pangs of despised Love, the Law's delay,
The insolence of Office, and the spurns
That patient merit of the unworthy takes,
When he himself might his Quietus make
With a bare Bodkin? Who would Fardels bear,
To grunt and sweat under a weary life,
But that the dread of something after death,
The undiscovered country, from whose bourn
No traveller returns, puzzles the will,
And makes us rather bear those ills we have,
Than fly to others that we know not of.
Thus conscience does make cowards of us all,
And thus the native hue of Resolution
Is sicklied o'er, with the pale cast of Thought,
And enterprises of great pitch and moment,
With this regard their Currents turn awry,
And lose the name of Action.

– William Shakespeare, Hamlet's soliloquy
from *Hamlet*, act III, scene I

No Traveller Returns
Book three in the Hindsights series

Stan Erisman

CONTENTS

CHAPTER 1: Crossings 1

How we initially delighted in a trans-Atlantic voyage in an Eastern European environment, before entering the hell of seasickness; how we survived by clinging to each other, reached a shore of utterly unfamiliar similarity; and how we made our final crossing into the unknown, secular world of Malmö, Sweden.

CHAPTER 2: The first eight days 18

How all the naiveté we'd borne inside us was drawn to the surface by the gantlet of barriers to starting a new life in a new Old World with a new old language, a lack of experience and of money; and how our continued naiveté rendered a daunting series of events too improbable for us to recognize as obstacles.

CHAPTER 3: Living with uncertainty 48

How we were batted between hope and despair; how our amazing Swedish teacher and new-found friend helped us in numerous crucial ways; how we thrived in our new, bizarre life, despite setbacks; How Jeanette's twin brother Michael joined us; how we began learning a new language, bought an old car, and came to see our hope and future in our new world; how our geographical distance to the old one helped us to accept and enjoy isolation.

CHAPTER 4: The grand European roadtrip 77

How our perseverance with the authorities freed us to make a long, somewhat picaresque, mid-winter roadtrip through eight countries on a miniscule budget; how much we learned about how little we knew; and how we began to feel at home in Europe and in Sweden.

CHAPTER 5: Settling in, down and up 111

How we moved from one sub-let to another, established contact with my renegade cousin Bob in Basel (Switzerland); how I began learning how to teach English at a private language school; how we finally got a primitive apartment of our own and sent for the rest of our things from Canada; How Michael finally left us on our own; and how I disregarded my order to report for US military service, thereby becoming a fugitive from my native land.

CHAPTER 6: Cleaning up the mess 151

How our first encounter with Bob (in Sweden) led to a second (in Switzerland), and how he'd also come to be a renegade (from the Meeting and religion) and an expatriate; how the shambles of his life were threatening to destroy him; and how

Jeanette and I took it upon ourselves to rescue him, and how the three of us began building an incredible friendship.

Chapter 7: Inside and out 180

How our friendship with Bob grew, as did our knowledge of Swedish; how we began undertaking the renovation of our apartment; how our understanding of Swedish ways led us to question the assumptions of our American upbringing; and how we reacted to my parents' visit in May 1971 (the last time I would ever see my dad).

Chapter 8: The feeling of freedom..207

How a brief visit behind the Iron Curtain aroused thoughts about the meaning of freedom; how Bob introduced me to classical music and how it awoke in me a veritable explosion of artistic expression; how Jeanette became my muse; and how teaching English became the way to buy my freedom to paint.

Appendix 1: The floorplan of our apartment in Malmö 239

Appendix 2: Paintings 13-18.. 240

No Traveller Returns

CHAPTER 1

Crossings

At about 4 PM on Thursday, August 14th, 1969, about four hours behind schedule, the smokestacks finally belched into serious action and the huge horn blared, making us jump involuntarily, then start laughing with nervous excitement. Quickly building up steam of our own, we burst into whoops of joy. After hours of emitting mere wisps of brown-gray smoke from its stacks, the *Stefan Batóry* was now generating clouds, the engines were roaring, the water below was churning, the tethering lines were cast away, and the ship at last slipped free to embark on its mission: to carry Jeanette and me across the Atlantic Ocean, to Copenhagen, for our final leg to Malmö, Sweden.

All kinds of thoughts and feelings were racing through us, far too many and too fleetingly for us to understand them or even be aware of them. They weren't just about leaving our parental homes, our hometowns, our home states, our native country; we were leaving our entire native continent, North America, with the realistic possibility of never returning. To some, our move may have appeared impetuous. Not to us. But any way you looked at it, it was a big deal. And even though we *couldn't* look at it in any way anyway, it *was* a big deal. But we were both well protected by thick layers of naïveté, particularly me. I'd never even been to Europe before; the aspect of the unknown was total.

The similarities were clear between what I felt now and when I boarded that Greyhound with Norm just over 62 months earlier: both meant huge steps into the unknown, ripping up the roots of everything my life had been previously, heading for a place I'd never been, with the focus on where I was going rather than where I'd been, and the sense and thrill of adventure. But there were also significant differences: the break from our families and past lives was more profound now (the frequency of visits and phone calls would be sharply reduced – and in some cases eliminated – due to the expense); we were now facing a new and entirely unknown culture and language; and the barriers to returning to Vancouver were perhaps just as high as any barriers to staying in Sweden.

(In one sense, I'd uprooted myself again when I split up from Norm five months after we got to San Francisco, but there wasn't much positive about that; a stupid mistake on my part, more a sense of failure than of adventure, and a bad aftertaste. But I got over it, sort of.)

My next major uprooting was Jeanette's first. And on the city level, the move from San Francisco to Vancouver was easy: a mere change of venue, the kind of move young married couples often take to set up a life of their own, on their own. On the country level, however, the move from the United States to Canada had been much bigger. Especially the *from* part. The choice of a new city was ours; the choice to stay in our home country was *not* ours; my only options were Vietnam or prison or exile.

Although our move to Vancouver had been a bit of an adventure, perhaps it wasn't adventurous enough to satisfy me, and certainly not Jeanette. For her, moving to Europe meant returning, at least a little bit, and she could hardly wait to get *back*. What surprised me most at the time (and even more so in retrospect today) was/is how willingly and eagerly she severed the ties with her family and her past. It seems to me now that a lot (understatement) was going on in her head that I never understood – and that she refused to share.

In my geographical uprootings, I'd probably been shielded from fear of the unknown by my nearly boundless optimism. Problems were simply the obverse sides of solutions, and those solutions would always turn out to be good, wouldn't they? Although I'd outgrown my mid-teen expectations that I could simply show up on a street in Hollywood, and producers would start lining up to provide me truckloads of money and limos full of outrageously beautiful women, my imagination still had hyperbolic tendencies. After all, we would soon be welcomed with open arms by Swedish strangers eager to be our friends, wouldn't we? Interesting jobs would be there for the asking. And a breathtakingly cozy apartment in some quaint and historical neighborhood of Malmö would be instantly available to us and easy to afford. Something in that direction.

There can be no adventure if you know in advance precisely what will happen. I'm sure I had some mental images of what things would look like at our destination, but since those images were probably crafted out of a few old movies (which may not have been filmed on location), or the imaginary pictures I created when reading books or hearing tales, I was more thrilled than informed.

Jeanette was thrilled too, in a much more down-to-earth way, though possibly buoyed by my effervescence. She *really* wanted to be in Europe again, to show me Europe, to live in Europe. The material aspects and practical obstacles seemed to be of no more interest to her than they were to me. Yet we were both well aware that this voyage entailed a sea change, at least on the surface. We would not be submerged in the greater depths for some time to come.

How long do uprooted roots continue to grow? Five years earlier, my first uprooting – from my childhood home in Oak Park, Illinois – meant making a clean break from a life of loving repression and fundamentalist indoctrination. The clean break was, at least, my intention. Yet it took me two years to break free from my mother's well-meant despotism. It took several backfired attempts on her part to oppose Jeanette in my life to complete the break. And it took another two years for Jeanette and me to understand the impossibility of believing in organized religion, although many stubborn roots would remain for another five years. But we were active gardeners.

We had no pangs of remorse or regret, no anxiety of separation, no fear of the great unknown we were facing. We had each other. As we'd become so deeply inter-dependent and co-reliant, our departure felt more like we'd washed two slim nuggets of gold from the gravel of a riverbed.

Standing on the sun deck, side by side, we clung to the well-worn, nervously vibrating wooden railing, and to each other, as the rumbling, churning engines were slowly moving us, foot by foot (or meter by meter as we would soon be saying) away from the dock and out into the waters of the Montréal harbor and on into the St Lawrence River. We didn't want to miss a second.

Although the *Stefan Batóry* was far bigger than any of the ferries we ever took to and from Vancouver Island (which meant it was by far the biggest vessel either of us had *ever* been on), it didn't take us very long to explore it fully. There were several decks of cabins; ours was down several steep flights of narrow stairs to one of the lower decks, where we found our tiny interior non-posh cabin, i.e. with no portholes, the cheapest available. The ship had a capacity of over a thousand people, including the crew, but it didn't feel like we were anywhere near that many on board, perhaps because we had no experience of what that many people would feel like on a ship that big.

We spent most our time out on the sun deck that first afternoon, feeling the constant, faint vibrations of the ship's engines through our ears and skin, and the lightly rocking, swaying deck beneath our feet. Following the St. Lawrence River to the Atlantic, we were literally going with the flow. The views of the river, with the trees, towns and villages that lined it, were pleasantly pastoral and idyllic as the afternoon sun deepened behind us. The bright sunshine, the fresh air, being on the water, the excitement of this major milestone in our lives, all worked together on our metabolism and enabled us to think about the dinner hour – the prospect of another round of the magnificent menus of delicious free food, even while lunch still distended our bellies.

The upper decks not only housed the restaurant, but also a couple of old lounges, a 1950s-style bandstand-equipped entertainment room that had once aspired to be a low-ceilinged ballroom, and a flat-floored folding-chair movie theater. We noticed a poster indicating that a Peter Sellers movie – *A Shot in the Dark* – would be shown later that first evening, after dinner. It never occurred to us that it might be dubbed into Polish. As it turned out, we couldn't understand a word, but Jeanette and I had seen the movie before and still found it funny. What was even funnier to us was that most of the time we were the only two people laughing. Maybe something (such as humor) was lost in translation, or maybe there were too many Poles who were as despondent as we were joyous about leaving North America behind.

After the movie, we played some checkers and listened to the ship's Polish dance band. We were keenly aware of the fact that the ship was sailing smoothly along through the darkness, never hesitating, and we made frequent forays out to the deck to help assure its progress. Although we knew we would have to make an early start for breakfast the next morning, it was after midnight by the time we went to bed in our tiny cabin. We were almost too full of excitement and new impressions to sleep.

I don't remember if it was because the dining room on the *Stefan Batóry* wasn't big enough to accommodate all passengers simultaneously, or whether there were too few staff members to serve us all, but passengers were assigned to either early or late seatings for all meals. We had the former, the earlier, which meant that our breakfast hour began at 5 AM. But we were young and resilient and didn't need much sleep. After a substantial morning meal to match my insatiable appetite – which amused Jeanette – we did some further exploring of our vessel. In the aft part of the sun deck there was a small, strange, seemingly abandoned swimming pool, about eight-by-eight meters, as I recall. It was almost uniformly deep, but there was no water in it. Two ladders went unusually far down into the empty pool; you would almost be standing on the bottom of the pool by the time you reached the lowest step. There were no diving boards.

Along one side of the ship we found a couple of outdoor ping-pong tables – tricky footing, even when the ship was hardly rocking or rolling at all. There was also a primitive court, nominally for floor shuffleboard, that was about a quarter of the normal size, almost more suitable for ambitious hopscotch. There were no sticks, nor were there any discs. Instead, there were hard rubber rings about fifteen centimeters in diameter, in faded colors that matched the faded and fragmented lines painted on the well-worn surface of the deck. A plaque on the wall stated that the object of the game was to throw these rings into certain squares. The crew insisted that this was shuffleboard, which made no sense to us; we called it "rings". We were soon joined by a couple of Polish boys whom I'd noticed playing cards near us while we were playing checkers the evening before. Together we invented some amusing rules of our own.

Wojciech Fiałkowski from Warsaw and Krzysztof Pawałowski from Poznań had been over for the summer to visit relatives living in Canada, and were heading back to the bleak heaviness of their homes in Poland. They were a few years younger than us, probably close to 20 years of age, and had only just met each other on the ship. Wojciech had rather rough, coarse facial features that could easily have made anyone guess he was at least 10, maybe even 20, years older. He smoked far more than Jeanette and me combined. His English pretty much matched his features. His stated ambition was to drive trucks around Europe, but to keep Warsaw as his home base.

Krzysztof was his opposite, which was in a way fortunate. Otherwise we might have rashly concluded that Wojciech was the typical Pole, but having met his counterpole in Krzysztof, we could avoid the all-too-easy stereotyping and its over-simplified views that close eyes and minds to anything that doesn't fit one's preconceptions. Krzysztof was extremely mild-mannered and timid, weighing each question for a considerable length of time before answering it. This may have been because he wanted to formulate himself correctly in English, which in turn may have accounted for his seeming to have a far greater command of our language than Wojciech. But it also seemed to be because he was concerned about first considering the philosophical ramifications of his answers, which were almost painfully earnest. He was studying mathematics at the university in Poznań.

Jeanette and I were eager to learn about different European cultures and ways, and to avoid viewing the Old World as a collection of theme parks created solely for the amusement of American tourists. We didn't want to be tourists. We didn't even want to be seen as Americans, given our disgust with the Vietnam War. We felt that our now-ended 13 months of Canadian residency might be more representative of how we felt and thought than the 23-24 years of US residency that preceded it. We wanted to learn about the world and to understand, and then to learn some more and keep on learning. We naively assumed it would be easy, as long as we wanted to badly enough.

In our discussions during the voyage (with certain interruptions due to high seas...), we probed many topics, including politics. The 1968 Soviet invasion of Czechoslovakia was still horrifying to us, as it was to our two new friends. It had hit much closer to home for them: Poland shares a long border with the Czechs, and Polish troops had been commandeered under the Warsaw Pact to participate in the invasion. Early on in our discussions, I put to them a tough question: *"If you'd been serving in the Polish Army and were given a direct order to shoot me, would you?"* They each thought about it, long and hard. Wojciech answered first: *"Yes. I would have no choice."* Krzysztof needed several more minutes. He was clearly struggling. Finally he said: *"No. I could not."* He had tears in his eyes. I think he'd already thought about the consequences either way.

We also understood that Polish people who felt like visiting relatives in the US or Canada (or any other country, for that matter) couldn't simply buy a ticket and jump on a plane or ship. They had to get permission from the government, and the government didn't make it easy. The intended host in the West had to sign Polish Government forms guaranteeing full financial support of the visiting Pole. The would-be traveler had to fill in numerous forms, undergo rigorous background checks and submit to invasive interviews – just to earn the right to be issued a passport. He or she would also be given to understand that should they decide to abscond or defect to the West, severe penalties would be meted out on the loved ones they left behind. Traveling from Poland was thus easiest if one stayed at home.

Sometime during that second day, while we were still safely cruising along the St Laurence River, which was now too wide for us to see both shores (and slightly rockier and bumpier for it), there was an announcement over the loudspeakers, first in Polish, then in English: safety drills were about to be held on each deck. All passengers were to report immediately to their assigned stations (as indicated by a card we'd found in our cabin). Jeanette and I hastened to find the way to our station, more out of curiosity than obedience. Some 30-40 passengers were at our station, and presumably equally many at the other stations. We were all issued life jackets and shown how to put them on. Then an officer greeted us and began reviewing the safety procedures. All of this was explained in Polish only. We looked at each other, then all around us at the others, who were listening intently. We seemed to be the only ones who didn't understand a word. Jeanette later wrote: "*We all stood in an enclosed deck with life jackets on. No one told us what to do and the lifeboats were on another deck???*" We tried to limit to controlled smiles (with only an occasional chuckle) our amusement at the absurdity of our situation. We also tried to discern any body language by the speaker or among the Polish listeners that would give us some indication of what was being said. Something may or may not have been mentioned about which stairs to use. Perhaps playing charades was not a favorite pastime in Poland.

After a superb multi-course dinner, we spent most of that evening in one of the lounges, Jeanette crocheting and me playing my guitar. We were in a world of our own, high on our adventure, high on each other, much more content than either of us could have realized. We didn't retreat to our cabin until around 2 AM.

Sex had hitherto turned out to play a surprisingly small role in our lives, far smaller than the *desire* for sex played before we got married. Marriage had been the hated prerequisite for having real sex, in accordance with the Catholic doctrines that Jeanette paradoxically didn't believe, yet felt bound by. During the voyage, sex played an even smaller role. Fumbling with condoms was never going to add to the fever, and the narrow bunk beds in our tiny cabin offered little in the way of comfort or room for maneuvering. Moreover, Jeanette still retained vestiges of the other effects of the Catholic prudery that inhibited her verbal or other communication on the subject. Moreover, she'd always astutely avoided public displays of affection, even holding hands. Yet I don't think either of us felt particularly frustrated, perhaps because of all the other excitement that the trip itself entailed. Or maybe something was wrong with our libidos. Yet I felt so close to her, as she seemed to feel towards me (our thoughts, feelings and reactions often seemed to be as synchronized as the flight of a flock of starlings). The borderline between us as two individuals often felt blurred.

On the third day, August 16th, we entered the huge Gulf of St Laurence, which we at first thought was the Atlantic because for a long time there was no land at all in sight, but the weather was still balmy and the sea was calm.

They were filling the swimming pool. It might have been with seawater; it was clearly unheated. The few who entered the pool left it almost immediately, shivering. The pool wasn't filled anywhere close to the top, which explained the need for the long ladders, because if one chose not to jump or dive in from the side at considerable risk, one had to climb several steps down from the level of the surrounding deck to reach the water surface. We later realized that the low water level was to minimize the amount that would slosh out when the waves got bigger. But right now the only waves were those generated by our ship's forward thrust into the blue waters of the Gulf.

We'd already explored the ship's few amenities as much as we wanted, played enough "rings" to last us a lifetime, and were beginning to feel the symptoms of boredom. Since nobody showed any interest in immersing themselves in the icy waters of the pool, they emptied it the next day, and it remained that way for the rest of the voyage – another eight days to go before our arrival in Copenhagen. We filled much of our time between meals sitting comfortably in the lounge, with Jeanette crocheting, me playing the guitar, and both of us reading and discussing myriad topics with Krzysztof and Wojciech.

Late that evening, several hours after dinner, when we were informed over the loudspeakers that we would soon be passing the last sight of land before Europe, we hurried out on deck to have a look as we entered the waters of the mighty Atlantic, the open ocean. It was incredibly dark and still, with no moon, but with billions of stars visible overhead. Just after midnight, we were informed that we might be able to spot a few small icebergs slightly to the north; and sure enough, we did. They were glowing faintly and magically in the starlight. We were thrilled beyond words.

The ocean felt, sounded, smelled and looked different, a totally new experience. (Or were we looking differently, a totally new perspective?) Even in the deep darkness, its vastness was almost tangible. It moved differently. There were no more small, choppy waves like on the river or in the bay. These had been replaced by great and slowly rolling swells, causing the ship to heave slightly upwards, then slightly to one side, then downwards, then to another side and back again in irregular patterns, all the while creaking gently, as if everything were running in slow motion – yet without a trace of white water on that powerful and vast liquid void. It was terribly exciting and majestic. We peered into the night as if bewitched.

About half an hour later, we noticed that someone (presumably crew members) had placed stacks of waxed cartons (the kind we'd gotten for take-home Chinese dishes from the Village Inn on Oak Park Avenue) in strategic locations near the doorways, stairways, corridors etc. We couldn't understand why. A short time later we understood. Several cartons had already been liberally filled (in a few cases people had missed them). The sound of retching was now accompanying the increasing creaking of the ship, and the acrid smell of partly digested dinners began to overwhelm the indoor air.

We hurried back outdoors to escape the sights, sounds and smells, but we couldn't escape the heaving of the ship as the swells intensified. I felt cold sweat breaking out on my forehead and saw that Jeanette was pale and glossy. We looked at each other and remembered our bravado the day before in dismissing the offer of Dramamine. We decided that the best course of action (actually the worst one) would be to head straight to our cabin and try to sleep our way through it. It was a race against time.

We made it all the way down to our cabin, hurriedly undressed and climbed into our bunks. We put out the lights to encourage the speedy arrival of sleep, but the heaving and swaying and creaking and groaning were not to be ignored. The cold sweat was all over us now. Nausea was climbing roughly, inexorably upwards in our throats. Our noses burned. Then our synchronized cascades began and we no longer found life at sea exciting.

It began with the return of dinner. Then lunch. Then breakfast, and possibly the previous night's dinner as well. Everything came up, in increasingly advanced states of decomposition, putrefaction and stench. When there was nothing left to come up, the dry heaves began, although they weren't exactly dry. It wasn't possible to disregard the stinging, burning, yellowish acidic fluid we were continuously disgorging. My whole body was attempting to turn itself inside-out. My feet were about to come popping out of my wretched mouth. If we slept at all that night, it was only because we collapsed until our bodies felt that we were sufficiently recovered to endure another round of ejecting whatever acid our stomachs had managed to produce in the meantime.

We didn't show up for breakfast the next morning – we were "indisposed". The kind, wizened old man who was our waiter, and who had shown such delight in witnessing and temporarily satiating my phenomenal appetite, was alarmed, and appeared at our cabin door with some tea and toast, the panacea for upset stomachs. Perhaps he was the one who sent for someone to summon us to the sick bay, where we were given shots of something whose name I only ever heard in Polish, and cannot remember. If there was any effect at all from the shots, it was negligible and far from immediate.

We tried to be up and about, outdoors – to avoid the smell of stale vomit in our cabin – but we still couldn't keep anything down, nor did we have the strength to stay up, nor a porthole to open and get some fresh air. We slept from 10 AM to 4 PM, then again from 6 PM to 11.30 AM. Sleep was all that seemed to work, oblivion was the only relief.

Gradually over the next 24 hours (or was it longer?), the heaving of the vessel began to subside, and our retching eventually became less wretched, and stopped, although the nausea would remain for days. One evening we were able to nibble at a little fruit and a couple of salty crackers, and drink a little tea with honey. It was a conscious effort to obtain sustenance, not a question of morsels taken for pleasure. Our stomachs and throats were raw and tender. Moreover, Jeanette slipped on the steep stairs, scraping her knee and bruising her leg. This was *not* how our trip was supposed to be!

On the 18th, with a third of our voyage behind us, we didn't bother to get up for breakfast. We did, however, show up in the dining room at lunchtime. Our waiter seemed genuinely thrilled to see us back at our table, but we could only manage a very light lunch – to his great and theatrical disappointment. We took another easy afternoon of crocheting and guitar playing in the lounge, and were served tea at 4 PM. In the evening we tried watching a Polish film (in Polish), called *The Adventure of a Song* (Jeanette wrote in her diary, "It would have been worse if we could have understood the dialogue"). After the film we talked with Wojciech until nearly midnight. Or, more correctly, we listened to him pour his heart out to us about a romance that had blossomed during his last seven days in Canada, and the girl he had to leave behind.

The succeeding days were successively bearable, to our great relief. At least there was no jet lag on this long west-to-east haul; we normally just set our clocks forward an hour each day. We were gradually able to eat a bit again, but my enormous appetite of the first couple of pre-ocean days of the voyage would not return for months, well after reaching our destination. We were informed by the crew that we should count ourselves lucky that the ship had such gloriously effective stabilizers, which reduced the rock (or was it the roll?) from 40 degrees to a mere six degrees. At least we had just three more days until we could get off the damn ship and walk around on *terra firma*, in Southampton.

We passed those days playing chess, checkers, and guitar; Jeanette crocheted some more. Outside, everything was blue, nothing but blue, one shade for the ocean, one for the sky, with a few white swatches appearing and disappearing on both. Jeanette wrote a letter to her parents and one to Marilyn to be mailed as soon as we got ashore, and I wrote one to my parents. In so doing, I failed to follow the prevailing family tradition (perhaps the prevailing American male tradition or even the global male tradition?) of turning over correspondence to one's wife on getting married. But Jeanette invariably added a note to my letters to Mom and Dad. And Jeanette and I continued our discussions with Wojciech and Krzysztof, about life and war, Poland and America, integrity and duty.

The 20th was for some imperceptible reason declared Polish Day aboard the *Stefan Batóry*. The only significance we could discern was that the food was exclusively Polish that day. We were only just beginning to recover some of our taste for a very limited range of foods, and were therefore insufficiently hungry to overcome the spontaneous squeamishness that arose when we began sampling the ship's version of what stodgy Polish cuisine had to offer. (We were probably in no state to pass fair judgment on food at that time!) Before we went to bed, we were informed that we would have the coast of Ireland within sight – during the night when no coastline farther away than 50 meters would be in sight, which meant out of sight. My reaction was mostly of wonderment, how unreal everything seemed; Jeanette's reaction, just knowing that Ireland was so close, was wordless bliss.

Despite the good news, our stomachs and throats still felt raw and sore from all that stomach acid washing over them; we skipped breakfast the next morning too. Three more-than-substantial meals a day, with very little exercise to work it off, would have been overdoing it, even if our digestive tracts hadn't been shot. We hadn't drunk any alcohol on the entire trip (maybe *that* was the problem?). It wasn't included in the fare, and we had to be *very* frugal, particularly about what we spent on things that weren't absolutely necessary. Besides, we were already giddy with excitement – we needed no kick from Champagne.

We had another long and interesting discussion with Wojciech, and we said we'd have to make sure we got both his and Krzysztof's addresses for future correspondence. Because of Wojciech's dominant presence, Krzysztof never said much when Wojciech was present; but on his own, Krzysztof had a lot to say, provided we maintained the patience to wait for him to overcome his timidity, think through the ramifications, and find the right words.

That evening the ship held a farewell dinner for all passengers who would be disembarking in Southampton the following morning. But since over 90% of the passengers (and all crew members) were Polish, not many would be getting off in England, except to walk around on land for a few hours. Beyond that first port of call, only a handful would be leaving the ship in Copenhagen; all the rest would continue on to the final port in Gdynia. The farewell dinner was perhaps merely an excuse for most passengers to enjoy the last couple of days in the West – and an excuse for the officers to hold an "extravagant" Captain's Ball. Jeanette and I had a pretty good time in our street-casual clothing, and we danced a couple of times. Before retiring, we were told that we would be passing Land's End during the night, our closest proximity to land since the Bay of St Lawrence. And now it felt like this whole thing was really happening.

Early the next morning, as we approached the port of Southampton, we followed the English coastline with great interest. So many of the far-away places in the novels of my favorite authors – Virginia Woolf, Thomas Hardy and others – were set in Cornwall, Devon (including the town of Plymouth – remember the Plymouth Brethren?), Dorset and Hampshire. But they were no longer far away. I was giddy with amazement. We got passes to go ashore until 11.30 AM, and as we headed for the city center, we walked past the *Queen Elizabeth II* herself, at a berth near our ship. Her immensity made the *Stefan Batóry* look like a fishing boat.

We intended to spend the morning walking around central Southampton. It was the first time I'd ever set foot in Europe. We were both charmed, but within an hour something felt strange, unsettling; the ground seemed to be moving, as if we were walking on an enormous springy, spongy air mattress. It felt only slightly weird at first, like the ship felt the first few days, and then it began to feel like the ship felt when we entered the open sea. At the first signs of a cold sweat, which hit Jeanette and me simultaneously, we realized we'd better hurry back aboard the ship, convinced that we were about to become seasick on dry land. We later discovered that we weren't the only ones afflicted by this phenomenon, known as landsickness or disembarkation syndrome. It began abating as soon as we reboarded.

About 30 of the passengers were late returning to the ship and it left without them, or at least it left the quay. It waited out in the harbor until 4 PM for a tugboat to bring the stragglers aboard again. We were told that they were fined to cover the cost of the tugboat service, or maybe it was just a shot across the bow to prevent anyone from doing likewise when we got to Copenhagen. As we headed through the remainder of the English Channel towards the North Sea, we spent most of the late afternoon and evening talking with Krzysztof. In the dining room that evening, everything turned Polish. All traces of everything but Polish food were gone, to our considerable disappointment. And since most of the announcements were no longer being translated into English, but were only in Polish, we kept having to ask Krzysztof what they were saying.

We caught some glimpses of the cliffs of Dover and of France as we headed through the English Channel. I was amazed to actually see them instead of merely reading about them in literature, as I'd done countless times as a student. After leaving the Channel, we would be heading mostly north and slightly east, passing Belgium and the Netherlands, towards the mouth of Skagerrak, the wide arm of the North Sea that separates Denmark from Norway, before it bends back downwards like an elbow over the northern tip of Denmark's Jutland peninsula and becomes another arm of the sea called Kattegatt, separating Denmark from Sweden. Kattegatt eventually narrows into a strait called Öresund. Near the end of this strait is Copenhagen on the starboard side (and Malmö on the port side), after which the strait would widen again to become the Baltic Sea, but that was not part of *our* voyage.

We awoke early the next morning, August 23rd, to new and strange sensations of queasiness. The waters of the North Sea were rough in a different way from the Atlantic; severe choppiness replaced the huge swells of the big billowing ocean, and the ship was jerking and banging in response. We didn't mind not being tempted by the new Polish-fare-only menus. Now we simply ached to survive until we got to our destination the following day. The skies were leaden. Traces of cold sweat were causing mounting desperation, a growing fear that a new wave of that abominable seasickness was beginning to hunt us down, like a flock of hyenas stalking a baby antelope, and we longed for the rocking to stop, we longed to disembark, to avoid all sea voyages forever, and we were sure – we promised ourselves – that we wouldn't become queasy on dry land again. Arrival had been scheduled for the next morning, Sunday, August 24th, but due to the four-hour delay caused by the stragglers, we wouldn't arrive until the early afternoon. And shore leave was cancelled for all passengers except those disembarking. We tried to keep ourselves busy with packing, and had our last evening conversation with Krzysztof, who was visibly dreading our imminent departure from his world.

After breakfast, we did our final packing and then spent most of the morning making arrangements for having our cabin bags picked up and placed together with the other bags we had in the hold, so they could all be put ashore together when we arrived. (I refused to relinquish the tube of my rolled-up paintings.) I think we were fewer than 10 people disembarking in Copenhagen.

We exchanged a couple of our precious traveler's checks for some Danish currency – at what turned out to be a very poor exchange rate – and received a tourist map of Copenhagen. Then we began planning where to go on arrival, and how to get there. According to the map, it would just be a few blocks' walk from the dock to the central station. We decided to head there with our bags strapped to the little dolly – our wheeled pillar. Then we went out on the sun deck and met Krzysztof and Wojciech.

The sea was wonderfully calm our whole last day. The air was warm, and there was some sunshine, but clouds that might bring a little rain were gathering. It was nearly lunchtime when we began to see land – the ridge of the Kullaberg peninsula in Sweden – on our port side as we were approaching the Öresund. A Danish pilot boarded the ship to guide us through the strait we were now entering. He piloted us all the way to Copenhagen. We were finishing a light lunch as we sailed through the narrowest part of the strait, just a couple of miles wide, with the towns of Helsingborg on the Swedish side and Helsingør on the Danish. We found out that the English name for Helsingør is Elsinore, the setting for Shakespeare's *Hamlet*, more specifically the Kronborg castle. We noticed the castle itself on the point protruding out from the town into the Öresund as we sailed past. For the final part of the voyage to Copenhagen, we could see both Sweden and Denmark at all times, and the strait was dotted with a few tiny islands, most of which belonged to Denmark.

The final approach was terribly exciting. It not only marked the end of a long and irrepressibly unforgettable voyage, but the start of what we hoped might be an entirely new life for us on an entirely new continent. Could we foresee the ramifications of everything we were seeing, of *anything* we were seeing? Not a chance. But from the ship we *could* see that Copenhagen offered a scattering of old buildings with green, copper-patina roofs standing out like bits of greenish turquoise jewelry in a latticework of red-tiled roofs and lush green trees. And there were no skyscrapers.

We were expecting to arrive at some kind of terminal where we could get a more detailed map, as well as some information about cheap hotels, sights to see that afternoon and evening, and where we could go to catch a ferry to Malmö. But the dock we arrived at, Langeliniekaj, had no terminal, no information office, no nothing. It was just a wide section of street with tracks in it for harbor cranes between the water and a brick wall about 10 feet high (totally unlike the tidy, fashionable row of boutiques found there today). We made this somewhat alarming observation from the deck before we disembarked. We were also watching anxiously for signs of our baggage to be unloaded onto the pier. Danish customs and immigration people came aboard the ship to process the few who were disembarking and not continuing on to Gdynia. Although only a handful were disembarking, the unloading process took quite a long time. At last we said our goodbyes to Krzysztof and Wojciech. We looked around us with big eyes and sighs, and then we headed down the long ramp to the nearly empty street, leaving the *Stefan Batóry* behind us forever.

We could have done without the light rain, more like a mist, that began to fall and blot out the sunshine. Our bags were there, and so was Krzysztof, who somehow managed to get shore leave just long enough to help us get all our bags strapped onto the dolly we were intending to push the few blocks to the central station. "*What a perfect friend he would make –* " Jeanette wrote in her diary, "*how we both like him. We hope to see him again someday.*" Krzysztof looked completely forlorn and resigned. His boyish shoulders were drooping, his smooth brow wrinkled and his pleading eyes moist. And all we could do was wave and mouth "goodbye" heavily as he reboarded the ship. (Krzysztof had told us of a Polish word – żegnaj – that he said was much stronger, much more melancholy than the English "goodbye", more like "goodbye forever". He said he never wanted to use that word with us. It still brings tears to my eyes.)

The tourist map we received on board turned out to have little to do with the territory, the real streets of Copenhagen. The map showed only the main thoroughfares, not all of the myriad side streets between them, with their high curbs that amplified the many shortcomings of the little dolly we naively thought would solve such problems. The dolly proved to be no match for our unwieldy pillar of seven different-sized suitcases, all with bulging, slightly convex sides, plus my guitar case and my cardboard tube of rolled-up paintings. And the rain was no longer limiting itself to a mere mist. Finding a taxi to hail became our only option, but finding one in that relatively deserted part of town on a rainy Sunday afternoon wasn't easy.

When we reached the first somewhat busier street, we finally succeeded, and asked the driver to take us to the central station. He didn't speak a lot of English, and we didn't know a word of Danish, but we did get to where we wanted to go (possibly because the taxi driver knew the English "central station" even though it sounds nothing like the Danish "Hovedbanegård"). Since it turned out to be more than four kilometers away (about an hour for an unencumbered pedestrian), we were glad we decided to spend the extra money on a taxi.

First we found a place at the station where we could check in all our bags except for my tube of paintings and a single small bag we would need for the night. It was my first-ever evening in Europe, and we didn't want to have to haul that blasted pillar around with us when we went to find a hotel and look around the city center.

We also found a tourist information office at the station and they pointed us to the simple, clean, and rather cheap Mission Hotel, just a block or two away. Although we were both weary from the already long day's overload of impressions, we went out strolling and spent the rest of the evening in the Tivoli Gardens, walking around full of wonder like two very small children. It was an amazing introduction to Europe and Scandinavia.

We couldn't really understand it – an amusement park, right in the heart of town, between the central station and the City Hall? Or was it an amusement park? Certainly it was nothing like any amusement park we'd ever seen in America. There were only a few rides, really tame ones at that, but there were lots of restaurants, cafés, bars, shooting galleries, parkways with beautiful flowers, and open-air stages. Each winding pathway was marked with colored lights. It was as if the entire park was a party inside a Christmas tree. At one of the stages, we stood and watched a ballet – free of charge – on our very first night in Europe together.

That night in Copenhagen was a magical experience, but we didn't feel it was really us; we had yet to reach our true destination. We were originally planning to stay in Copenhagen for several days, but we were far too excited to wait any longer to get straight across the strait to Malmö. Copenhagen felt crowded, and we were overwhelmed by the many strange faces after 10 days of getting to recognize nearly all of the faces we encountered onboard. Besides, we felt it would be easy to come back to Copenhagen once we'd settled in Malmö (in this we presumed correctly). Unlike how easily we seemed to fit in in Southampton (apart from our burgeoning nausea), we couldn't understand the Danish signs and voices around us, and we preferred to try to accustom ourselves to just one new language at a time. In short, we still had one more crossing to make.

We found out that we could get a ferry to Malmö from a place called "Havnegade". The Danish pronunciation sounded very exotic, something like "HOW-neh-GAAA-theh" as if spoken by an inebriated actor over-acting; but it just meant "Harbor Street", plain and simple. (But original Danish pronunciation is much more fun.)

So after an unhurried Monday morning, August 25th, we checked out of the hotel and headed to the station to collect our bags. Having learned from our experience the day before, we didn't hesitate to take a taxi to the ferry terminal. The ferries ran almost hourly, and the crossing would take about an hour and 40 minutes. Our ferry, a black-and-white vessel that also took a few cars, was called the *Absolon*, which I correctly guessed might be the Swedish name for the ill-fated son of King David. It was a well-worn ferry, tiny compared to the *Stefan Batóry*, but not too much smaller than some of the ferries we took on Puget Sound.

We couldn't do a lot of walking around on board; we had our pillar of bags to look after, and we stayed with them, close to the gangway, trying to tighten the straps on the dolly to make our final leg more manageable. We were bursting with excitement. Fortunately, the crossing was very smooth. We peered eagerly out to see the first signs of Malmö. Most of the buildings were low and made mere irregularities against an otherwise flat horizon. Only a few taller structures were visible: a couple of church spires, a lone 27-storey building and a big harbor crane. [I should point out that since two correct spellings exist – story (plural stories) and storey (plural storeys) – I have unilaterally and unanimously decided to seize the opportunity to use the two spellings to distinguish between the two meanings of the word. In my writing I thus use "story" to mean "tale, narrative" and "storey" to mean a level or floor in a building. Thus: "This is a *story* about a 10-*storey* building." Readers who have issues with this distinction may address complaints to: Stan c/o Santa Claus, North Pole, or email *santa@claus.np/stan*.]

The ferry pulled into the Malmö harbor, the gangway was put down and the rope barriers were taken away. We were free to step ashore, with all the freedom that pushing a tipsy tower of suitcases on an under-dimensioned dolly would allow. Were we home?

CHAPTER 2

The first eight days

We now saw ourselves as immigrants, not tourists. Copenhagen was the foyer. We were anxious to enter, even though it was all new, strange, confusing, foreign, alien. But it was our possible future. We saw Malmö with the awed and trepidatious eyes of would-be immigrants with uncertain status. As holders of US passports, we needed no visas for entering Sweden as tourists, even though we weren't. We approached customs and immigration building full of the obeisance of lowly, nervous suppliants – supplicants – as if some new groveling, ingratiating hormone had just been released within us to effect a degree of metamorphosis. It was a warm day, almost balmy, but it had been raining a little. It looked like there might be more to come.

We entered the drab, single-storey brick building, which seemed to consist of a single, large, pale room, with less-than-adequate fluorescent lighting, walls that may once have been white, a stone floor, and a few long benches or low burnished stainless-steel counters designed for spreading out suitcases for inspection. Several somewhat bored-looking uniformed men were standing in front of and behind these counters, perfunctorily scrutinizing every solemn and silent person who passed by. The only ones they stopped were the few whose shopping bags were both bulging and clanking. I thought of Kafka. But we were no longer expecting a welcome wagon or even a red carpet; we were settling for the absence of hostility, and not too many hours of grilling.

It turned out to be a complete anti-climax. The customs officer (a policeman) more or less waved us through without a second glance (or a smile), despite our preposterous, almost comically absurd pillar of luggage. Instead, we had to buttonhole him and hand him our passports. He looked at them with scant interest, stamped a three-month tourist visa into them, and nodded for us to go on through. But I remained where I was, standing there in front of him. He looked quizzically at me. I asked about work permits. His dark blue uniform with brass buttons looked strange to me because it was different from the uniforms we'd seen before, but only slightly different. I couldn't put my finger or my consciousness on *what* was different – a subconscious reaction Jeanette and I would be having repeatedly, hundreds of times, over the next few weeks. The impact of these reactions was cumulative, and the aggregate aggravations would prove to be very tiring, mentally.

He gave me a strange look, the way people do on being asked a question they don't really understand, or don't have the answer to, or are too indifferent to be bothered with. He said something about a "special office" for work permits and residence permits, making it clear to us that as far as he was concerned, the matter at hand was now closed.

Then we broached a new subject: where to find accommodations – you know, hotels, a place to stay. He directed us to an office (not the aforesaid special office) on the other side of the canal, on the corner just a block beyond the central station, which in turn was down a block and across the street from the ferry terminal.

The line of ferry passengers going through the terminal (more like a wide corridor) was now showing signs of congesting behind us, and our laconic official seemed eager for us to move on. Since we were equally eager to please our first real Swedish Person (a *bona fide* Official at that), we left the building and crossed the street, staring wide-eyed all around us, the way Norm and I stared at downtown San Francisco just over five years before.

So much had changed during those five years. The Meeting was behind me forever, but that turned out to be only the first step in my decompression from a childhood and youth of intense, purposeful and insidious religious and political indoctrination. I assume that many of the basic fundamentalist Christian doctrines were still with me when I stepped off the bus in San Francisco. The ensuing five years showed me numerous other paths to explaining the universe and coming to terms with my own existence, and the nature of existence itself, thereby enabling me to continue peeling and tearing off more and more layers of the myths in which I'd been kept immersed. Yes, the strictness of the Meeting provoked me to rebel. But more importantly, it also primed me for *questioning* – not just the Meeting, but anything at all that I could discern to be making unfounded claims of Truth.

Although I'd learned that the truth of an idea needn't have anything to do with how widely it was held to be true, it was never going to be easy for someone as naïve and gullible as me to see through the smooth-talking charlatans, sincere con men, sociable snake-oil salesmen, earnest tricksters, cynical swindlers, and foolish nice guys I'd already met and had yet to meet. My education gave me a whole set of valuable tools, but I was only just beginning to learn how to use them. I still viewed myself as some sort of Christian, a vague Believer, but since indoctrination is emotional, there were emotions I was still unaware of, and that

I would have to become aware of in order to find out what sort of beliefs might really merit making me a believer in something or anything.

Our feet were young, rested, yet still sufficiently calloused – ready to explore this new strange dull gray-brown Malmö, this small underwhelming city, with an overall nothing-sensationally-new-here look that was enhanced by the comfortable warmth and brightness of this late-August Monday. The details were disorientingly different and in stark contrast to the overall seen-this-beforeness. For starters, the signs were nearly all in Swedish, of course, which not only meant we didn't understand them, but we could only guess at how the words and names might be pronounced correctly. Most of the car models were ones we'd seen before (except for the older Saabs), but only rarely, while most of the ones we were used to seeing all the time were nowhere to be seen: the Fords, Chevys, Buicks, Dodges, Oldsmobiles, Plymouths (Brethren included for me), Lincolns and Cadillacs. The architecture was generally much older than what was typical in North America – many red-tiled roofs and a few copper-plated roofs with pale verdigris patina. Many of the traffic signs used different symbols than we knew, but they tended to be self-explanatory and were similar to those we'd seen in Copenhagen the day before.

As we'd noticed in Denmark, the average person seemed to be slightly taller than the average in North America, but none were taller than the tallest we'd seen in the New World, and there were quite a few short Swedes as well. Most were of fairer complexion. There seemed to be a predominance of blonds, with fewer redheads than we'd seen in Denmark. Most of the people dressed differently; again, it was not that we'd never seen people dressed like the Swedes before, but they were never in such a majority before, and there was hardly anybody in jeans and tennis shoes. Many of the elderly men wore hats. My dad wore a hat when I was a kid, but by the 60s it was no longer his constant companion when we left the house. (Since I began losing my hair in my 60s, I took to wearing a cap to protect my scalp from sunburn, and a hat in winter to keep my head warm.) In many respects, the outward signs of Sweden in 1969 felt to us a bit like the US as we remembered it in the 50s.

The pace of life was noticeably slower. People moved purposefully but leisurely. Few were noticeably hurrying. Although there were a few muted smiles, hardly anyone was laughing out loud, nor were they shouting angrily, gesticulating wildly, or looking at others with hostility. In fact, the people we encountered tended to avert their eyes (sometimes even their faces) and tread onwards, minding their own business – all behavior we'd seen before, but never before as the rule rather than the exception.

Despite being Sweden's third largest city, Malmö had a population that was a remarkably steady quarter of a million, making it the smallest metropolis we'd ever thought to live in. Jeanette had already experienced how different a significant population downsizing felt when we moved from San Francisco to Vancouver, and I'd felt it in the previous step as well, with my move from Chicago to San Francisco. Apart from a lone, distant 27-storey "skyscraper", a large traverse shipbuilding crane (marked "Kockums", the name of the shipyard) just across the inlet from where our ferry docked, and a church tower a few blocks away, we could see no buildings taller than five or six storeys. It was unintimidating, kind of the way we both liked it.

We pushed our suitcase pillar across the street, then into the next block to the train station, correctly assuming there would be lockers or a baggage room in which to stash the bulk of our luggage while we got oriented. We'd packed in such a way that one suitcase each would see us through at least a week, possibly two or more. We checked in five suitcases with the dolly, plus my guitar case. I kept the tube of paintings with me.

Then we located the tourist office, about a block away, across the canal. We entered, bursting with curiosity. The weight of the major unknowns on our shoulders was increasing by the minute, primarily because of the shortcomings of our financial reserves, and also because we both began to realize the implications of setting out on such a venture without having sorted out any of the practicalities beforehand. We would gladly have done so, but we didn't know how. We knew nobody at all – not in Malmö, not in Sweden, not even in Europe. Though surrounded by the entire populations of Malmö, Sweden, and Europe, we felt totally alone.

But we had each other.

Our top priority was to find a place to stay that night (at least). We knew we had to go for the cheapest possible accommodations, probably not a hotel. Perhaps a bed and breakfast? After nervously inquiring whether the lady at the counter spoke English, which she did, we told her what we were looking for, and she suggested a room in an apartment belonging to an elderly couple. Breakfast was included, and the price was 30 kronor per night (roughly six dollars at that time). It would be only our second experience of a rooming house (we spent two nights in such an establishment in Montréal), and it was far cheaper than the small hotel in Copenhagen the night before. We said yes. She phoned the proprietors and presumably told them we'd be along shortly. She also gave us a street map and marked our present location and that of our destination: the unpronounceable "Föreningsgatan", number 53.

"*Just walk up here hundred meters to deh big square,*" she explained in nearly fluent, accented English, and started pointing to each place on the map. "*It's called Stortorget, and you cross it. Keep to deh left and you are in Södergatan, and you are walking dare tills you come to Stora Nygatan – dat's where Gustaf Adolfs torg is – about tree streets, I tink. Den you are going left two streets to Djäknegatan.*" The last word sounded to me like "Yeck-neh-gawtun", quite unlike what the name that she was pointing to on the map looked like to us.

"*Dare you are going to deh right one street and across deh canal and going straight, straight, now it's Amiralsgatan, and you are going dis vay tills you coming to Föreningsgatan, and you turning left. It's about six blocks, and it's number fifty-tree right across from deh big churchyard, you can't miss it.*" I was prepared to disagree with that last assumption, but instead I watched her write the name of the proprietor on the map. We were to ring the bell next to that name at the entrance to the building.

We had a couple of other important questions to ask her before heading off to find our room. The first was where we could go to see about finding jobs. The immigration man told us something about a special job office, but since her English was clearly better than his, and perhaps her helpfulness as well, we hoped she would be able to provide more information. She looked puzzled at first – perhaps the question was not typically asked at a tourist information office, after all – so I had to reformulate it several times before she suddenly realized what I meant and said, "*Oh, yes, arbetsförmedlingen!*" Now it was my turn to look puzzled. She wrote the word down for me. I couldn't remember ever having seen such a long word in my life, except for the rather artificial *antidisestablishmentarianism* we used to joke about as kids. Instead of trying to figure out the exact meaning of her word, I just hoped she'd given us the name of a place that would help us find work. I asked her to show us where it was on the map. It was only about five blocks from the rooming house, almost along the way we'd soon be going.

The second question was where we could find the American Express office. We wrote our families that they could write to us care of that office in Malmö.

She told us that American Express didn't have an office of their own in Malmö, but apparently there was a travel agency that represented them, and it was along the way, at the big square, which was where we had to go first, before continuing on to the rooming house.

We started off in the humid weather, hoping it wouldn't rain, walking along all the old newness, carrying one suitcase each, plus my tube of rolled-up paintings, grateful that we'd stashed most of our unwieldy pillar of luggage, in view of the countless challenging curbs there were to battle.

In those first 100 meters to the big square, we noticed three fashionable galleries. One had some works by Miró and Chagall on display. Most of the buildings around the big square were old and impressive: the majestic yet darkly ugly City Hall; a very old red brick building in one corner, with a cellar restaurant; a couple of auspicious-looking hotels; a fabulous pharmacy ("*apotek*" – the "apothecary" in *Romeo and Juliet* came to mind) guarded by the image of a lion, full of exquisite woodwork and old porcelain medicinal vessels; and an exclusive-looking clothing store with timber-framed upper floors. A couple of the buildings were from the 1400s, centuries older than the US itself, older even than the presence of Europeans in the long-since-discovered New World. In the middle of the square was a big bronze statue of a pompous-looking fat cat of some kind, astride his bronze horse, staring at things he'd never be able to see. (Charles X Gustav was his name, a 17th century warrior king for five years. He died at the age of 37.)

We found the Nyman & Schultz travel agency, where we were pleased to find a letter waiting from my parents. However, it contained an ominous envelope from the Selective Service: the draft board was informing me that I was reclassified as 1A, ready for immediate induction. *They* may have thought I was ready; I knew I wasn't and never would be. But I did know that as soon as we had an address in Sweden, I would have to notify them. It was a federal offence not to, and since there was always a very slight chance that I wouldn't get drafted after all, I didn't want to have exposed myself to other ludicrous felony charges just for failing to report my address. The notice strengthened our resolve but weakened our knees.

As we proceeded along a relatively bustling street called Södergatan, we admired a couple more very old timber-framed buildings. There were also some modern buildings, and everything in between. The short street seemed far too narrow, or far too busy, to accommodate both vehicles and pedestrians safely. It also had a bank, and we stopped to cash a traveler's check in order to have some Swedish currency handy. At the end of Södergatan, at the corner of the next square where we were to turn left, we saw a couple of trams and lots of buses, and a lot of greenery at the far end of the square. Two blocks to the left we came to Djäknegatan (How the hell did she pronounce it?!), turned right and soon came to a bridge across another canal. From the bridge we got an almost unobstructed view of that 27-storey building in the distance. Many of the buildings seemed not too dissimilar to those we'd seen in North America; the differences were in the details, and we weren't yet seeing those details, at least not with our eyes.

We paused on the bridge to take a long look and soak up the feelings. Was this canal, lined with lovely leafy trees on either side, the same canal we'd crossed before, or was it a different one? This one seemed much wider, but both were still – and much cleaner than we expected canals in a city to be. Perhaps it made a loop, like a kind of moat? The water was clear and shallow enough to see the bottom, about two meters deep in the middle. The embankments were covered with large, carefully laid stones or boulders that sloped up to railings along either side, at street level. On the far side, there was a sidewalk between the railing and a bigger street, Drottninggatan. Malmö seemed to us like a very civilized place.

After crossing the canal, we headed on up Amiralsgatan, a moderately trafficked street with tram rails in the pavement. A set of large buildings on the corner, just across Drottninggatan, turned out to be an old high school – Latinskolan – that seemed unusually more devoted to learning than to sports in that it wasn't surrounded by vast practice fields and stadiums, although to me the building itself bore a vague resemblance to Oak Park High. Just past the school, we came to a beautiful, wide, tree-lined parkway down the middle of a street called Kungsgatan, with charming old turn-of-the-century five-storey apartment buildings along the far side. The exquisite brickwork on the buildings seemed to bear witness to the professional pride of the builders. Several blocks down, the parkway was interrupted by a copper-green-roofed, multi-spired church that I immediately associated with an orange squeezer. The parkway appeared to continue beyond the church.

The next street was Föreningsgatan, the address of our accommodations. We turned left as instructed. So did the tracks in the street, although we'd seen no more trams since that last square. After about three blocks, we saw a big cemetery on the other side – what the lady called a churchyard, although it held no church. But I remembered the cemetery setting of Thomas Gray's *Elegy Written in a*

Country Churchyard – and knew our rooming house was not far. We also saw a laundry on the corner of the block just before ours, and made a mental note of it.

Outside the entrance of the building there were some names and buttons mounted next to the door. We found the name of the proprietor of the B&B, and pushed the button. We were soon buzzed through to a passageway, and we took two flights up to the third floor, where we were received by a very nice elderly couple who seemed every bit as nervous as we were. They were perhaps mostly nervous about having to speak English, which they couldn't, and we were mostly nervous about mostly everything else. With the help of sign language and gestures they showed us to our room, which overlooked the cemetery and the busy street. The room was small but light, immaculate and comfortable enough to rest and sleep in. The bed was just big enough for both of us, and didn't leave more than a narrow strip of floor space along the two long sides, but since it was fairly high, there was room under it to stash our luggage. The closet space was limited to a rather small free-standing unit with a couple of drawers below and a few hangers above. There was also a small round table with two chairs at the foot of the bed – our breakfast room, as it would turn out. The toilet was out in the stairwell. There was no shower.

The lady turned to me, then to Jeanette, then said "*brake-fass?*" with a markedly struggling and interrogatory rise in tone, accompanied by a gesture of eating something invisible, followed by another gesture pointing to her watch. Using our dazzling powers of deduction, we agreed that she was trying to ask at what time we wanted breakfast and I held up eight fingers. She nodded and smiled. New question, in Swedish: "*Kaffe oder te?*" For some reason she used the German word for "or" (*oder*) rather than the Swedish (*eller*). Maybe she thought it would be easier for us to understand any non-Swedish words, even though we knew even less German than Swedish, meaning none at all (except in retrospect). Anyway, I replied "Coffee, please." I paid her the 30 kronor for the room; she seemed terribly relieved not to have to try to ask me that question without words. Then she left us, and we were on our own.

We sat on the bed for a while, looking at each other, smiling with wrinkled brows, our minds racing in all directions at once. It seemed very real and yet very unreal. We'd planned to move to an unknown country, to a totally unknown, unheard-of place called Malmö, and here we were. Here we really were. For some time (I have no idea how long), we were speechless, numb. Then we began talking, babbling, swelling into two torrents of words about our feelings and impressions of everything so far, trying to take it all in and let it all out and grasp what it all meant now and what it might mean for our future, both immediate and possibly for the rest of our lives. This felt more like a water*barn* than a mere watershed.

It was already late afternoon by the time we emerged from this haze. As we were now unencumbered by baggage, we decided to plunge right in and start exploring the city that might possibly become our new home, starting with the exact location of *arbetsförmedlingen*; we wanted to be sure of finding it easily the next morning, and if possible to see when they opened.

Then we began walking around the central parts of the town, up one street and down the next, finding all kinds of charming buildings and lanes, some covered with old cobblestones. The more we walked, the more we liked what we saw: big beautiful parks and a few canals, remarkably tidy and litter-free, an amazing library. Nothing about the town was sensational; it was kind of low-key and down-to-earth, but the overall impression was of a very civilized place.

We passed a bookstore and bought a much more detailed map of Malmö. We figured we'd be needing it sooner or later. The store sold stationery as well, and we got a package of aerograms – a single sheet of thin paper that could be folded in such a way as to constitute both letter paper and envelope in one, pre-marked as international air mail. Only stamps would be needed; we found those at a post office. We simply showed the woman at the counter our aerograms. She understood that we wanted international postage, the lightest weight.

We decided to try the corner laundry and brought a small pile of our dirty stuff from the trip – socks, underwear, a few sweaty shirts and blouses. Again, the lady behind the counter spoke only a few words of English. We hoped we'd managed to communicate what we wanted. We read on the ticket stub that we could pick it up the next day, but as soon as we'd left, we realized that we had no idea what it would cost.

As evening approached, our feet were beginning to get tired, and our heads were exhausted. We returned to the train station and picked up two of our five remaining suitcases, plus my guitar. Three to go. We were hungry and stopped at a bakery to get some French bread, as well as a couple of pastries for dessert. Then we headed back to the rooming house for a meal of bread and water and decided to make an early night of it – our first in Sweden! We didn't sleep like babies; we slept very well.

The next morning at eight o'clock sharp, there was a light knock on our door.

After hurriedly pulling on some clothes, I opened, and our landlady smiled and handed me a breakfast tray. I took it from her and put it on the table, and she waited nervously in the doorway. When I turned back to her, she made a round, encompassing gesture that suggested she wanted to say or ask something about the room itself. Then she made a waving-goodbye gesture, while looking like a big question mark. I guessed that she might be asking whether we were going to leave that day or stay another night. I responded with some vigorous gestures of my own, raising my hands high, but parallel with the floor, fingers extended straight down, as if to play three rapid crescendos on an invisible piano, to indicate that we weren't going anywhere. To reinforce that message, I took up another 30 kronor from my pocket, and her face brightened. We *did* understand each other.

Breakfast consisted of a pot of strong coffee – *very* strong compared to the American dishwater we were used to – accompanied by a small pitcher of real cream and a small bowl of sugar cubes that were extremely hard and took a lot of persuasion to dissolve. There were also two strange-looking open-face sandwiches each. Thick slices of rather stodgy sweet off-white bread were coated with about a quarter-of-an-inch-thick layer of butter (I'd never liked *any* butter on my sandwiches, and even though Jeanette did, she only liked a very thin layer – essentially what remained after applying butter and then scraping it off again).

On top of the butter was an even thicker slab of cheese. Although we both liked a bit of cheese now and then, neither of us were *aficionados*, and certainly not for breakfast. There were also some sliced tomatoes on the side, which we guessed were for putting on top of the cheese, but can one really eat tomatoes for breakfast? It was something new for us Yanks. There was also one boiled egg each, in egg cups. I'd always hated eggs. Jeanette liked eggs all right, and had eaten boiled eggs in egg cups the previous time she was in Europe. She knew the procedure. But we both longed for the breakfast room on the *Stefan Batóry*.

We first removed the slice of cheese and scraped off whatever butter was clinging to it. Then we scraped off all the butter we could from the bread, giving Jeanette the right amount for her taste, while I had to settle for an excessive and barely edible amount for my taste. Then the cheese went back on and we ate the sandwiches, and the sliced tomato, which wasn't bad at all. Even after removing all the butter, however, the sandwiches were still heavy and stodgy enough to fill us up for quite a while. Although we felt a little embarrassed to be returning the tray with a big mound of uneaten butter on the plate, the thought of eating it made us both gag. Jeanette got both eggs. The coffee was great.

Now it was time to get the ball rolling, to get over to this famous *arbetsförmedlingen*. They opened at nine, and we were there a few minutes after, armed with our passports. There was a waiting room inside the door with the long name on it. Along the wall to the left there were several service windows, like at a bank, and there were numbers above them. There was a small dispenser by the door. We took a number and sat down to wait our turn.

A couple of people were already waiting in the room. Only two of the windows were manned. The room itself was light and cheerful. There were brightly colored walls, a high ceiling and a linoleum floor. Yellow and orange dominated. Nothing about it felt strange except for the fact that nearly all signs and notices were in Swedish – of course. But a few were also in English, one of which made it clear that *arbetsförmedlingen* meant "labour exchange". How lucky for us, as it turned out, that English was our native language, through no fault or merit of our own!

After about 20 minutes, one of the visitors left and our number came up. A buzzer sounded to indicate when this happened, and possibly to arouse anyone who may have dozed off. We were glad it went smoothly, so we didn't have to spend hours of anxious waiting, mulling over what we were going to say.

The young man (not much older than us, I guessed) behind the window greeted us with a friendly *"Hi!"* (Actually, he said "Hej!", which in standard Swedish means "hi" and is pronounced "hey", but in the dialect of southernmost Sweden "hej" is pronounced "hi". The standard Swedish word that is pronounced "hi" is spelled "haj" and means "shark". See how much fun we were about to have?) I immediately asked whether he spoke English, apologizing for not being able to speak the language of the country we were in. His English turned out to be pretty good. I told him we were eager to find jobs. He asked what kind of jobs. I told him I had a degree in English from the US, and that Jeanette had experience as an executive secretary, but that both of us were willing to do just about any kind of work, including washing dishes.

He looked somewhat confused, as if he were thinking several thoughts at once. Suddenly he said, *"Could I see your passports, please?"* We had them with us, pulled them out of our pockets, and handed them to him. He thumbed through them carefully, pausing for a closer look a couple of times. Then he looked up and exclaimed, *"But you haven't got any work permits!"* I told him that when I enquired about that at the Swedish Consulate in Vancouver, they told me that we'd have to find jobs first, which was what we were trying to do now. His brow wrinkled, and he leaned back, his brain whirring. The seconds were ticking. Each second seemed to make the room tremble.

Finally, he leaned forward, looked at us again, and said, *"I'm afraid it's kind of complicated, tricky, and I don't really know how to explain it, but I think you need to take your passports with you to the police station on Sallerupsvägen and they will be able to tell you."* He looked very worried, almost as worried as we were rapidly becoming. I asked him to show me where this police station was on our map. It was about five blocks further along Föreningsgatan from our rooming house, not terribly far. We thanked him and left.

The police! What had we done?! Were we criminals now? Then we remembered that the immigration control in the harbor the day before was conducted by the police, so maybe it wasn't a criminal offence to ask about jobs if you didn't have a work permit. But we were very agitated. Mirroring the day with its scattered showers, light rain and occasional sunshine, our minds were now filling with dark, threatening clouds.

We began walking along Föreningsgatan, which was flat but felt like a steep hill. We passed a synagogue, which for some reason surprised us. A block later came the cemetery, and across the street we saw the entrance to our rooming house. After the long cemetery came a block with buildings on our side too. One of them was a bakery, with a big window full of ridiculously delicious-looking breads, rolls, sweet rolls, cakes and cookies. We knew from the evening before that this country offered some mighty fine bakery goods. The door was at the far end, and we resisted temptation until just a few steps beyond the open door, halfway to the next corner, when the smells ambushed us from behind and we swirled around, went in and bought a couple of large, spiral-shaped cinnamon buns each. We'd wolfed down half of them by the time we crossed the street.

There was another school in the next block, an elementary school, and we could see that it was already in session, even though it wasn't yet September. Then again, why should Swedes follow the American schedule? Maybe they didn't even have Labor Day on the first Monday in September, when we were used to the opening of school doors the following day? We crossed the following street, called Ehrensvärdsgatan, and noticed that many street names ended with "gatan". We began to suspect that "gatan" might have something to do with "street".

One block later, we came to another big square filled with and surrounded by busy busses. To our right was a relatively tall and rather modern dark-red-brick-clad building, 12 storeys high. The façade facing the square was almost as wide as the square itself, with 36 identically sized windows across on each floor (at least on the top 10 storeys), and a fairly big grocery store at the street level. But the building was narrow in the other direction, and there were no windows at all on the narrow side. It reminded me a bit of pictures I'd seen of the tall UN building in New York. In fact, apart from the many differences, it was identical.

We consulted the map again. The police station we were looking for was on Sallerupsvägen, which was the next corner. In fact, that's where Sallerupsvägen began, to the right only. And that's where Föreningsgatan ended, although both streets clearly continued beyond that corner in their perpendicular directions, under assumed names. After Värnhemstorget (*Aha! "Torget" probably means "square"!*), what used to be Föreningsgatan was now Lundavägen (*Why weren't all of these streets called "gatan"? What the hell does "vägen" mean?*) as it headed east on its way out of town, while Sallerupsvägen became first Östra Förstadsgatan, then (according to the map) Östergatan, then Adelsgatan as it headed back into town the other way, almost right back to the tourist office we'd visited the day before. Were these street-name changes just to confuse the tourists? Why couldn't a street keep the same name from beginning to end? We didn't have to search for sources of confusion. They found us.

When we rounded the corner onto Sallerupsvägen, we found that the big redbrick building complex continued the entire length of a long block, first as a short three-storey section, then as a longer five-storey part. At the far end was the entrance to the police station, on the third floor, if I remember correctly. We entered a small waiting room with a small reception area and a window where we understood we were to announce our presence and state our business to the woman behind it.

She beckoned, and we told her that it was the guy at the – I couldn't possibly pronounce the word – "job place" who sent us; that we'd been told by the Swedish Consulate in Vancouver that we had to find jobs before we could get work permits, but that the job man told us the opposite. We were pretty confused. She looked puzzled too, for different reasons. I also mentioned that I'd heard that Swedish towns adopted artists and that I was an artist, and then I wouldn't even need a work permit, would I? She looked for a moment like I'd told her that cats could fly, then even more puzzled, not because she didn't have the answers, but because they were presumably too complex and surreal for her to explain in English. She asked us to take seats, and somebody else would see us shortly.

After a 10-15-minute wait that seemed many times longer, a gray-haired man – no uniform – with a kind face came out and motioned to us to follow him into his office. He had a couple of extra chairs on one side of his desk and asked us to be seated, while he sat down on the opposite side in his small, tidy, paper-filled room. Then he asked to see our passports, which we had ready to hand over. He looked at them, his brow creasing increasingly, and asked what we wanted. I first told him about the adoption thing. He wondered *where on earth* I'd heard such a strange thing. I realized that Lee Whitehead's colleague was either greatly mistaken, or had fed me a very tall tale, or that I'd only understood what I wanted to hear. Then I told him exactly what the Honorary Consul told us, which I'd also told the job guy and the receptionist, and he looked around and up at the ceiling and back at us. He gave a deep sigh.

"*OK, it's like this. They were both right – the Swedish consul and the man at arbetsförmedlingen.* [I'd failed to teach him how to say "job guy".] *The thing is, you've got to find an employer who's willing to hire you, then get a letter from them promising you the job. Then you can send this letter together with your application for a work permit to the immigration department, and then – maybe – you will get the work permit.*"

"*Great!*" I exclaimed, relieved, "*so we just go out and find jobs, and then it's settled?*"

In the face of my unbounded, unfounded optimism, his brow wrinkled again, this time even more, like he was about to tell us something that he didn't want to have to (the kind of look my dad used to get when he was told he had to fire someone at work). He sighed again, deeply, and said softly, "*I'm afraid it's not that simple. You see, the rules are like this – not my rules, you understand, but it's the rules we have to follow – that when you make your application, you can't do it from here, from Sweden. You have to make it in your own country....*"

Our jaws dropped, our hearts sank; we must have turned very pale. Thoughts were flashing: We won't be allowed to stay, what *the hell* do we do now?! We just got here and spent most of our savings to get here and sold everything and had no home to go back to and the US isn't an option because of the draft and Vietnam and where do we go now and how do we get there and are we going to stay on for a while anyway and see something of Europe first and what's the point of a crazy rule like that and there must be something, some other way, anything?!

Our agitation must have been written all over our faces and made him even more uncomfortable than before. "*Our 'own country' is across the ocean,*" I observed pleadingly, almost whispering. "*We'd never be able to afford going back and forth like that.*" He shook his head and squirmed in pained sympathy. "*And besides,*" I added, "*we can't go back!*"

At this, he suddenly sat upright in his chair and hurriedly asked what I meant: "*Why can't you go back?*" I explained that I was about to be drafted into the US Army and sent to Vietnam, and that I had no intention whatsoever of letting that happen. I showed him my reclassification notice from the Selective Service. He studied it, nodded vigorously and he averted his eyes slightly upwards, as though he was searching for some information in the space in front of the top of the wall behind us.

"*Well, you don't need political asylum at this point – you haven't been drafted yet. And there's a chance – a very small chance, but still a chance – that you could apply for a residence permit, from here, when your tourist visa runs out. And if you got it – a big IF – there's a chance that you could apply for a work permit from here too. But please understand that it's not a promise; you'll have to take your chances!*"

I'm sure he could see how crushed and disheartened we were, and he seemed to be trying desperately to find ways of helping us. He asked where we were staying. We told him about the rooming house. He recommended that we attempt to find something cheaper – some sort of cheap apartment – as soon as possible. He told us another very long name – *bostadsförmedlingen* (the housing exchange) – and of course we asked him to write it down. The last four syllables were just like the ones in the word for the employment office, so we thought it might mean "office" or "exchange", but it seemed too complicated a word to mean something that simple. We also asked if he could show us on the map, and he was only too happy to point it out. It was only a block or two from the employment office. At least our rooming house turned out to have a very convenient location.

He had one more piece of advice: sign up for a course to learn Swedish, as soon as possible. It was free for immigrants, and he happened to know that the fall term would be starting very soon. The name of the place – *Kursverksamheten* – was unexpectedly a syllable shorter than the other two official places, and the location – Regementsgatan, along the canal – wasn't too far away either, and we could even figure out that it might mean something like "Regiment Street". In fact, we'd probably walked right past the building on our stroll the day before.

It was clear that he was doing everything he possibly could to be helpful, and we were very grateful for that. We were still in a major quandary, but some of it had melted away ever so slightly in the warmth of his words. It was enough for a confirmed optimist like me to manage a smile as we shook his hand, thanked him profusely for his helpfulness, and left the building, full of doubts and fears and hopes and more confusion than ever.

As we headed out, our voices slipped into high gear and we couldn't stop. The implications of what we'd just heard were huge, and our clamoring speech was like pumps running hot to bail out the inundation of disturbing news. We took turns bringing up questions for consideration: Although our chances of being allowed to stay look slim, do we want to give it our best shot? *Yes!* Do we want to see as much of Europe as we can afford before heading back to Canada if we can't stay? *Yes!* Is the situation hopeless? *No!* What do we do in the meantime? *Take his advice: find cheap housing and start learning Swedish!*

The rooming house served us well for the first night, and could even be a good emergency solution for a few more nights. But at 30 kronor per night, that would add up to 900 kronor per month (about $180 at the time), plus the major extra expense of not having a kitchen and having to eat out all the time, in a town where eating out wasn't cheap. And there were the obvious discomforts of cramped quarters, no shower and no toilet of our own. Surely we can find a place where the rent is less than 900 kronor a month!

We headed back towards our quarters and decided to pick up our laundry and leave it in our room. The laundry was ready, shirts and blouses neatly ironed and folded, everything pristine. They'd even ironed my underwear. And it cost a small fortune, giving us a harsh but practical lesson in how right the policeman was in also urging us to learn Swedish if we were going to stay here. We would also have to find a laundromat, presuming that Malmö had one. We based that presumption solely on the fact that San Francisco and Vancouver had them.

We needed no further persuasion to tackle the language problem forthwith, particularly in view of the fact that Swedish classes were free. Knowing some Swedish might also help convince the authorities of the sincerity of our intentions to become upstanding members of the community, and also help us find work if we got lucky. Moreover, learning a new language would never be a waste of time – it's brain candy! When do we sign up? *Today – right now! We'll deal with the housing office first thing tomorrow!*

Full of most of the emotions in the spectrum known to man or woman, each of them seemingly generating energy, we hurriedly left our room, made our way back to Amiralsgatan, then down to Drottninggatan where we'd seen that high school the day before. We noted on our map that after four short blocks, Drottninggatan would become Regementsgatan – another of those tourist-defying name changes – and we would be at the school, Kursverksamheten.

The ground floor of the four-storey building had been modernized, with big plate-glass storefront windows, while the other three storeys retained their old red-brick charm. We went inside to enquire and were thrilled to find that we could enroll in a Swedish-for-immigrants course beginning on September 15th, just over two weeks off. That buoyed our spirits a great deal, at least temporarily.

From there we decided to return to the train station and pick up the rest of our suitcases. There were just three left, plus the dolly, and we could always stick them under the bed at the rooming house, where we would remain until we had somewhere better to go. On our way to the station, we passed a kind of supermarket-department-store combination called Tempo, and they seemed to have a cafeteria upstairs. We went in for a hot meal, taking advantage of being able to see what we were getting and how much it would cost before we got it. It wasn't too bad; it filled our stomachs for a while, and we could sit there among the mostly empty tables and study the map, talk about our precarious situation, and rework our plans without being bothered by the staff.

By the time we got back to the rooming house with our remaining bags, we were both exhausted again. It seemed like every hour brought new and urgent problems and obstacles. Between the physical strain of all the walking and the mental strain of running an invisible gantlet, we were struggling. And our chances of staying looked slimmer all the time. We stayed up to use the first of our aerograms to write extensive accounts of our trip since Southampton, but abandoned those efforts halfway through; we feared we might cause the recipients (our parents) unnecessary alarm because of the gloomy way we were feeling at that moment.

The next morning, after an equally punctual and unappetizing eight o'clock breakfast, followed by another 30 kronor payment to see us through the coming night as well, we left our luggage-filled room and walked back to Amiralsgatan, turned left two blocks to Henrik Smithsgatan, to *Bostadsförmedlingen*, in a building that looked like it might have been constructed in around 1900. Inside, there was an expected reception counter and waiting room, but this time, when our number came up, we were ushered into a large modern open-plan office with many desks, bookshelves, typewriters, stacks of papers, racks of forms, and people sitting at desks or standing at filing cabinets. There was little noise – all sounds were muted and hushed.

We were shown to a desk that was the workplace of an enthusiastic, spry young English-speaking man who asked how he might help us. *We're looking for an apartment.* Good, he said, pulled out a form and asked for our names. What kind of apartment? *Not too big, maybe one or two bedrooms.* Location? *Fairly central would be best – we have no car and would be dependent on public transportation, and we don't yet know Malmö very well.* Modern, unmodern or half modern? These were new terms – new concepts – for us, and he was obliged to explain. "Unmodern" was the cheapest but the most primitive; it entailed no central heating or hot water. Some unmodern apartments had toilets in them, but some you would have to go out into the stairwell or even to the courtyard. "Half modern" meant an apartment that had its own toilet, central heating and hot water, but was kind of old-fashioned, not up to the latest standard. And "modern" indicated a good standard all around, but the rent was highest.

We decided on either unmodern or half modern. He smiled and filled out the form for us, writing with speed and determination, based on everything we said. Then he looked up, stood up and said, "Good! Now I have all I need, and I'm sure we'll be able to help!" We grinned enthusiastically, stood up and exclaimed, *"Great! When can we see what you've got?"*

His smile vanished, his brow wrinkled (we were seeing a lot of that) and he sat down again, abruptly. "Oh, I'm sorry. We have nothing *now*! This is for a waiting list. It takes maybe one or two years...." Our spirits deflated in a flash like a silently bursting balloon, fortunately not bursting through our rectal orifices, or we would have shot around the room like rockets without guidance systems. *"We need something ... like ... now...!?"* I ventured.

He seemed very sympathetic, as if we were toddlers who had with the utmost sincerity just asked for the moon. "I should have made that clear, very sorry. We're a government, uh, thing, and we don't have those kinds of possibilities," he explained apologetically. "You have to go to the private ones – maybe they can help you."

Then he pulled out a phone book and turned to the yellow pages. We matter-of-factly observed that phone books in Sweden also had yellow pages, and then realized that it was not at all obvious that they would. He opened to the page where the private apartment rental agencies were listed and showed us how many there were. There must have been 50, all over Malmö, but predominantly in the central area. Then he got up and took the phone book over to a photocopier, made a copy of the spread and kindly handed it to us.

It felt like setbacks were quietly forming a long line, patiently waiting their turns to assail us. Neither the work permit nor the housing question was turning out anything like the way we'd hoped. But at least we were already enrolled in a Swedish class. And although they often gave us bad news, most of the people we met were extraordinarily kind and polite, even if we perceived their manner as somewhat stiff, formal and abrupt.

We now had a long list of rental agencies and a detailed map to find them. We decided to plunge right into it, starting more or less randomly near the top of the list, but we also tried to find those nearest to where we were. First we stopped back at our rooming house to pick up my tube of paintings; if we passed any galleries while searching for rental agencies, we could always go in and sound out those opportunities.

The first two galleries showed no interest at all, and they managed to do so haughtily. I shrugged, but Jeanette was livid: *"They're so goddamn stupid! Assholes! Don't they understand?! Don't they know <u>anything</u> about art?!"* I had to calm her down and remind her that our task right now was to solve our housing problem. Then we came to the first rental agency on our list, which consisted of a somewhat dingy office run by a somewhat gruff and semi-hostile man – quite unlike the preponderance of people we'd met so far. He looked up at us from a desk behind a counter as we came in, and barked something at us in Swedish. I explained in English that we unfortunately didn't know Swedish yet, but that we needed an apartment. Switching to English, he stood up, came over to us and asked what we were looking for. We now knew what "unmodern" and "half modern" meant; we were prepared. I spelled out the same criteria we gave the man from Bostadsförmedlingen. He thought for a minute, ruffled through some file cards, and pulled out a couple. Sure, he had what we were looking for, just right, half modern, the rent was a mere 360 kronor a month.

Our hearts soared. *"We'll probably take it,"* I said, *"but could we see it first? And can we move in right away?"* He indicated that both requests could probably be arranged. Then he added that it cost 125. I stared at him blankly, uncomprehendingly. *"I thought you said 360...?"* He nodded, and smiled a little sarcastically. *"Yeah, 360 kronor a month, that's the rent; and 125 – 125 <u>thousand</u> kronor – that's for the furniture."* I protested that we didn't want any furniture, that we would furnish it ourselves, and that it sounded like awfully expensive furniture anyway. He just shrugged, turned away, sat back down and muttered, *"That's the way it works here."*

We left that first agency and took another look at our list. After two more agencies and two more galleries in the central area gave us almost identical stories respectively, we were feeling kind of desperate. We couldn't understand what the hell was going on. It made no sense at all. And we weren't getting any closer to finding an apartment. We'd run into a wall, in addition to which Jeanette was still feeling a bit sick to her stomach and generally under the weather.

Our day felt like one rebuff after the other, and it was wearing us down, but we noticed another rental agency on our list – Rörsjöns Bostäder – that was close to our rooming house, and we decided to give it one more try that afternoon. It was on Ehrensvärdsgatan, the small street we crossed that morning, just a block or so before coming to the building where the police station was, facing the elementary school; we'd almost walked right past it. Our expectations were rock bottom.

The entrance was at number 18, about three steps below street level. It housed a modest office with a large window facing the street. The office itself was about five meters deep and slightly more than four meters wide. A narrow counter (or wide shelf) around 40 centimeters wide and 120 cm high divided the office lengthwise, ending with ample space to walk around behind it where there were two desks. The part of the office one entered first was filled with a somewhat shabby sofa, a couple of chairs, a coffee table strewn with magazines and pamphlets, and a small bookshelf. Behind the counter sat a man I guessed to be his late 30s. He jumped up with a smile when we entered. I asked if he spoke English. He responded by stretching out his hand to shake ours, and said with an even bigger smile that he *loved* to speak English, and wondered what he could help us with.

He wanted to know all about us, and to tell us all about himself. (We would later discover that he bore a striking facial resemblance to a young and well-known Swedish singer named Sven-Bertil Taube.) He'd learned English when he worked as a seaman in his youth. He told us he was married and had a very young child – a boy named "Andos" – but sadly his wife had just left him and taken the baby with her back to her mother's place in Tingsryd, and now he had this business to run, and they had a new and wonderful apartment themselves – six rooms and a kitchen – and everything would have been great if she hadn't left, but what can you do, and he owned the place where he had his apartment rental business, and the premises were divided into two, since he owned another business in that other one just through the door in the far corner behind him, although the real entrance to that other business was next door, from the street, a business that was a hairdresser's for dogs run by a girl named Ingrid, but people called her Misse, and she rented the room from him, and it was fantastic that we were from America – he'd been to America on ships he was working on, and he liked Americans, and he didn't know what to do about Margaretha (spelled with an *h*, but pronounced without it, as a T; there are no *th* sounds in Swedish) – that was his wife – and how he liked us instantly and knew that we were good people – and he was a great judge of character – and what kind of apartment were we looking for anyway?

No one could say he wasn't fluent in English. He seemed genuinely friendly and genuinely helpful. We were instantly bowled over by his effusiveness and thoroughly convinced that he was the Typical Swede, the archetype of all Swedes. His name was Bruno Nyman. He explained that his last name meant "new man" in Swedish, so he was always jokingly telling his wife that she had a new man every day.

We told him all about how and why we left North America, and thus why we were hoping to settle in Sweden, even if we hadn't worked out the how part yet, and we asked if he could explain the totally bizarre stuff we were being told at the rental agencies. It seemed that Sweden in general and Malmö in particular were suffering from an almost brutal housing shortage, he said. The system was supposed to work like this (at least as Bruno explained it): landlords were supposed to notify Bostadsförmedlingen when an apartment in one of their buildings became vacant, and Bostadsförmedlingen would then offer it to someone on their waiting list, and they could move in. No commissions, no dirty deals, shorter waiting lists. That was the theory. To get what happens in practice, add greed, that great enemy to ideals and kindness everywhere. Suddenly a relatively small shortage opened up opportunities to hang on to vacant properties, and the wheels were set in motion: let the shortages become critical, start offering shortcuts past the queue to people with cash, under the table ("for the furniture"), and dirty deals abound. OK, Sweden wasn't a utopia after all – but at least it had nice theories.

Bruno talked and talked, asked us questions – he had many – and answered ours – we had many. It was dark by now, and our feelings of hopelessness were dissipated by the lively conversation. Bruno seemed gravely discomforted that he had no apartment anywhere close to meeting our criteria among his current listings. Instead, he offered us to stay that night at his place – his and Margaretha's huge apartment – but we'd already paid for the night at the rooming house, and we didn't really feel comfortable about leaving our stuff there. Then he excitedly said he had a brilliant idea: the dog barber shop next store (he reminded us that he owned the premises) had a room at the back! He led us through two open doors to have a look at the little room. We had no idea what he had in mind.

The windowless room was about three by eight meters. Along the far long wall was a stainless steel countertop with a double sink, some kitchen cabinets and a tiny fridge. It was where he and Misse made their coffee. The short wall to the left had a door. Bruno explained that the door led to the stairwell, where there was a toilet. Along the short wall to the right was the room's only piece of furniture: a single bed. Then Bruno said that if we wanted to use this room instead of our rooming house, we could stash our bags there – and have the full use of it until a suitable apartment became available – and that this little room would be, for us, absolutely free of charge. Access to the room was through a flimsy curtain.

We were flabbergasted by the generosity of his offer. We thanked him profusely until he almost looked embarrassed. But it was kind of late, and we were mentally and physically worn out, so we agreed that we'd show up – pillar of suitcases and all – the next morning at around ten. We shook hands vigorously, big smiles all around, and said goodnight. As far as we were concerned, this confirmed that Bruno Nyman was the Typical, Ideal Swede.

Back at our rooming house that evening, we were trying to digest the day's emotionally intensive roller-coaster ride. We couldn't get over it. We finished our letters home, leaving out the creepier details, leaving out our imminent move to the back room of a dog barber shop, then went out to get our aerograms into the mailbox before the evening's last mail pick-up. Although we were dead tired, we were too wound up to sleep, and Jeanette still felt a bit ill. We found great comfort in each other's arms, which is how we finally fell asleep.

The next morning's breakfast routine was different in one respect. We woke up early – before our landlady arrived with breakfast – and were busy packing our bags when she arrived. We thanked her – *tack så mycket!* (thanks so much) – and indicated that we'd be leaving soon after breakfast. I pointed to my watch, held up ten fingers to indicate the hour of our departure, waved the key, and she seemed to get the message.

We quickly ate the parts of our breakfast we could manage, enjoyed the coffee, then began carrying the first three of our bags down the stairs to the passageway just inside the big door to the street. Since Jeanette was still feeling lousy, she waited downstairs in the passageway between the street and the stairway with the three bags while I ran up and down with the remaining bags. When I'd retrieved the last of them, I knocked on the landlady's door and handed her the key. She looked a little surprised, possibly disappointed. She didn't show her cards much.

Down in the passageway, it took some effort to get all our bags strapped back onto that little dolly. We had only about five blocks to go to Bruno's, but there were twice that many curbs, plus the two we would have to conquer to get to the other side of Föreningsgatan. Each curb was a monumental task. Jeanette was carrying my guitar case and the tube of my paintings, but she had to put them down at every curb to help me get that unwieldy and increasingly wobbly pillar down one curb and up the next. Things fell apart. The center couldn't hold. Mere suitcases were loosed upon the sidewalk. Jeanette's dandelion-yellow suitcase – the one she'd bought for her first trip to Europe in '65 – got damaged.

But we got there. Our collapsing pillar would never make it down the steps into Bruno's office; we had to bring in the bags two at a time and set them down temporarily just inside the doorway. Bruno stood up as we entered, but he was busy on the phone, agitated, and he waved us on through to "our" back room. His eyes got wider and wider with each new round of bags. We went through the door out of Bruno's office, through the back end of the tiny barber shop, making several trips. We stashed a few bags under the bed. The rest had to stand on the floor, close to the wall. We looked at the single bed (more like a cot) and decided we wouldn't mind the extra coziness for a while.

As soon as Bruno got off the phone, he joined us. He told us very apologetically that he had an awful lot of work to take care of that day, but we told him he didn't need to explain or excuse anything; *we* were the "intruders", and besides, since we had to explore Malmö, we'd keep out of his hair. He seemed relieved about that, but asked us to be sure to be back by four that afternoon to continue our discussions from the previous evening. Or was it his way of telling us that he wanted us to *stay out* until four? We couldn't be sure.

Acting more on our inference than on Bruno's implication, we took our map and left somewhat reluctantly; we were actually still too worn out to do any more exploring, but the weather was decent, and we could always go and sit in a park or something. Since we had no real agenda or urgency that day, for a change, we could take it easy rather than charge about like crazed rhinos, and we could begin to notice some of the details in our new surroundings.

We saw many cars with an upper-case H decal on the back, and made a mental note to ask Bruno about it sometime. The horse chestnut trees were already beginning to turn golden brown – a new sight for Jeanette. I remembered them from Illinois, but there were few such trees in Northern California, if any, or at least none she could remember. And we couldn't remember having seen them in Vancouver. Or did we simply fail to notice them there?

Some of the streets and sidewalks were paved with square or rectangular stones that looked to me like granite, ranging in size from two by two inches and up to ten by four. Most were gray, but some were reddish, some nearly black, some nearly white, and in many places they were laid in beautiful patterns – concentric, interlocking arches or sections using stones of different sizes and shades. A few of the oldest streets had rounded, uneven cobblestones instead of the flat paving stones. The cobblestones were beautiful and charming to look at, but not terribly pleasant to walk on. We were glad not to have encountered any when we were pushing our dolly!

We now noticed that there was also some fine print on the street signs. Beneath the street names, there was usually a small "kv" followed by a different name than the name of the street. We later learned that these were the names of the blocks – even the blocks had names in this country! – and that the "kv" stood for "kvarter", which meant "block" and that the word had the same origin as "quarter", like the French Quarter in New Orleans.

In fact, we were beginning to realize that there were rather many words that were identical or almost identical to English (like *buss, taxi, park, kanal, salt, potatis, papper, soffa*), and many others were similar if you let your mind associate freely, such as *dryck* (drink, beverage) and *penna* (pen or pencil). *Skriva* was "write", but by associating it with the older words "scribe" and "inscribe" it suddenly became easier to remember. Butter was *smör*, related to the English "smear" which is easily done with butter. We also learned that the letters with diacritical marks – å, ä and ö – are separate letters that come last in the Swedish alphabet. The å is pronounced something like the *o* in "open", although more exaggerated; ä is a bit like the *a* in "at"; and ö is something like the *oo* in "room" (if you were Inspector Clouseau). That helped a little when trying to read signs. It also helped to identify some words that are similar to English (*gå* is pronounced something like "go" – which is what *gå* usually means). Maybe learning is about self-defense. Strange, incomprehensible things can feel threatening. Learning makes things less strange. That seems to apply to people, too.

But the process of becoming aware of details and the many differences in them – linguistic, architectural, physical, geographical, culinary, cultural, behavioral, monetary, and everywhere else our overworked perceptions took us – required us to sit down frequently and just be, something we hadn't been doing a lot of lately.

We were back at Bruno's office punctually, just before four. He'd had a rough day, he told us, and he and Margaretha were still fighting. He said that although we'd stashed our bags in the back room, there was no reason why we should sleep there, that night at least. The three of us drove off to his place.

It was in a newly built apartment building in a completely new part of town called Rosengård – Rose Garden – on a street called Bennets väg (*väg* turned out to mean "road" or "avenue," pronounced similar to "vague" and probably vaguely related to "way"). With its six rooms, plus a large kitchen, a big bathroom and a separate lavatory, it seemed almost cavernous to us. There were hardwood floors everywhere, and although the furnishings were somewhat gaudy and definitely not in our taste, everything was clearly brand new and costlier than anything we'd ever been able to afford. He had a few original paintings that looked a bit like Max Ernst imitations to me, by a local and rather prolific local artist named Max Walter Svanberg. They seemed to be in vogue, in Malmö at least, which was why Bruno said he'd bought them; they would be appreciating, if not appreciated.

We talked for a bit, had some sandwiches with Bruno, and then he turned on the TV. Only three channels were available in Sweden at that time: two non-commercial Swedish channels and one non-commercial Danish channel. Jeanette and I didn't understand a thing, but after a while there was an English-language program that wasn't dubbed, but had Swedish subtitles. Suddenly, abruptly, Bruno stood up and announced that he was going to the movies, and he left us sitting there. To us, it was *very* strange behavior, especially from a host, but who were we to question it? After all, wasn't Bruno the Typical Swede?

The next morning I felt awful, probably having taken over the same bug that was bugging Jeanette. We rode with Bruno in his VW Beetle to his office, and found that Ingrid was already there, trimming a poodle. Bruno introduced us and told us that everyone called her Misse, *"which means kitty – or <u>pussy</u>,"* he added with a smirk, a leer and a wink, which Jeanette reacted to with something similar to hostility. Misse was cute, blond, probably around 20, half Swedish and half Finnish, and rather coquettish, especially towards me, which Jeanette didn't like one bit either.

But we all went about our respective businesses, ours being to hit the streets again. Before we left, Bruno handed us a key, to enable us to get in and out if he wasn't around, like on Saturdays and Sundays. We tried taking my paintings to a few more galleries, *"but they are still not dealing with art,"* Jeanette wrote in her diary. It was generally a frustrating and depressing day, exacerbated by gloomy overcast weather. However, when we returned to our little room, Misse was cleaning up for the day, and she and Jeanette had a good chat, after which Jeanette's impressions of her changed completely. Jeanette and I spent our first night alone in the room at the back of the offices, on that single bed.

The next day was Saturday, and since nobody was stirring in the offices, we got up late and repacked our things. We washed out our best Samsonite suitcases with a view to selling them. We were completely worn out from having to deal with all of the debris of our dashed naiveté, and decided we might as well return to Canada. Nothing seemed to be working out the way we'd planned, and we couldn't foresee having enough money to travel anywhere, plus if we did, we'd probably jeopardize our chances of being allowed to stay in Sweden, and we weren't sure we'd have enough money for tickets home to Vancouver – they would have to be plane tickets – because there was no way we were crossing that ocean again in a goddamn boat! – and then we couldn't take all our bags, and we could just leave the excess clothing, since I'd gotten nearly all of it cheap at The Emporium anyway.

We went for a long walk into and around town, discussed our options back and forth so intensely that we stopped making mental notes of where we were. We looked up to find ourselves a bit lost. We'd left our map behind but eventually found our way.

Just after going to bed at 11, we heard noises out in Bruno's office, and somebody laughing. I threw on some clothes and rushed out to find Bruno there with a woman I first presumed to be a prostitute. She had blond, heavily sprayed hair, lots of makeup in spite of being around my age, fleshy lips and the shortest miniskirt I'd ever seen. Then Bruno introduced us to his wife, Margaretha.

They'd brought along a thermos of coffee. In the meantime, Jeanette also dressed and joined us, and the four of us sat there in the office drinking coffee and talking. Their infant son Andos was still at her mother's place in Tingsryd. (Was "Tingsryd" the name of a part of town? Another city? Another country? A suburb of Tashkent? The Swedish word for jail? We had no idea.) Since Margaretha didn't speak English very well, Bruno had to do a lot of interpreting. She couldn't seem to understand how anyone couldn't understand Swedish. I guess we were surprised she didn't know English, in the way that English-speaking people everywhere seem to assume that English is the default language of *homo sapiens* and – in my mom's world – God and the Bible.

By around one in the morning, they suggested that we all go back to their place, and then leave for her mother's place – *Tingsryd* – in the morning. We'd developed the habit of just saying *yes* to anything Bruno the Typical Swede suggested. Back at their place, they served some booze, and we stayed up drinking until around 2:30. Strangely enough, we actually ended up having had a very nice day.

After breakfast on Sunday morning, August 31st, the four of us squeezed into the Beetle, Jeanette and Margaretha in the back seat, and we took off. Tingsryd, it turned out, was a small town about three hours' drive northeast of Malmö. It was a pleasant ride, and we got to see something of the clean and sparsely populated southern Swedish countryside. There seemed to be many more similarities between Sweden and Canada than between Sweden and the US (and not just in terms of the topography).

Margaretha's mother was very sweet and hospitable, and had a hot meal ready for us all when we arrived in the early afternoon. She spoke no English and seemed far too old to be Margaretha's mother. Her weary manner was the polar opposite of her daughter's: no make-up or flashiness at all, no vulgarity, no ebullience or volcanic temper. The reunion of little Andos with his parents seemed strangely nonchalant or indifferent. Andos was even younger than we expected, still in infancy. He couldn't have been many weeks old, but he was very cute and good the whole time.

After lunch, Bruno took the four of us to a nearby lake, where they had a small motorboat that we drove around in for a while. It was beautiful and peaceful (apart from the roar of the boat), especially when Bruno was approaching a tiny island and shut the engine off to show us how beautiful and peaceful it really was. Jeanette called it *our* island – hers and mine – and hoped we'd come back to it some day. The sun was beginning to set when Bruno started the engine again and took us back, to the pier, to the car, to the others.

Bruno and I sat watching *fotboll* on TV while all three women were preparing dinner in the kitchen. Jeanette really seemed to hit it off with Margaretha's mother, even though they couldn't speak to each other in words. To me, "football" always meant American football or its close Canadian cousin. What we were watching was "soccer" to me, and yet it seemed to make a lot more sense to call it football, since it was actually almost entirely about kicking, unlike American football. It was the first time I'd ever seen a game, and I had some difficulty following parts of it. Just when it looked like one guy was going to break free and score a goal, the referee would blow the whistle and the other team would get a free kick. It made no sense to me. Bruno tried to explain the offside rule, but I wasn't convinced that he really understood it himself.

Most of the conversation during dinner and the rest of the evening was in Swedish; Jeanette and I didn't understand a word. We just absorbed the very different melody of the language, trying to identify as many words as we could. It was easier with written texts.

We spent the night in Tingsryd and remained there for most of Monday morning, September 1st. They apparently had some planning to talk about concerning the forthcoming christening of little Andos. Then Bruno told us that since Margaretha would be staying on in Tingsryd to help her mother and Andos for a few days, the three of us would drive back to Malmö. Along the way home, we stopped at a farm. Bruno said he owned it and that he'd rented it out to some tenants who didn't seem to be taking very good care of it. They didn't appear to appreciate the surprise visit.

As we drove on, Jeanette commented that farm life looked very desirable. Bruno leaped on this and exclaimed that we ought to take over his tenant's farm and raise chickens. He painted glowing pictures of how rich we could soon be from breeding chickens for both eggs and meat, and we could cash in all our remaining traveler's checks to make the investment. (He sounded us out about our finances enough to know that we were living off our traveler's checks, but he clearly had no idea how little we had or he wouldn't have suggested a property investment!) He was a very smooth-talking salesman, which tends to work pretty well on naïve listeners. He made the idea sound very tempting, but there were just too many obstacles – like the lack of money, the lack of residence permits, the lack of anything resembling *any* business experience, let alone running a poultry farm!

We made another stop on the way back to Malmö, this time in the old university town of Lund. My mother's uncle Carl[1] visited it some years before; his daughter studied nursing there. We found Lund to be as charming as Carl did, not that I had a great deal of respect for his opinion about anything.

That evening, we went with Bruno to a movie theater and saw a forgettable American movie. Shortly after we got back to his place, at about 10 o'clock, we were starting to think about retiring when Bruno announced that he had to go out to meet a business partner in the harbor, and did I want to come along? He was hinting unmistakably that he wanted just me to join him. I looked at Jeanette. She shrugged and said "go on", so I continued following my habit of saying yes to everything Bruno suggested.

On our way in the dark to a remote part of the harbor that was nowhere near where we'd arrived on the *Absolon* just over a week before, Bruno told me that his new business partner's name was Percy, and that he (Percy) was rigging up an old fishing boat with a false bottom for use in "importing" contraband booze and cigarettes. Although an alarm bell went off in my head (*it couldn't be typically Swedish to break the law like that, could it?!*), my absolute faith in Bruno remained unscathed; it was Percy who wasn't the Typical Swede, not Bruno.

When he and I got to a dimly lit part of the so-called Free Harbor, Percy leapt out of the boat at the sound of Bruno's approaching car, relaxed when he saw Bruno climb out, then tensed up suspiciously when he saw me too. Percy spoke no English. When Bruno explained who I was (I've often wondered what he told him; I could only pick up the word *amerikan*, with the stress on the last syllable), Percy immediately asked Bruno to ask me whether I knew how to manufacture LSD. I think I must have gasped, both at the realization of what kind of underworld character Percy was – but not Bruno! – and at the ludicrousness of the notion that all Americans are somehow born knowing chemistry.

Their conversation soon came to an end, and Bruno and I drove back to his apartment. Even though I still really wanted to believe that Bruno was the Typical Swede, my ill-founded faith was shaken. Then Bruno told me that he

---

[1] Readers of Book 1 (*Natural Shocks*) may recall this duck murderer from the chapter "Pets".

and Percy were going to be starting up a business together in the near future. He didn't mention anything about what it was, but at least it wasn't LSD (I asked him). I could hardly wait to tell Jeanette all about my mysterious little outing. Then we would try to figure out whether the world we entered eight days earlier was surreal or just absurd.

CHAPTER 3

Living with uncertainty

The next day, September 2nd, we went with Bruno to his office (and our little room) and had breakfast with him there. Then he left to drive back to Tingsryd and would return on Thursday. We suspected that a lot of things were going on beyond the reaches of our linguistic barriers, and perhaps beyond our cultural ones as well.

When half-barbered toy poodles began sniffing around in our room later that morning, we said goodbye to Misse and headed downtown to find a letter waiting from Jeanette's mom, informing us that Michael had already booked an open-ended ticket to fly over to see us in a couple of weeks. Although we welcomed his visit and understood his need to get out of the parental home, and their need to get him out, we thought we'd agreed to let him know once we had a place to stay, and *then* invite him to join us. But we had no place to stay yet. In fact, we were so full of uncertainty that we hardly knew what was happening in an hour or two, much less what would be happening weeks ahead. Perhaps Michael's outsider's perspective on the issues that were plaguing us might be of help. At least we could speak freely to someone without having to explain everything or find easy words all the time.

Then we took a ferry to Copenhagen and visited a couple more galleries with my paintings, an experience that once again ended up infuriating Jeanette. In spite of that, we had a nice day, and actually enjoyed being on the water for the crossings, to our surprise.

When Bruno returned on Thursday, he'd brought Margaretha and Andos back with him. He'd dropped them off at their apartment and then came to pick us up to bring us there to help unpack their things; they appeared to be reconciled.

We were glad to be able to be of help, both on Thursday and Friday, and we got to use their facilities to do our laundry. We spent the nights there as well. On the Saturday, their apartment was full of visitors: two of Bruno's aunts and their husbands and a few cousins. We had crayfish for the first time ever for either of us. The eating of crayfish in late August or early September was a strong Swedish tradition, we were told, and comprised a variety of rituals. The crustaceans were accompanied by bread, beer and *snaps* (Swedish aquavit). The crayfish themselves, cooked first (in salted water with a little beer, sugar and plenty of crown dill), then eaten cold, looked like miniature red lobsters. We were shown how to break off the abdomen from the hard shell that covers everything else, then slurp the shell like hell to get the briny, dill-flavored juices out. We then had to peel or pry off the hard shell over the abdomen, revealing the meaty tail – most of what there is to enjoy. But there is also meat in the two main claws, and with some patience, tiny wads of tasty meat can be extracted from the even tinier legs, preferably while drinking a *snaps* and singing a Swedish drinking song from a little song booklet printed for the occasion, to celebrate each successfully consumed crustacean. Jeanette and I just laughed and noted how the singing evolved from timid to bold to raucous to totally smashed with each new *snaps*.

For dessert there was a strange-looking cake (*spiddekauge*, a specialty of Skåne) made of yellowish, rather eggy meringue and sugar glaze that was spun round and round, as if someone emptied one tube of toothpaste after another to make a tall basket. It looked kind of festive, but didn't have a lot of flavor beyond the sweetness of the sugar, although by that time our taste buds might have been a bit numb from all the *snaps*. We had a very nice time. There'd been no further mention of Percy for several days now.

On Sunday Bruno took us for a long drive to a number of scenic places in Skåne, Sweden's southernmost province that includes Malmö. We saw beaches and manor houses and Skanör (a charming village with a goose crossing). We were really impressed with what we saw – and even more by what we didn't see: no slums, almost no littering, country roads not uglified by billboards. Everything was green and lush and well cared-for. Even the television programs were free from commercials.

Jeanette told Bruno and Margaretha that her twin brother would soon be coming to Malmö to spend some time with us. For some reason we never understood, they both seemed really displeased about that. In the evening, our hosts went to the movies while we looked after Andos. I wrote to Dad and Mom that it was hard to know what to write when we didn't even know what to think.

On Monday morning we rode with Bruno to his office and found Percy there, busy with something. He looked up and glared at us suspiciously as we slipped through to our room to change clothes. We hurried, since we didn't feel that our presence was entirely welcome. As we were leaving again a few minutes later, we couldn't help noticing that there were about five or six TV sets stacked in the reception part of the office. And Percy couldn't help noticing that we noticed.

Jeanette and I ended up having to spend most of the day pushing Andos around town while Margaretha continued to shop. In the late afternoon we headed back to the office to meet Bruno, since Margaretha told Jeanette that he would drive us out to their place for the evening. The TV sets were gone, but in their place there was a stack of pricy stereos, still in their cartons.

Tuesday was pretty much a repeat of Monday, but Percy wasn't there and instead of the stereos, there were piles of small boxes about the size fine watches come in. As we were leaving, Bruno stood up from his place behind the counter and called me over. His eyes were sparkling. He pulled his shirt sleeve up a few inches (or centimeters now), revealing a very expensive-looking gold Rolex watch. He asked me what I thought he'd paid for it. I told him, quite honestly, that I didn't have a clue. He seemed disappointed, but insisted that I guess. He was greatly disappointed that I guessed a figure that was only about a tenth of the retail value, but it turned out that what he'd paid was only about half of my figure. I thought of Burly and Slim and shuddered.

Then Bruno decided to explain to me the nature of the plans for his new enterprise with Percy: they were going into the money-lending business. Swedish law, or bank practice, or both, allowed anyone to cash checks for up to 300 kronor without clearance, he told me. He and Percy were going to lend money in increments of 500 kronor, for which they would receive two checks of 300 kronor each, post-dated one month. That way, they would always be certain of getting their money back – along with 240% annual interest. But they needed more seed capital, and they presumed that we had plenty of money in the form of traveler's checks. They had no clue how close to the bottom of our barrel we were. Maybe they were doing a little stereotyping of their own – *Americans* means *rich* Americans, right? In any case, Bruno was very eager for us to cash in our checks and put the money into the lending business. He claimed we'd be millionaires in no time; he had it all figured out. We declined as graciously as we possibly could, but he was not amused. And we realized that Percy would be even less so.

On Wednesday, Bruno told us that Margaretha had to visit Ronneby, a town near Tingsryd, to take care of some important business at a court or something, but since she had no driver's license, I would have to drive her there, in their VW Beetle; Bruno had to work. Fortunately, I had a little practice driving Al's Beetle during our last couple of weeks in North America, but I still didn't feel comfortable with a stick shift, nor with somebody else's car, nor driving to an unknown destination in a new country, without a map, entirely dependent on directions from someone who could barely speak English. Nevertheless, Margaretha and Andos (in the insert from his baby buggy) got into the back seat and Jeanette got in front next to me in the front. And Margaretha was going to guide me to Ronneby and back.

It was pretty straightforward. All we had to do was find a certain highway out of Malmö, and then stick with it all the way through the beautiful countryside. I learned that the "H" stickers I'd seen on many cars (and on the dashboard of Bruno's Beetle) were reminders to drive on the right (*höger* in Swedish). Sweden switched from left-hand to right-hand traffic only two years before our arrival, and we were very grateful to them for having done so. (But it didn't explain the fact that small delivery vans were just about the only vehicles with steering wheels on the right, even among older ones. Bruno said something about how often Swedes drove in Denmark and on the Continent, but that made little sense to me either.)

After Margaretha took care of her errand in Ronneby, she wanted to stop at lots of places to buy things, and then said we'd go over to Tingsryd to see her mother briefly. I was getting pretty weary from the anxiety of driving a strange car on strange roads to strange places, following strange instructions in a strange language. I just longed to get back to Malmö and leave the car behind me.

We eventually returned to Malmö in the early evening dusk along a street called Södra Bulltoftavägen, in accordance with Margaretha's lucid guidance. The end of said street seemed to me to split into different directions, something like a T-crossing. At the far side of it there was a rounded, slightly raised part paved with granite stones, beautifully patterned in the manner I'd seen before. I was convinced I had to turn either left or right. I asked Margaretha which way I should proceed. "*You driving straight!*" "Straight" would, in my interpretation of a word I thought I knew, have meant driving up over the raised stone mound, which somehow didn't seem plausible. I repeated my question, demanding to know if I should turn left or right. *No, no, you driving straight!!* I turned around to make eye contact with her, giving her a most uncomprehending and agitated look, as cars behind me were beginning to show signs of impatience for me to move on. "*Straight!!! Straight!!!*" This time she roared urgently and gesticulated, chopping the air in front of her with her open hand. She was a Swede, and this was Sweden. I wasn't Swedish; who was I to contradict her? I drove straight, up over the roundabout – the first roundabout I'd ever encountered in my life. (I'm glad she didn't say "Left!" because then I'd have entered the roundabout going in the wrong direction, against traffic. That particular roundabout/traffic circle, whatever, at the end of Nobelvägen in Malmö, has since been raised further from the street level and the stone paving removed. It now has grass and a few trees growing on it, thanks to me?) Margaretha screamed. Car horns blared around me. Other motorists drew up beside me, leaned over to stare and glare at me ostentatiously, reproachfully tapping the sides of their heads with their index fingers. At least I understood the body language. By the time we arrived back at their place it was nearly 9 PM, and I was completely frazzled. Bruno was at the movies.

The next day, September 11th, my brother John's birthday, we awoke to the sounds of Bruno and Margareta fighting again. His mood was dark and hostile, towards us as well. We rode in silence with him to the office, where Percy was already working. They spoke to each other in hushed tones, as if they assumed we'd learned Swedish overnight and their language was no longer a sufficient guarantor of privacy. We hurried out to the travel agency to see if there was any mail for us, and to discuss the sudden turn of things. When we got back, Bruno tersely announced that he'd found us an apartment that was available for immediate occupancy. It was less than a block away, also on Ehrensvärdsgatan, just across Föreningsgatan, number 14. It turned out that the building had a name – *Ensamheten* (Loneliness) – as it was originally the only building on the block. It has since been razed, thus making its former site the only gap in the block; number 14 no longer exists.

Our new apartment was unmodern – no central heating, no hot water – but at least the toilet was in the apartment rather than out in the stairwell or the courtyard. The apartment was furnished; we would be sub-letting it for a relatively affordable 300 kronor a month. Bruno informed us that the person holding the lease – to whom we would have to pay three months' rent in cash the next day – had just taken a new job in Trelleborg and didn't want the long commute. We were also informed that even though we wouldn't get to move in until the next day, the 12th, we'd have to pay the rent for the full month of September.

We ignored Bruno's sullenness. We were far too excited to finally have a place of our own, sort of. Bruno took us to see it. The building had a cavernous and gloomy stairwell, and our apartment was on the third floor. On entering, there was a small vestibule with the door to the lavatory straight ahead. The lavatory contained a small sink, as well as a toilet bearing the brand name "Frontanus" sealed in the vitreous china. I, of course, immediately associated the name with an anatomical anomaly.

The ceilings were very high, well over three meters. There was a kitchen to the left, with a small Formica-type table and four aging, cheap, Windsor-style chairs, a very small fridge, a gas stove and a stainless steel sink with faucets for hot and cold running water – both of which were cold. To the right of the entry was a living room with horrendously garish bright red floral wallpaper and fairly cheap post-war furniture, including a sofa big enough for Michael to use as a bed when he arrived, as well as two armchairs and a few lamps.

To the right was a doorway to what would be our bedroom, furnished with a couple of single, cot-type beds that we could move together, a chest of drawers, a nightstand and two lamps. Unfortunately, the doorway was not covered by a door, but by a mere drapery. In our enthusiasm about getting a place of our own (and free of sniffing poodles that left their hair everywhere), the privacy problems that would arise once Michael arrived hadn't occurred to us yet. There was a heater in each room, but they weren't on, as there was no need of them in the warm and summery September weather that we of course presumed was typical for the Swedish climate. Without exception, every September we'd ever spent in Sweden had had weather exactly like this.

We now had a very busy day ahead of us, first to clear our bags out of the dog shop and get them across Föreningsgatan to our own place. Then, for the first time in more than a month, we could unpack. We also had to go to Tempo to get a few groceries. We would at last have a fridge and cupboard that contained edibles. Jeanette was eager to start cooking again, albeit with some unknown ingredients. When we'd completed our errands, we went out with Bruno for coffee and cake, even if we were celebrating something quite different from him. That evening Jeanette and I went out for dinner to try out one of the two Chinese restaurants in Malmö at that time – the nearby Shanghai on Östra Förstadsgatan – before coming *home* to try out our bed.

Bruno came by for coffee the next morning. On his own, without Percy, he was still a very congenial guy. Without Margaretha, he was calm and not quite so interested in status symbols. And he loved speaking English with us. Margaretha was supposed to come by and leave off Andos "for a while" – a timeframe we'd already learned had little meaning in the context of Margaretha. Jeanette and

I waited for her arrival, then I had to get to the bank to cash a few traveler's checks to pay our new landlord; Bruno brought him by in the afternoon (still no Margaretha in sight). His name was Bror Landin (Bruno told me that *bror* meant "brother", which sounded both familiar and odd to me; familiar because of all the "brothers" I'd grown up with in the Plymouth Brethren, odd because there was no equivalent English name I could think of. I knew that in the old Swedish naming system, the father of someone named Sven Larsson might have been Lars Nilsson, whose father might have been Nils Andersson, etc.

Anyway, Bror Landin was a gaunt, weary, middle-aged man who spoke almost no English. He showed us how to turn on the heaters, with Bruno interpreting. We paid our three months' rent, plus an extra 100 kronor for some extra heaters that he said he'd deliver later that day but didn't. We were now paid up to December 15th, and thereafter we would pay by check, to an address he gave us. It reminded us that our tourist visas would have expired by then, and how many uncertainties we were facing about what would happen after that. As they were leaving, we asked Bruno why Margaretha hadn't shown up, but he waved off the question. Then we asked if we could take him and Margaretha out to dinner that evening, as a token of our gratitude for his help. He said sure. In the evening he, Margareta and Andos showed up, and the five of us dined at the Shanghai. No mention was made of Margaretha's disappearing act.

During the meal, they were at each other's throats half the time, in Swedish. During the other half, they told us that Andos was to be christened on Sunday, and could we please come along to St. Paul's Church to be "witnesses". We expressed some surprise about the christening, not having been aware that they were at all religious. They laughed and said it wasn't about religion, it was just a tradition. I offered to bring my camera to record the event for posterity, and they seemed to think that would be a good idea. Afterwards, Jeanette and I went for a long walk; we had much more to digest than our dinner.

The next day, Saturday, was my 24th birthday. Unannounced, Margaretha came by with Andos in the morning and announced, "*I going for shopping Copenhagy, you passing Andos!*" Before the meaning of what she'd just said registered fully, and before we could ask questions she wouldn't have understood, she held up Andos' bottle and a package of infant formula, and added, "*I coming tobacks clocken one!*" And off she went.

Jeanette and I stared at each other, dumbstruck. We guessed that she'd told us she would be returning to pick Andos up at one o'clock. And we soon discovered that she forgot to leave any diapers. Since I had to get to the post office to register our address and mail our latest round of aerograms to our parents, I also picked up some diapers at the supermarket. When I got back, Jeanette changed Andos, and we discovered that the directions for the formula were in Swedish only. I grabbed the package and ran down to Bruno's office, only to find it closed. We had to guess, and Andos eventually got something sufficiently satisfying for him to get to sleep. Then Jeanette and I had lunch and a piece of birthday cake. The hours went by very slowly.

One o'clock came and went. Margaretha did neither. We knew that the shops in Copenhagen closed at one, so we figured that she might be as late as 3:30. We tried to read as long as Andos slept, and do whatever seemed to cause him the least distress when he didn't. At 3:30, I again tried visiting Bruno's office. Still not there. I tried calling their apartment from a phone booth on the corner. No answer. We were becoming more than mildly irritated, and also slightly alarmed.

I repeated the procedure – check Bruno's office, phone them at home – every half hour for the rest of the afternoon, and then for the entire evening. No response anywhere. We finally decided that whatever happened, we would have to bed ourselves down when Andos went to sleep for the night (we hoped he would sleep) and try again in the morning. Fortunately, Andos did sleep rather well, which was more than we did.

Early the next morning – the morning of Andos' scheduled christening – we still hadn't heard a word from either of them. I again went down to Bruno's shop, quickly ascertained that nobody was there, then phoned their apartment from the pay phone on the corner. This time it was busy. I waited a few minutes and tried again. Still busy. Then I rushed back to tell Jeanette, then rushed back to try again. Still busy. I kept trying for close to an hour, returning to Jeanette once to let her know what wasn't happening. Finally, we decided to put Andos in the buggy and wheel him as quickly as we could across town to their place in Rosengård. When we arrived in the corridor outside their door, we could hear them screaming at each other even before we had time to ring the doorbell. They finally opened, saw us, saw their son in the buggy, and just motioned towards an alcove where Bruno said we could park Andos and the buggy, and they continued their screaming match. Bruno screamed towards us, in English, that he'd found a condom in her bed. She screamed back that he had a new woman. Then she left, slamming the door behind her. After talking long enough with Bruno to feel certain that he wouldn't go rushing out too, and reminding him of the christening just an hour or two away, we left and walked back home, hoping for the best.

Jeanette and I walked down to the church at the appointed time (we were actually a bit early – I was my mother's son) for the christening. To our surprise, Bruno and Margaretha were both there, suitably dressed up, with Andos in a christening gown. Margaretha's face was puffy, and she was wearing a dark wig, in honor of the masquerade. The christening was to take place at the tail end of an ordinary Sunday church service, but apart from the five of us who were there solely for the christening, the only attendees were about half a dozen elderly ladies, all of whom looked weary and withdrawn. Apparently this was the typical congregation for Swedish churches except at Christmas, when they would suddenly be crowded, not due to a sudden peak in religious fervor, but because in Sweden, to most people, the church stood for tradition, not religion, and Christmas (*jul*, pronounced *yule* and with the same meaning) was all about traditions.

The minister was a woman, another new experience for both of us. I was running around among the pews and around the altar taking pictures from all kinds of angles. As soon as it was over, Jeanette and I were asked to accompany Bruno and the minister into the vestry, where Bruno told us we had to sign some papers as witnesses. We were very surprised to see on the papers that the little boy's name was actually *Anders* – their southern Swedish accent had made it sound to us like *Andos*, which we'd assumed was a Greek name. We were even more surprised to discover that the document we'd just signed made us more than "witnesses"; less than three weeks after arriving in Sweden, we were now the godparents of a Swedish boy!

We all went back to their apartment for a lunch of sandwiches with shrimps and smoked salmon, accompanied by beer and snaps. A dozen or so family members were there as well, few of whom spoke any English or seemed to know who the hell we were, or seemed to know anything about the raging battle between *Anders'* parents. It seemed to Jeanette and me that our highly mysterious relationship with them was coming to an unforeseen end, and we felt fortunate to have gotten a roof over our heads while it lasted. But we also felt distraught about the fate of that sweet little boy. (Jeanette was so upset by this traumatic event that she omitted the whole thing from her diary and wrote something nicer instead.)

When we got home to our apartment that evening, just the two of us, Jeanette reminded me of her previously stated intention: that she never, ever wanted kids. She felt strongly that the world was neither a good nor a safe place for them, with its innumerable wars and cruelty, and bringing children into it would be nothing short of irresponsible. She could see that I was kind of shocked by her unexpected outburst. She asked if not having kids would be a problem for me. I couldn't find anything directly reproachable in her reasoning, and I guess I didn't mind having a way out of the hateful vow I'd been forced to make to the man in the dress. I said I couldn't miss kids I never had, that she was all I ever wanted, and that I sure would miss her if she ever left me. She swore she never would.

Then I set about writing my appeal of the 1-A draft classification my parents forwarded to me, and also to inform the Selective Service of my change of address, no longer care of my parents in Oak Park but care of Landin in Malmö. Some years earlier, I appealed for conscientious objector status (1-O) on the basis of the fundamentalist Christian views I never quite held. Now I was writing to appeal for 1-O status on grounds of being a pacifist – but this time with no mention of religion:

> *I understand from various sources such as news media that the major reason draft boards are reluctant to grant 1-O classifications is that those people did not request such status from their initial classification. [...] In the six years since I first registered with you many things have changed. When I was 18, I would have loved to go to war and kill as many "commies" as I could. I would have (and did) scorn the idea of war being immoral. Therefore I would hardly have requested 1-O classification. Likewise I would hardly have advised you of marital status because I was not only unmarried, but I scorned the idea of marriage. But* people change *and now I am married and a pacifist. [...] Yet you are asking me to be part of a military whose principal function is to take lives (call it murder, "defense" or whatever; it adds up to the same.) I tell you I cannot do it!*

The next day, Monday, September 15th, we attended our first Swedish lesson. Our teacher was a friendly, maternal, somewhat stocky, neatly dressed, middle-aged lady named Elsa Braun. She had short, curly graying blond hair, and told us she had two children our age. She spoke English well. She also spoke French, German and Italian, and showed great interest in all of us, including why we came to Sweden. Since English seemed to be something of a common ground, she conducted the introductions in English, with the occasional support of German or French. There were ten other students in our class, besides us, from a variety of countries. Although I may have forgotten someone, I do remember Urs, a heavily bearded young man from Switzerland, who came to Sweden to escape the Swiss draft (he already had the knife); Jütte, a pretty blonde from Germany who was helping her German husband in his business in Denmark and wanted to be of more help with his Swedish clients; Temenuschka, a girl our age from Bulgaria, who was joining her family in Sweden and escaping Bulgarian oppression at the same time; Maria, a stocky, middle-aged, bleach-blonde woman from Spain whose Swedish husband was tired of living outside Sweden; Gaylee Gaye (I'm not making any of this up!), a thirty-ish American woman whose husband worked in the oil business and kept getting different postings all over the world, and she tagged along for all the rides; Man Kai Man from Hong Kong, who was working at Malmö's (and Sweden's) oldest Chinese restaurant (Kin Long); Mila and Milka, teenage twins from Yugoslavia who appeared to be identical despite being of different genders, and were joining their family in Sweden; and the multilingual Boris, 17, also from Yugoslavia, who came to live with his Hungarian mother who'd left his father a few years before.

After the brief introductions, Elsa then explained that the classes would be conducted almost entirely in Swedish, starting with a basic vocabulary and a few of the most common phrases, in order to achieve a foundation on which to build. She then plunged right in and spoke only Swedish, pointing to tables, walls, floors, books, etc, carefully enunciating the words for them in Swedish and getting us to repeat after her. She followed with things like *My name is... What's yours?*, and got us to ask each other. The class lasted for one and a half hours, and we would be attending on Mondays, Wednesdays and Fridays. We found it rather boring for quite a while, but Elsa was outstanding.

There were two short routes to school, and they were very pleasant walks. Both started with half a block's walk from the entrance of our building down to Kungsgatan, then along the tree-lined parkway, where we could either continue to Amiralsgatan, make a partial loop around St. Paul's church, and proceed down a block to Drottninggatan at the corner of Latinskolan; or we could leave Kungsgatan after a block and a half and cut diagonally through a small park (Rörsjöparken) to Drottninggatan, in which case we'd have a view of the canal as it bent around the inner part of Malmö. Drottninggatan turned into Regementsgatan at Södra Förstadsgatan, and our school was only half a block away.

Living with uncertainty

Before returning to our apartment after the first session of our Swedish course, we stopped by Bruno's office to see whether Bror Landin had been in touch about the heaters. Bruno interrupted a fierce ongoing fight with Margaretha, both of them standing there seething at each other, to ask what we wanted, and replied that we shouldn't expect to hear from Landin. The only thing Bruno told us about his ongoing fight was that Margaretha lost him his dream house, yet we got the impression that she was the one who was furious with him and that he was mostly defensive. We were perhaps fortunate that our first lesson hadn't imparted fluency in Swedish. The violence seemed to be verbal only, apart from a lot of slamming of things (a couple of relatively small objects may have become airborne). We melted out the door.

Jeanette and I slept in the next morning. We hadn't been prepared for the mental weariness of dealing with Bruno and family, a new dwelling, a new language everywhere we looked and listened, truckloads of anxious uncertainty about our immediate future, the imminent arrival of Michael, new foods, the absence of familiar sights, sounds, smells, peanut butter and hot water. The outlets and light switches were somewhat different, and we had a toilet called Frontanus. We also realized that we'd have to cash a few more traveler's checks and find some sheets and blankets, both for ourselves and a set for Michael. There were many little things we needed, things that were ganging up on our budget and coming dangerously close to overpowering it, which didn't do a lot to assuage our anxiety.

I got a birthday card and $10 from Jeanette's parents in the mail that day, as well as a brief letter and greeting from John and a short note from Nancy. (I must have been deeply disappointed, because Jeanette's diary described my reaction as "...poor Stanley!!!") That evening we heated some water on the stove and took our first sponge baths since our camping trip to Vancouver Island with Michael, who would be arriving the next evening. I could see that Jeanette was really looking forward to that, which I found a bit puzzling, even though I'd witnessed the intensity of her desire to maintain contact with him while he was in Vietnam – all the letters she wrote, all the packages she sent, all the anxiety she expressed to me verbally or indirectly. Yet none of that intensity was ever present whenever we met him, nor was any reciprocated. There always seemed to be a great distance between them. Or maybe there was a different type of closeness I couldn't see or understand.

I thought again of Remarque's character Paul's response to his family when he was home on leave from the front[2] – his nearly total alienation as well as his inability and unwillingness to connect with anyone. I hadn't come close to understanding the book well enough, at least not in terms of what Michael was likely to be going through, groping through. Jeanette and I did our best, reaching out in darkness, to show him we cared, to be approachable, but he'd unwittingly and unwillingly entered a world from which there was no escape. We had it easy. I never had to agonize over my decision to take whatever steps were necessary to avoid serving in an army fighting a war as unjust as the one in Vietnam. Seeing what had become of Michael – and he wasn't even listed among the casualties! – only strengthened our resolve and commitment to our decision to uproot ourselves from the unchosen land of our birth. (PTSD – a condition that used to be known as battle fatigue or shellshock – wasn't identified as such until 1980, and is not included in the official military statistics of the Vietnam War casualties, despite well over a quarter of a million victims among US troops.)

On the morning of Michael's arrival, we went to our second Swedish class. When it was over, Jeanette told Elsa that her brother was coming to stay with us and asked if he could join. Elsa said that would be fine. She seemed to take a special interest in us, especially regarding my situation relating to the war in Vietnam. On our way home from school, we bought more food and a four-liter pot, which would be needed for the unusual dual purposes of taking sponge baths and cooking pasta. We also bumped into Bruno a couple of times. He told us that Margaretha was in Copenhagen for the day, that they now hated each other, and that Anders was with a babysitter.

Michael would be flying to Copenhagen, then changing to a 15-minute flight to Bulltofta, Malmö's tiny airport, arriving at 6:30 PM. We could take a bus there from Värnhemstorget, just a block from our apartment, out Sallerupsvägen, almost door-to-door service. Since we didn't know that the bus ride would take less than 15 minutes, we ended up arriving two hours early. He arrived on time, we took the bus home and had Jeanette's delicious spaghetti and meat sauce, then sat up talking for a while. He told us he preferred using "Mike" now, especially when his dad wasn't around to lay claim to that form of their shared name. He also announced that his army benefits gave him considerably more financial

---

2 See Remarque's *All Quiet on the Western Front*.

freedom than we had, and that it was his firm intention to share expenses with us – a third of everything – which we were kind of hoping for if our budget was to stand a chance of surviving. We also explained our precarious and highly uncertain status in Sweden, and how we intended to proceed to maximize our chances for being allowed to stay. Since we wouldn't know anything for sure until our tourist visas expired and we explored how to extend them, if that was at all possible, Jeanette and I would have to remain in Sweden – although excursions to Denmark didn't seem to jeopardize anything – until December, but if he wanted to travel around in Europe before then, he shouldn't feel bound to wait for us. Jeanette also told him that she'd enrolled him in our Swedish class, in case he wanted to join it. He said he would, but that now his jetlag was overwhelming him. We called it a night.

The next day the three of us walked all around central Malmö (we already knew it well enough to serve as Mike's guides), and we started bringing him up to speed on the single page of Swedish words we'd learned in our first two lessons, in preparation for his first class the next day. Early that evening, there was a knock on the door. The first to greet us was a poodle that marched straight in as if daring us to object. It was delivered to us by Misse and her boyfriend, whom she also had in tow. The owner of the poodle was unable to pick it up before Misse's closing time, and she felt we would be more willing dog-sitters than she was. Joining her were Bruno and a rather vulgar-looking young woman, whom Bruno told us was his new fiancée. The four of them were going out dancing. Misse and her boyfriend stayed for a while to talk to us, perhaps because she felt guilty about dumping a poodle unbidden into our laps, but more likely because she wanted to get to know Mike better. She hardly took her eyes off him. Then they left to join Bruno and his new flame. The bizarre aspects of our lives in Malmö seemed to have no end.

On Friday the three of us attended Mike's first Swedish lesson, our fourth. Since Mike wasn't the only new member, Elsa told us she'd be splitting up the class into two groups. Of those in our original group, everyone but Urs and Man Kai Man would remain, and Mike was the only additional student. We also each received a textbook and a workbook, *Svenska för er* (*Swedish for you*). We still found it very boring. The idea of learning a new language was extremely exciting, and Elsa was a great teacher, but the beginning part, collecting the essential building blocks, was just drudgery.

After class, Elsa wanted to talk with us a bit more. We gave her a brief account of the strange comings and goings of Bruno and Margaretha, and we could see from the angle of her dropped jaw, her audible gasps, the increased diameter of her eyes, and the additional furrows in her brow as she shook her head in disbelief, that it could no longer be considered consistent with the truth to regard Bruno as a Typical Swede.

On the way home, we encountered Margaretha and Anders. She looked at Mike with suspicion, which didn't abate noticeably when Jeanette told her who he was. She explained that she had a new apartment and was planning to go back to school. Jeanette and I had such a lot to explain to Mike that we ended up walking to the outskirts of town, at a tangent from where we lived, paying scant attention to where we were going. We were pretty exhausted, for multiple reasons, by the time we got home.

The next day we took Mike to Copenhagen, where we walked and walked some more, all day long. The pastry shops were very difficult to pass by. We asked for a dozen Danishes and were informed that all pastry in the shop was Danish, this being Denmark and all. It took a little concentration to accept the fact that Danes (and Swedes) called the pastries we meant *wienerbrød* (literally Viennese bread!). Anyway, we came home with a big bag of them and continued devouring them decadently, together with good, strong Swedish coffee.

In the evening, Misse stopped by to see us – at least that's what we thought at first, until it became apparent that she was there to see Mike. She was dressed very seductively – an extremely short skirt and a blouse which she must have put on in a hurry, because she'd forgotten to button half of the buttons – and was flirting with him openly. But Mike wasn't biting in the least, not even when she managed to extract from him that he liked the Beatles, and she promptly invited him back to her place "to listen to her albums". (Jeanette and I weren't included in the invitation, but wondered if "albums" was the Swedish word for "etchings".) He was certainly in a small minority of guys who could have resisted an invitation like that from a girl like Misse, but he just squirmed in discomfort and declined her every attempt to cajole and entice him. Even Jeanette found his refusal incomprehensible. Eventually, Misse could no longer endure the rejection and left in distress. Jeanette and I felt really sorry for her.

Mike refused to talk about it, and his silence was accompanied by the same symptoms he showed back in San Francisco when the subject of Vietnam came up. Jeanette and I vowed to ourselves not to belabor him with it, but at the same time we were driven by a consuming desire to help him get free from the prison of memories and feelings from which he seemed not to want to escape, or maybe to express feelings he didn't know he had. We all went to bed, disturbed and wordless.

We spent Sunday talking about what trips we would make once Jeanette and I got our permit situation resolved. Mike made no mention of attending a Catholic church; perhaps he'd given up that stuff too. But Jeanette seemed strangely irritated with her brother, as though his dismissal of Misse was in some way also a dismissal of her. His presence began to weigh heavy on her. He never went out without us, and we could never go out on our own. He never took any initiatives to do anything but sit in the living room or kitchen and read, yet never discussed the books he was reading. Literature seemed to be more of an escape hatch from (rather than a door to) communication and broadening of the mind.

Jeanette occasionally mentioned (to me) how she'd hoped that Mike's being with us and out from under his oppressive father would be able to do him good, to free him, to open him up to life, to find his wings. He would join in certain conversations readily enough, but he seldom started one. Jeanette began to realize that the pattern of life at home that Mike adopted after Vietnam, and that was driving her parents crazy, was beginning to drive her crazy too. And finding her hopes unrealized, her disappointment was all the greater, and quickly began turning to frustration, irritation and despair.

On Monday after class, we went to the Nyman & Schultz travel agency office, not only to check for possible new mail for us, but to see if they could help us with information regarding possible trips to Helsingør and Hamburg. Such nearby destinations, however, seemed to be beneath their dignity (especially on budgets like ours).

The glorious weather we'd been experiencing nearly every day since our arrival four weeks earlier suddenly turned into fierce winds – so fierce that the outer pane in one of our bedroom windows broke. The elderly lady who served as the caretaker for our building came to see which one was broken, and we had to assume she would do something about it. Jeanette and I spent the rest of the day studying Swedish and writing letters. We were powerfully motivated to learn Swedish quickly. Mike wasn't, and read Dostoyevsky.

On Tuesday, we went to the train station to find out about train tickets to Helsingør and Hamburg and discovered that it would be beyond-budget expensive. Mike, however, felt he could afford it without a problem, so we urged him to go ahead on his own, but he backed down. Instead, we thought we'd start looking into buying a used car in which to do our traveling.

Wednesday was a beautifully temperate day, and Jeanette told me she had to go for a walk on her own after class. She explained that if I accompanied her, Mike would join us, and she was beginning to suffocate. As a result, Mike and I went home; I studied Swedish and he read. In her diary for this day, Jeanette wrote, "Michael finished *The Idiot*!!! [He] has been here a week today."

We continued treading water for the next couple of days. Nothing was happening, Jeanette and I were in constant anxiety about the evaporation of our money and the non-evaporation of Mike. We looked into buying a radio to rescue us from the deafening silence of not being able to speak and act as freely as a young married couple might wish to do, nor being able to discuss anything of substance with Mike. In our rather open and noise-transmitting apartment, with Mike sleeping just outside our bedroom, separated only by a drapery, Jeanette and I were feeling pretty inhibited; Mike never went out. Although we'd been financially extended in Vancouver, now we felt poor. We couldn't afford a night at a rooming house (for just the two of us). Even the cheapest radios we could find were beyond our budget.

A degree of temporary relief from the internal tension came on Saturday, September 27th. The three of us took the ferry to Copenhagen at 9 o'clock, then walked to the central station and took a train up to Helsingør to visit Kronborg Castle, the somewhat dismal real-life venue for the even more dismal fictional *Hamlet*. Although Shakespeare never visited Denmark, he somehow seemed to have captured the setting with surprising accuracy. The castle was located on the edge of town, along the water (we'd spotted it from the *Stefan Batóry* just an hour or so before the end of our trans-Atlantic voyage). After a couple of hours of wandering around the halls, chambers, dungeons and grounds, we took a train to the Fredenborg Castle, then on to the lakeside Fredriksborg Castle, which we found to be the most enchanting of the three. We didn't get home until 9 PM, pleasantly exhausted, and stocked up with bread from Denmark's fabulous bakeries.

Elsa told us that we needed to register our presence in Sweden in order to get a Swedish civic registration number, which would entitle us to free medical care. Such registrations were handled by the Swedish Church, which surprised us greatly. Elsa explained that it was the centuries-old duty of the Church to keep public records – births, deaths, marriages, etc – and that since they had little else to do, due to extremely low church attendance, due to even lower religiosity, they retained this function. There was no link whatsoever between religion and this function.

So Jeanette and I went to the church where Andos – no, *Anders* – was christened just two weeks earlier, but we were told that we had to visit the parish office instead, about eight blocks away, and that they weren't open on Sundays, but had normal office hours. Early the next morning Jeanette and I walked a few miles across town to the only laundromat in Malmö, at the corner of Mariadalsvägen and Kronborgsvägen. (Mike decided to stay at home, sleep in, and read, which meant that we were on our own, alone, together!) After our laundry was ready, we walked back home to drop it off, then walked on to the parish office and registered, then went with Mike to our Swedish lesson. (After Elsa divided her growing class into two, we were in a group with lessons from 11.30 AM to 2 PM.) Then we went grocery shopping and returned home.

During the next week or so, the weather turned noticeably cooler. The trees also started turning, and some leaves were beginning to fall. We were glad we'd also brought warmer clothing. Jeanette and I filled our days studying Swedish. We were slowly beginning to make some progress, which made it less boring and it pleased Elsa enormously. We also took time for grocery shopping and reading (Mike wasn't the only reader among us!). On October 8th, Jeanette and I celebrated our third anniversary, which meant that at this point we'd celebrated each of our anniversaries in a different country. Mike and I began looking for a used car to make excursions with, and even a trip or two if we ever got residence permits – or found we would have to leave. And on Saturdays we continued to make our trips to Copenhagen to shop for budget-friendly food and to see the sights.

A lot of the shops in the Havnegade harbor area in Copenhagen seemed to cater specially to shoppers coming from Sweden to buy goods that were significantly cheaper in Denmark, particularly cheese, meat and alcohol. (Swedes were so prominent among the customers that prices were more likely to be indicated in Swedish kronor than Danish.) The competition among the stores was fierce, and by going for the specials at each shop, it was easy to save a lot of money on certain staples. Moreover, most purchasers were awarded free tickets for the various ferry lines between Malmö and Copenhagen. There were three different lines: Öresundsbåtarna (the Öresund Boats), Centrumlinjen (the City Center Line) and Flygbåtarna (the Hydrofoils, which took only 35 minutes, compared to nearly two hours for the other two lines). As a result, we were soon awash in free tickets, and trips to Copenhagen became free of charge. It was just a matter of grabbing a handful of tickets, heading for the harbor, and picking the boat we wanted to take that day.

One of the special sights involved a climb to the top of Vor Frelsers Kirke, a church with a spiral staircase on the exterior of the spire. It was an exciting climb that gave a fabulous view all around Copenhagen and across the strait to Sweden. But we found the zoo too expensive – 95 cents each – and didn't go in. We also bought bread on our trips to Denmark. Most of the Swedish breads we'd tried were heavy and sweet, and for our taste they were only edible toasted. Our supply of the Danish bread tended to run out quickly, which ended up requiring us to splurge on a toaster, our first European appliance. Our typical breakfasts consisted of cereal with milk, some artificial-tasting orange juice, and good, strong coffee. Lunches usually consisted of bread (if it was fresh from Denmark) or toast (if it was local) with mustard and cheese, either Danish Danbo or Port Salut. We were only just beginning to discover the non-Velveeta world of cheeses that was now available to us.

All three of us liked wine. We soon discovered that in Sweden, alcohol was only sold in special government-run shops, called *Systembolaget* ("The System Company", a.k.a. *Systemet* or even *Bolaget* for short), roughly the same arrangement we'd experienced in Vancouver. They were only open on weekdays, and never in the evenings. Our nearest outlet was on Pilgatan, a side street off Värnhemstorget, marked by a dark-green sign that only became visible after looking hard enough for it (or perhaps having the experience to spot it in a crowd of other signs). Inside the door was a world of silence – a large open room, lit by fluorescent tubes, and a long L-shaped counter with 6-8 cash registers manned by somber-looking, mostly middle-aged women dressed in dark-green uniforms.

Their selection was listed in discreet dark-green catalogues, and sample bottles were displayed in glass cases along the wall opposite the cash registers. The bottles for sale were kept at a safe distance behind the counter. People in line didn't speak to each other, but shuffled slowly forward in silence, and when your turn came up, you would state your request in a low, muffled tone, or present a list (pale yellow forms for writing lists were available). You weren't expected to make any big purchases – customarily two or three bottles at most. Dark-green unmarked plastic bags were available, but many men (most of the customers were men) brought their own leather satchels along, in which to hide the fact that they'd been to *Bolaget* once they'd left it.

Bruno told us that until 1955, sales of alcohol were controlled by personal ration booklets that allowed the purchase of no more than a few bottles a month, and that privileges could be withdrawn for people who overindulged. Naturally, that arrangement almost obliged people to purchase their full ration even if they might not otherwise have been interested. Moonshine abounded in Sweden's forests, according to Bruno, and most people with easy access to Denmark smuggled a bottle or two extra each time they visited the neighbor country. When rationing was abolished, people continued their small-scale smuggling due to the significantly higher prices in Sweden. The duty-free quota was just one liter of distilled alcohol and two liters of table wine. Anyone taking a day trip to Copenhagen and not bringing home his or her full quota was viewed as stark-raving mad; smuggling in a few extra bottles was a local sport, or possibly a national pastime.

A couple of times, Jeanette and I crossed Föreningsgatan to visit Bruno for a chat. His money-lending business was now in full swing. (Elsa said it constituted usury and was illegal.) He told us he still saw Margaretha once in a while, whatever that meant. And we got a post card from Wojtchek to which we replied with a letter.

We applied for a residence permit in mid-October, at the police station near us, when we still had over a month to go on our tourist visas, just to make sure it would get processed before our tourist visas expired. We were alarmed to hear that the processing time could be around *two* months, and we were worried about ending up in some kind of limbo. Worse, they told us that our chances of being granted an extended (3-6 months) stay were pretty slim. All our anxiety returned.

At our next Swedish lesson, Elsa noticed how anxious we'd suddenly become; she wanted to speak with us about it. We explained the new status of our situation: how slim they'd told us our chances were for a residence permit; my new draft classification, how risky (and unaffordable) it would be to go back and forth to the US, and how desperate we were to stay. She listened with great concern. Then she told us that maybe the immigration police didn't really grasp our situation, and that because her husband was a judge in Malmö, she was personally acquainted with most of the people who worked at that police station, and how much she'd like to go and speak with them on our behalf, if we didn't mind (!). Our faltering hopes revived. We turned her loose, with *carte blanche* to plead our cause.

A couple of days later, Elsa knocked on our door. She'd just been to see the immigration police two blocks away, and felt she'd been able to get them to view our situation in a rather different light. She cautioned us that she couldn't be certain of the outcome, but said that we could expect a summons to the police station for a new interview within the next couple of weeks. Rays of hope were streaming in, and we were overwhelmed by Elsa's kindness and unexpected willingness to intercede.

Since Mike was now more urgently advocating the purchase of a radio, we intensified our search and finally found a very cheap one. We then spent the better part of an evening finding a way to hang up the wire antenna in the kitchen window in such a way as to enable us to receive signals from Radio Luxembourg, a kind of "pirate" station set up on a small ship in the English Channel to circumvent the monopoly of the dull BBC in Britain, which refused to play enough of the popular music that young people like us were craving. Besides, we couldn't yet understand anything on the Swedish or Danish stations that dominated our local airwaves, and the music they played was highly successful in failing to appeal to our tastes.

On Monday, October 20th, Dad's birthday, Bruno told us he'd found us a good bargain on a car – a white 1961 Saab 95 station wagon with a two-stroke engine. It seemed to be in decent condition (not that any of us were knowledgeable about cars), and was, of course, a stick shift, with the gearshift lever on the steering column. We didn't really understand the meaning of the two-stroke business, but Bruno told us it used the same kind of fuel as mopeds, whatever they were. The fuel turned out to be one that contained four percent two-stroke motor oil mixed in with the gasoline. Since many cars in Sweden used such fuel, Swedish gas stations also had pumps offering a pre-mixed four-percent blend. The Saab also had a "free-wheel" function, something we'd never heard of except on bicycles. It meant that by pulling a certain lever on the dashboard, you could eliminate nearly all of the engine drag to save fuel, but it wasn't advisable on downhill slopes. We hoped our car wouldn't turn out to be a lemon.

Jeanette and I felt that the price (the equivalent of $400) was beyond our budget, but Mike was eager to get wheels, and said he'd contribute half instead of a third. We told him that in that case, he should feel free to use the car for trips on his own if we didn't have the time to join him, and that we'd pay him back a percentage of his share when he returned to the States. He smiled in unconvincing assent (but never used the car on his own).

The fact that it was a station wagon would give us the possibility to haul big things, like furniture, at some point in our optimistic future. In experimenting with the seat configurations for that possible use, we discovered a particularly exciting, serendipitous feature: the back seat could be folded down in such a way as to make a large, almost completely flat surface out of the entire area behind the front seat – long enough for any or all of us to stretch out fully to sleep. Suddenly, long trips down on the Continent could be within reach of our budget.

Mike had still never said how long he intended to stay with us. We knew that his return ticket was open-ended, yet we found it awkward to ask. He didn't, however, have any intention of applying for a Swedish residence permit, but said he would leave Sweden for at least a few days when his three-month tourist visa expired in mid-December, then return on a new one. Based on that, we sort of guessed his stay might last six months; the prospect of an even longer stay came as a surprise.

In the late morning on Thursday, October 30th, there was a knock on our door. We were greatly surprised to see a police officer standing there, and we invited him in for coffee. He said he couldn't stay, but just wanted to inform us (we had no phone) that we were to appear at the police station on Sallerupsvägen at 3 PM that same day for the interview, and that we were to bring our passports. Our hearts were pounding.

Just a few minutes later, there was another knock on the door and we jumped. This time it was Bruno and Bror Landin, who came to install our missing heaters – just in time, because the weather was now quite chilly and stormy. Bruno stayed on for coffee until we had to leave at 2:45 for our interview.

It's hard to know whether the police officer we met at the station wondered why we were getting such special treatment, or if it just felt that way to us. Whichever it was, he told us our case would be considered in the light of the heightened risk of my being drafted. We knew he'd received this information from Elsa, but he didn't mention her. He seemed rather impressed by our determination to learn Swedish, although we couldn't help demonstrating that we had little to show for it so far.

He told us that they'd stamp our passports to indicate that we'd applied for residence permits, and if our tourist visas expired before the decision came through, that stamp would entitle us to remain in Sweden until the decision was made. Further, he told us that under these circumstances, *if* we were granted a six-month residence permit, there was a *chance* that we would also be allowed to apply for work permits – after having found a willing employer – *without* leaving the country to make the application. We were stunned, dazed, relieved, thrilled, jubilant.

When we got back home, we were surprised to find that Landin had let himself in and was completing the installation of the heaters (we thought he'd already done that). Afterwards, Jeanette and I were emotionally exhausted and went with Mike to the movies. It turned out that unlike most other European countries, Scandinavian countries didn't dub foreign movies on TV or in cinemas, but used the original soundtrack and ran subtitles. This not only enabled us to keep in touch with our own spoken language, but to pick up quite a few Swedish words from the subtitles as well.

One of our classmates, Boris, spoke excellent English, which he'd learned back home in Belgrade simply by going to undubbed American and British movies. His skills with English as a foreign language far exceeded those of any other person we'd ever met. His native Yugoslavia had four official Slavic languages (covering two different alphabets), and Boris spoke them all fluently. His mother was from Hungary, so Boris learned that language too. (Since Hungarian does not even belong to the Indo-European family, it meant a considerable linguistic leap.) Russian was a required subject in his school, and with those languages in tow, he quietly added the remaining Slavic languages to his repertoire: Polish, Czech and Bulgarian. He knew a bit of Italian and some French. Oh yes, and a little German, of course. Always useful. He stopped by a couple of times to chat, which Mike also seemed to enjoy.

November was a month of anxious waiting, mostly for the decision about our residence permits. Jeanette and I were working hard on our Swedish and making progress. We had our little Swedish-English dictionary with us everywhere and were constantly looking up new words we'd see on signs and in shops. Mike, who wasn't bothering too much about his homework, was quickly falling behind, but seemed not to care. Elsa said she was particularly impressed by our progress and gave us a book of short stories, *Onda sagor*, by

Pär Lagerkvist, which was excruciatingly difficult, but ultimately rewarding to struggle our way through.

Common words or phrases in some languages, perhaps most, are seldom pronounced exactly the way they're spelled, particularly not in the vernacular. "*I am going to work*" becomes "*I'm gonna work*" or even "*uh-muh-nuh work*". Such shortcuts are also used in Swedish, for example "*Det är en bok*" is usually pronounced "*De e en bok*". Elsa taught us to use the shorter vernacular forms to enable us to communicate with people we encountered outside the classroom. One day the school's head teacher visited our lesson to check on our progress. She started asking us some simple questions, such as "*Vad är det?*" while pointing at a table. We looked at her with blank stares. Then Elsa cut in, repeated the question in the vernacular (*Va e de?*), and we answered immediately and correctly, also with the vernacular pronunciation, the only kind we'd learned. The head teacher practically huffed out. (Imagine pronouncing, exactly as it's spelled, with *no* silent letters, "*I would love some tea*"!)

The quest to learn Swedish made me aware of some hitherto unknown (for me) phenomena in how my brain worked. I couldn't help observing, for example, how frequently I would be searching in my new bank of Swedish vocabulary for a word and come up with a French one – hardly ever an English one. It was as though my brain had one section for my native language and another section for foreign languages, and the native-language section would tell the rest of my brain, "*Hey, if you're looking for a Swedish word, don't come looking around here. Down the temporal lobe to your right, second convolution on your left to find all that foreign stuff!*" I also noticed that I simply *couldn't hear* certain Swedish-only sounds – phonemes that don't exist in English, like the pronunciation of the Swedish vowel *y*. To produce that sound, you have to try saying a long *e*, as in *cheese* (when smiling for a photo), but exaggerate the length of it, which would normally be done by grinning broadly, *cheeeeese*. But instead of grinning broadly, you try to achieve an equally hyper-long *e* by doing the opposite – pursing your lips. Then you get something like that approximates the sound of the Swedish *y*. It took me a very long time, first to hear the difference, then to be able to produce the sound myself.

Thanks to my having studied French, I had no trouble grasping the difference between the meaning of *ja* (*yes* in English, *oui* in French) and *jo* (also *yes* in English, but *si* in French). It was a bit trickier for Jeanette. But the problem – in the sense of having to refrain (for social purposes) from bursting out laughing –

for both of us was that both Swedish forms of *yes* are sometimes "spoken" while inhaling sharply.

Then there was *ju*, a reinforcing word thrown in here and there, meaning something like "as you know" or "as you should know", but since *ju* is such a tiny word, it's used more frequently, even excessively, by some people. *Jo* is pronounced almost like *you*, whereas *ju* is pronounced more like it would be pronounced if it were French, which means with a vowel sound not found in English. If monolingual Anglophone readers are feeling a bit confused at this point, then I have succeeded in rendering a very small sample of the confusion we felt as we struggled to learn Swedish.

In mid-November, our tourist visas expired, and we still hadn't received The Decision. It was a weird feeling, even though our passports bore stamps indicating that we'd applied for residence permits and were entitled to remain in Sweden pending the decision. We were optimistic enough to start making contingency plans *in case* we got our permits – we really believed we would now. And we were itching to travel down through Europe, and make a real roadtrip of it. We started talking about a few musts: Hamburg, Amsterdam and London were at the top of the list, but not just the big cities; we wanted some small towns and rural areas too, for balance. But at this point it was still a dream. We also started taking the car on day-trips in Skåne – Helsingborg, Landskrona, Ystad – and were enjoying the now-barren countryside in between. We didn't even think of the alternative (if we didn't get our permits), which would have meant moving back to Canada and starting over.

On November 28th we had our first snowfall, and five days later our Swedish class went on a field trip by bus, starting with a visit to a locally well-known country inn in Spången (where we were disappointed to be served Swedish hash (*pyttipanna*) instead of being allowed to partake of the sumptuous and tempting Christmas buffet that dominated the dining room), then on to visit a 16th century paper mill in Klippan. The elderly gentleman who was our guide spoke to us in Swedish (slowly for our benefit), and to our surprise, we got the gist of what he was saying.

After the paper mill, we stopped at the Hyllinge glassworks and for the first time saw glass being blown. But even more mind-blowing was the scenery outside. The very flat ground was covered in glistening white snow, with a ground fog that added hoarfrost to every twig on every tree and bush, while the coral-red hue of

Living with uncertainty

the sun gave the entire scene a massive dose of magic. Even though it was only around three in the afternoon, the sun was very low on the horizon. We were prepared for Sweden to be colder than San Francisco, or even Vancouver, but not for the winter days to be so goddamn short. When we took a closer look in an atlas, the reason became clear once we realized that even southernmost Sweden was as far north as the Alaskan panhandle.

Our rent was only paid up to mid-December. After consulting Bruno, with whom our relationship had cooled to a severe chill, we arranged for payment of an additional two months' rent to Landin for our apartment, thinking that we might be home from our roadtrip before the rent was again due in mid-February.

Two blocks down from us, almost to Drottninggatan, was a store (*Friluftsmagasinet*) that sold all kinds of camping supplies. We found reindeer skins that gave great cushioning and protection from extreme cold, and were thus perfect for placing under sleeping bags, especially if we also bought the store's down-filled models. They were also reasonably priced. Looking at the expense another way, we'd just bought the cheapest possible hotels for our roadtrip.

A day or two later, we heard from some of our classmates and Elsa that some terrible massacre had just been discovered in Vietnam, apparently committed by American troops on civilians. We tried to find out more, but since we couldn't understand enough Swedish to get a very clear picture from the radio or the Swedish newspaper, we bought a copy of the next issue of *Time* from the newsstand. The sickening massacre in Mỹ Lai (a.k.a. Song My) not only gave us the chills, but sickened us – and made Jeanette and me enormously grateful to have left the US. When we told Mike the news, he broke out in a cold sweat. He was visibly shaken, but he only shook his head and said nothing. Neither did we. I thought of Colonel Chivington. We decided to get a subscription to *Time* as soon as we were settled. We couldn't be in the dark all the time about what was going on in the world, and it would take quite a bit longer until we could handle the complexity level of Swedish newspaper or radio reports.

At times like these, we understood how cut off we were in certain ways. In any situation where we had to rely on Swedish when speaking to anyone who wasn't fluent in English, our level of Swedish restricted us to a primitive vocabulary strung together with hopelessly incorrect grammar. This was like the standard Hollywood treatment of Indians, who were portrayed as incapable of expressing complex thoughts or reasoning, simply because Hollywood made them express everything in English; their grunts and grammar unfairly purported to reflect their intellect. The misrepresentation was in fact more about the presumed unwillingness or inability of moviegoers to read English subtitles. Having to read subtitles while allowing the eloquence of another language would put the shoe on the other foot, or perhaps the foot in the other mouth.

On Friday, December 5th, Elsa invited her entire class to her home on Norra Klockspelsvägen in a modestly fashionable western part of town (*Friluftsstaden*), approaching the even more fashionable Limhamn. The purpose was to have an informal get-together over some traditional Swedish Christmas treats like *glögg* (spiced mulled wine, served hot), and an impressive array of delicious Christmas cookies and candy. We also got to meet her husband, Sven, the judge. He may have been as interested to put faces on our names as Jeanette and I were to put a face on his. He was a tall, lumbering man, balding, with a bow tie and kind eyes. We felt indebted to him, even though we weren't sure how much he was aware of Elsa having dropped his name when she intervened on our behalf with the immigration police. (Perhaps he wouldn't have wanted to know?)

Elsa had fashioned the Brauns' modest row house into a beautiful and cozy home. Their son Lars, in his 20s, had already moved out (we didn't meet him); their daughter, who went only by her nickname (Mojsan or Moisan[3]), was in her late teens, very tall, and still living at home. She seemed unable to take her eyes off me that evening. We had a very nice time getting a glimpse of what a very comfortable standard of living we could aspire to if we ever had any weird notions about joining the Swedish middle class.

On Wednesday, December 10th, a card from the police arrived in the mail. We now knew enough Swedish to figure out that it said that the decision about our residence permits had been made, and that we should report to the police station with our passports within a week. But it didn't say what the decision was! We were trembling with excitement, held in check by fear. For all we knew, it could mean immediate deportation. We were shaking, possibly visibly, when we presented our passports at the police station the next morning. The woman took them, took out some papers and looked at them, then took a rubber stamp and began stamping away at those papers and at our passports like she was smashing at an

---

3 I'm uncertain both of the spelling (identical pronunciation in Swedish) and of her real name.

invasion of ants on her desk. We still didn't know what was going on. When she handed them back, we saw that we had been issued six-month residence permits! She also handed us a document with a great deal of difficult Swedish text on it. We asked her what it meant. She told us to wait.

A few minutes later the same friendly policeman we'd talked to the first day came out to the waiting room and sat down with us (there was nobody else in the waiting room at the time). He told us to regard our six-month residence permit as the next step. After that, we'd probably get a 12-month extension, then two years, then a permanent residence permit. "Oh, and by the way, if you find an employer who'll write a letter promising you a job, come back and we'll help you apply for a work permit – *and you can do it from here, from Sweden.*"

Gobs of complicated uncertainty suddenly and simply vanished. Waves of relief, joy and gratitude swept over us and we could barely refrain from hugging the vicariously pleased policeman, but we knew we'd most likely cause him more embarrassment than pleasure. We hadn't yet reached the point in our lives (or budgets) where such an event would automatically call for Champagne. Instead, we went out and bought the reindeer skins and sleeping bags, then went back and told Mike that it was time to start working on an itinerary for our Roadtrip. Mike's reaction to our news was dampened and largely inscrutable, although not overtly negative. But he knew at that moment we wouldn't be moving back to America. Although we strongly doubted it, we couldn't rule out the possibility that he'd been *sent* to us by his parents to persuade us to come back to North America. But then we were a little paranoid.

We'd hardly traveled at all since coming to Europe. Now we were nearly bursting to get out there. The timing was perfect; few companies would be hiring anyone but temporary Christmas help in mid-December, and we couldn't take any job without first getting a promissory letter on which to base an application for a work permit – a question of weeks, if not months.

On Friday we had our last Swedish class for the first term, and we hardly needed to tell Elsa our good news; it was written all over our faces, and she was nearly as thrilled as we were, on our behalf. We thanked her profusely; without her intervention, we considered it highly unlikely that we would have been granted permission to stay in Sweden. I've remained convinced of that all my life.

We spent Friday afternoon and evening, as well as Saturday, planning and packing, and writing a few Christmas cards, both to the folks back in the US, to a few in Canada, to two in Poland, and to some new friends in Sweden. We also sent one to my unknown renegade cousin Robert in Switzerland, along with a letter giving a brief outline of my own renegade status, in terms of the Meeting and Vietnam. I assumed I could write as witheringly as I wanted about the Meeting experience; he would either take offense and not wish further contact, in which case I wouldn't have wanted contact with him either, or he would respond with the enthusiasm of a fellow, like-minded renegade.

At some point during the autumn – my memory fails me here – Jeanette and I received certificates with our Swedish Civic Registration numbers, roughly the Swedish equivalent of Social Security numbers. The big difference was that in Sweden we were now entitled to free medical care and, if we wanted it, free education all the way through college (something that elicited very mixed feelings in Jeanette). The certificate itself was just a piece of paper, which could be folded to credit-card size, like a Social Security card. It took us a while to realize that it meant a great deal more in a country where healthcare and education are regarded as human rights, not the exclusive privileges of those who can afford them.

Although we wouldn't find out about it for nearly a month, on December 17th my name appeared on the front page of the *Chicago Daily News*, together with my old Oak Park address, in a story about my having been granted political asylum in Sweden. The following day a similar story appeared in the *Chicago Tribune*, whose reporter phoned my dad at work to ask him about it. Dad was shocked. "*Son in Sweden, Kin Shocked at Charge of Draft Evasion*" was the headline. When my parents sent me the clippings I was also shocked, mainly because the articles were simply untrue. I'd received a residence permit, not political asylum. I hadn't even been drafted yet, and my latest classification was still under appeal. I was traveling on a valid American passport. There was no need for me to receive asylum, even though I felt a very strong need to be allowed to remain outside the US. And, contrary to the articles' claims, I was no longer 20 years old and hadn't been for more than four years. I never did find out how the American press got hold of what residence permits Sweden issued, or why they failed utterly to fact-check instead of writing articles about me to elucidate and disseminate their fabrications to their readers. They clearly didn't subscribe to the famous slogan of the *New York Times*: "All the news that's fit to print."

CHAPTER 4

The grand European roadtrip

It was a week before the winter solstice, just four days after our residence permits came through. It was also a Sunday morning, December 14th, and we got up in the pitchiest of darknesses at 5:30 in order to load the car and make it to the car ferry terminal in the western part of Malmö – Limhamn – in time to catch the 7:50 ferry to Dragør on the Danish side. Our sketchy itinerary included Lübeck, Hamburg, Amsterdam, and eventually – if all went well – Christmas in London. Beyond that, we had no clear plans in terms of destinations or the length of our roadtrip, although we set one month as the maximum. The rest would be up to our budget, our travel-weariness, and our old Saab.

The crossing to Dragør was our first time on that car ferry, and we were surprised to find how modern and fresh-looking it was. It took just 50 minutes in the dim winter dawn that was struggling to become day. There was a biting chill. Dragør appeared to be a charming little village on the island of Amager, separated from Denmark's principal island, Sjaelland, by the same narrow waterway that split Copenhagen in two. But we would have to see more of Dragør some other time; first we had a scenic two-hour ride southward, crossing a couple of bridges connecting Sjaelland with a couple more Danish islands (Falster and Lolland), to reach the ferry terminal in Rødby, from where we would cross to Puttgarden on the tip of a German peninsula a bit north of the Medieval town of Lübeck. Jeanette kept a diary of this Grand European Roadtrip, upon which I have drawn extensively to complement and correct my own memories. (She interjected quite a few Swedish words into it, probably to keep in practice.)

The second, rather sterile-looking ferry took about an hour and a half and got us to Germany before one o'clock. Our lunch on board consisted of a large bag of sandwiches that Jeanette had made for the three of us, plus some beverages we bought in the cafeteria. The drive to Lübeck was enchanting. The cold white landscape dotted with picturesque hamlets and barren groves nearly fused with the gray skies and dim winter daylight. We saw several large hawks perched on fenceposts, and a few deer in the fields foraging for whatever might be edible beneath the thin cover of crusty snow.

We spent a couple of hours walking around Lübeck, the capital city of the 14th-century Hanseatic League, a union of medieval Northern European merchant guilds that banded together for mutual protection and promotion of commerce. Lübeck was also the birthplace of Thomas Mann, an author I knew fairly well, albeit in translation. The winter chill went from biting to bitter as we strolled among the quaint Christmas market stalls. We went into an old church to have a look, and when we found a heater inside, we became reluctantly grateful churchgoers. As it was already getting dark, we decided to drive on to our principal destination for the day: the big city of Hamburg.

The downtown area (*Stadtmitte*), incredibly decked out in Christmas lights, was full of people and traffic. After finding a place to park, we walked around in the crowded unknown. We eventually spotted a tourist office that provided a free city map, but by this time the sum of the day's experiences and impressions was already catching up with us, and the darkness above the lights was turning everything beneath them into a cacophony of sensory overload. Since we'd been up since 5:30, we decided to find the nearest campsite on our maps. But the tourist office map turned out to be nearly as sketchy as our first Copenhagen map was, and since the streets kept changing names (not just in Malmö!), we grew more and more frustrated.

We finally found an official, deserted site for campers on the edge of town. This was where we'd spend the night. We sat in the car with the engine running while finishing off Jeanette's sandwiches. Then we began preparing our "room" by opening up back of the Saab to make up our "beds". Since we couldn't leave the engine running due to the fumes, and since the car doors were open, the car quickly turned icy cold. With only the light in the car and some distant streetlights to see by, Mike and I squeezed all our bags into the front seat, made the back seat flat and spread out the two reindeer skins for padding and warmth, then unrolled the two arctic-weight sleeping bags, one for Mike, the other for Jeanette and me to share. Speed was essential, but we quickly learned the drill. While Mike and I were dealing with this, Jeanette found herself a place to pee in a dark corner of the campsite. Then I did likewise. Jeanette got into our sleeping bag first, and I followed and zipped us in. It wasn't designed for two, but since it didn't seem to mind (it didn't break), we didn't mind either. Finally, Mike climbed into his bag, beside us, and before zipping it up, he pulled the car door closed.

It was very dark, despite the streetlights in the distance, and the even more distant city lights. And it was freezing cold until our own body heat had time to heat up the insides of our sleeping bags and, to a lesser extent, the interior of the car. There was no room at all to move. It was absurd. We lay there, in complete sardinian stillness, and started to laugh, softly, almost muted, more like chuckling. As the windows steamed up, our soft laughter continued until we fell asleep.

Apparently we slept reasonably well; we didn't wake up until the pale winter daylight awoke us at around 8:30. Despite our youth, however, we were pretty stiff, and the chill hit us like a truck when we emerged from our respective cocoons. We hastily threw on all the icy outer garments we had, rolled up the sleeping bags and skins, got our bags into the back, and started the engine to begin dissipating the frozen condensation on the insides of the windows. Then we scraped thick layers of frost from the outsides. Mike and I tried dry-shaving in the rearview mirrors (since I still had my Van Dyke-style beard, I only had my cheeks to shave), one of us on each side of the car. We hurried back to *Stadtmitte* in search of a café for warmth, breakfast, and some kind of toilet. (The one we found barely met our most urgent needs.)

Once we'd thawed out, we went out to explore the town on foot, in something like daylight this time. For several reasons, we went into a big department store. The first priority was to find proper toilets. Then we looked around, mostly in the basement food department, which amazed us with a vast selection that was mostly out of our price range. We did stock up on bread, and bought a small block of cheese to ensure that the cheese slicer we'd brought with us from Sweden would feel fulfilled. We also bought a couple of liters of soda, some fruit, a jar of marmalade, a bottle of wine and some chocolate candy bars. Then we continued walking around the center of Hamburg, and finally went back to the car to head for Bremen.

Bremen was a lot smaller than Hamburg, wieldier. We bought some postcards, visited the cathedral and "*awed at all there was to awe about*," as Jeanette put it. An organ recital was underway. The acoustics were wonderful and they had heaters. From Bremen we drove on to Oldenburg, a lovely little place with a storybook, car-free center. Their Christmas market included a real elephant that sought to become better acquainted with me by sniffing at my sleeve. Crowds of people were enjoying their Christmas cheer by singing raucously in the keys of J major through L minor as they emerged from an establishment of intoxicating liquid refreshment. We remained there enjoying ourselves until night was falling – several hours after darkness fell, but still not late – and thought it best to head on out of town to find a shoulder (of the road) to lie on (in our car-bed).

Halfway to Leer, we found a roadside layby with picnic tables (for other times of the day and year), one of many such places we saw that were marked with a large *P*, some 30 meters into a grove and away from the worst of the highway traffic noise. Before preparing our "beds", we made sandwiches, shared the bottle of wine, and had a candy bar for dessert. It was still bitter cold, but we were becoming hardened (or just frozen solid).

Our morning procedure was already a routine after the first day, except that we now actually had some pale sunlight. We had breakfast in the small town of Leer, which showed few traces of devastation after the War. But we got the impression that many of the towns and villages in this area were fairly new, and wondered whether the original ones were destroyed in the War. There'd been an awful lot of bombing going on around here – the key city of Hamburg, the crucial port of Bremerhaven, close to the Dutch border and all.

Such reminders inevitably led us to muse about what the hell all the people we saw, particularly those who were our parents' age, were doing during the War. Yet was it fair to hold "ordinary Germans" accountable for the acts of their government? Most Americans I'd ever heard talking about World War II seemed to think so – the same ordinary Americans who were seething about the treachery of people like me for refusing to participate in their unjust war in Vietnam. Would recent revelations about atrocities like Mỹ Lai cause them to change their views? I doubted they would feel *they* were accountable, even those who avidly (or rabidly) supported America's stupid War in Vietnam!

A powerful momentum of public opinion had been building up for a long time in the US, particularly in the two decades following World War II, with the second "Red Scare". The first Red Scare, 1917-1920, in the years starting with and immediately following the Russian Revolution of 1917, when the Communists (the Reds) overthrew the Czar, and quickly replaced one absolute tyranny with another. Apparently the first tyranny had posed no threat to Americans and could be blithely ignored.

Although the Russians (the Soviet Union, the USSR) were on "our" side during World War II, once the Nazis had been defeated, Stalin began rapaciously grabbing most of Eastern Europe, giving the American right wing a made-to-order excuse for whipping up fear and hatred against any ideas that could be labelled "communist" or "socialist" (while blurring the differences), and the second "Red Scare" was underway.

The next major source of fuel for this scare came in 1949, when the

Russians – the "red devils" – got The Bomb, bringing with it the world's first threat of thermonuclear war. The threat was heightened the next year, with the beginning of the Korean War (1950-53). Korea had been partitioned into North (Communist dictatorship) and South (capitalist dictatorship) at the end of World War II. Then on June 25th, 1950, North Korea's self-anointed Great Leader, Kim Il Sung, decided to invade the South, and the counter-attack was on (officially under UN auspices). This was when the second Red Scare really got going, under its demagogical Republican champion, Senator Joseph McCarthy. People all over America (notably teachers, actors, writers) began losing their jobs if they were even suspected of present or past affiliation with the American Communist Party – including guilt by association.

The influence of the Red Scare continued unabated through the mid-war 1952 presidential election, in which a politically inexperienced but well-decorated WWII general, Dwight Eisenhower (Republican), roundly defeated the moderate Democratic Illinois governor, Adlai Stevenson. Although "roundly defeated" is reflected in the 55-44% margin of victory in the popular vote, it required the Byzantine and frankly undemocratic provisions of the Electoral College to make the victory lopsided: 39-9 in the number of states carried. Eisenhower's running mate was a guy called Richard Nixon (who would eventually play a role in the Vietnam War...).

As McCarthy grew bolder, his smear tactics became increasingly aggressive – and influential on the American public, who could witness them on the new medium of television. He eventually went overboard, and was officially censured by the Senate in 1954. But the Red Scare didn't stop there. The Eisenhower administration fanned the flames by applying the "domino theory" (if one Southeast Asian country "falls" to communism, all of the other countries in the region will fall too), specifically to Vietnam. Thus, in 1955 Eisenhower sent a "Military Assistance Advisory Group" to train South Vietnamese army personnel, marking America's first direct military involvement in that country. And we all know what that led to.

Getting back to our road trip in 1969,[4] Jeanette and I were hoping that the growing protests of the minority anti-war movement would become a majority one day, and sweep Nixon and Kissinger out onto the street in the next elections

---

4 As the author of this book, I am duly authorized to digress, according to article 5549623, C-section, of whatever.

in 1972. Hope is free, isn't it? And the Red Scare, or Red Menace, is still ongoing as I write this. Except that for some idiotic reason "red" is also the modern American term for the *conservative* Republican party, simply because both words begin with *re-*! Go figure.

Anyway, we reached the Dutch border at around 11 AM on December 16th, 1969, and entered a small country with a dichotomy that baffled me. There were *two* names for the country (Holland and The Netherlands), *two* names for its currency (guilders and florins) and *two* capital cities, Amsterdam (for domestic affairs) and Den Haag (for international affairs). And suddenly there were windmills everywhere, the farmland was now almost flatter than flat, and we crossed one canal after another, many with drawbridges of striking design. Sheep and dairy cows were in abundance. Sometimes there are real reasons for stereotypes.

The first town we stopped in was Groningen, a charming place with numerous quaint-looking restaurants we couldn't afford. But I was unable to resist the opportunity to reacquaint myself with Ritmeester Livarde cigarillos in the same small purple tin cases I sometimes enjoyed courtesy of The Emporium. This time I had to pay for them. We again stocked up on what we needed for our lunchtime and bedtime sandwiches, and cheap wine, and we stopped along the way to Leeuwarden to deal with the unabated hunger brought on by ocular inspections of the eateries of Groningen.

Leeuwarden was a real treat – amazingly picturesque and cozy. We bought some Dutch chocolate, and spent some time lazing about in the old town with its charming homes. We noticed, first in Groningen and even more in Leeuwarden, that very many Dutch homes were built abutting the sidewalk, yet had huge picture windows without curtains. They seemed to be designed to make looking straight into people's living rooms, kitchens and lives not merely possible, but unavoidable. The homes themselves were pristine, like showcases.

As the sun was approaching the horizon (not that it ever rose terribly high above it that day), we decided to head toward the locks that marked the beginning of the enormous dike (*Afsluitdijk*) that enabled Holland to reclaim quite a lot of land from the North Sea. We'd heard the legend of the boy who saved everyone from drowning by plugging a leak in the dike with his thumb, so of course we had to stop and have Mike take a photo of Jeanette and me doing just that (except that we had our thumbs in the *outside* wall of the dike…).

There was a campsite along the dike causeway, but it was gated and closed. As dusk was settling in, we tried heading out along a narrow, isolated road in search of a place to pull over for the night, but were unsuccessful. We were traveling in the general direction of Amsterdam, which we fully intended to visit, but we didn't want to spend the night there, since we felt it might be tricky to find a suitable campsite in town. We soon arrived at a little town called Edam, known for its spherical cheeses covered in bright red wax. As we drove slowly through the town, we were bowled over by its Lilliputian charm and fascinating personality. Since only a few establishments were still open, we tried to find a place to park our car for the night and have time to purchase some additional provisions. We saw a sign with a campground symbol out by a lake called Markenmeer, but the campsite was also closed. We decided to park along a small canal connected to the lake, only a few minutes' walk from the heart of town. Nobody else was around, and it was very cold and damp, but above freezing. First we walked around the little town, and got a big red Edam cheese to meet our cheesy needs for a week or two (we didn't need a fridge...). After a short, brisk tour, we needed no more sights or chill that evening. It was getting pretty dark.

When we got back to the car, the lights of Edam were glistening around us and there were lots of stars reflected in the lapping water of the canal as we ate our evening meal in the cramped shelter our car afforded. We were freezing in the chill. We'd already made a habit of procuring a bottle of wine during the day for a shared nightcap, and we scrunched ourselves into the sleeping bags, listened to the silence, occasionally breaking it with our comments, and fell asleep as only those can do who combine naïve youth with a lack of affordable options.

When we awoke the next morning, we couldn't see out our windows, not because they were steamy, but because of thick layers of ice, inside and out. Nor could we hear the lapping of the water in the canal. We opened the door of the Saab to a new landscape. The canal had frozen over. Huge icicles had formed on the posts and railings that ran along the canal. Thick white frost covered every surface of every visible object, and the lake appeared to be frozen as well, although visibility was limited to a few meters from the shore by a thin freezing fog. Mike almost fell into the canal trying to get some water to use for shaving (I didn't bother). An added difficulty was keeping the frost from reforming on the rearview mirror the instant he scraped it off.

Our plans were to head straight into Amsterdam – normally about half an hour's drive away – and we longed for a café in which we could begin thawing out, externally and internally. But the heavy, Sisyphean morning traffic into the well-worn and complicated streets and avenues of Amsterdam threatened to turn us, in our Tantalean quest for relief from hunger and chill, into three bundles of raw nerves. At last we spotted the desired combination of a café and a parking space with a long enough time limit to enable us to rejoin the more outwardly civilized ranks of the human race.

Our curiosity and spirit of adventure also returned as we drove on and we left our car in the next free parking space we happened to find, then headed on foot into yet another unknown: the streets and sights of central Amsterdam. Although it made a much dirtier impression than Malmö, and was still bitingly cold, there were plenty of interesting things to do in a city where the number of canals seemed almost equal to the number of streets, all lined with charming old buildings.

We joined a free tour of a diamond-cutting works out of purest curiosity. The tour ended in a showroom with staff waiting to serve anyone who looked like they might have even a little more money than we had (they didn't bother about us much). We took in the Municipal Museum as well as the National Museum, and were awed by the Rembrandts and the other Dutch Masters. When we stopped at a post office to send some postcards, Mike attracted some attention by getting caught between a wall and a swinging door. He emerged uninjured only to be attacked by a near-sighted pigeon. Then we visited major collections of paintings by Max Ernst and Vincent Van Gogh, before ending up at a Chinese restaurant that served delicious food in huge portions – our first culinary treat of the trip.

As Mike's pockets were considerably deeper than ours, he decided to spend the night at the Swiss Hotel (now renamed and refurbished), in central Amsterdam (a 2-minute walk from Amsterdam's Red Light District – no connection intended), while Jeanette and I headed back to our spot along the canal in Edam, happy to have the extra space and the privacy. The two warm sleeping bags we'd bought for the trip could be unzipped all the way, then re-zipped together to form a single large one that gave us enough room to move, which kept us warmer than ever that night.

On Thursday morning, December 18th, we converted our double sleeping bag back into two singles, then drove into the city and picked up Mike at 10. He seemed refreshed and pleased with himself after a night in the hotel. That made three of us. Then we continued on to Haarlem, where we visited a huge, cold cathedral that reminded Jeanette of a mausoleum. We ate gigantic, stodgy Dutch pancakes for lunch, with plenty of thick, sweet syrup to restore our energy. Then we looked for some additional outer garments as allies in our battle against the unrelenting chill.

Our next stop was Den Haag, where we took a tour of the Peace Palace, a.k.a. the World Court of Arbitration. Our elderly guide enunciated every syllable – especially the word "arbitration" – with such exaggerated clarity (he made it sound like some guy named R.B. Trayshun) and with such hard American *rrrr*'s that we could scarcely contain our laughter until we were out of his earshot. I continued, in our guide's manner and accent, to conduct a private tour of the city for Jeanette and Mike. Den Haag impressed us as being as clean as Amsterdam was dirty. That night, the three of us had a huge campsite on the edge of town all to ourselves.

On Friday morning, we drove back through Den Haag and on to the more touristy but pleasant town of Delft, where we had our breakfast and bought the provisions for our lunch. We then drove on to Belgium, through industrial Rotterdam, and were very disappointed to be waved through at the border without a new stamp in our passports. Needless to say. (Here I was going to say that our disappointment was only needless to say because we weren't very European yet, but since it was needless to say, I didn't.)

Our first Belgian stop was Antwerpen. Although we passed through some lovely countryside along the way, and visited the train station, the city center, the old town, the cathedral, a castle museum on the water, and were impressed by the bustle of the city, my most salient memory of that bitterly chilly day was the intoxicatingly warming effect of a paper cone filled with hot and perfect French fries, procured at a stand along some street in the heart of town. Nothing had ever warmed the frozen me like that since the hot chocolate my mom prepared for me at the halfway point of my Thursday morning paper route in Oak Park when the temperature was -20°F (-29°C). If I were the fabled lion, and the chill were the thorn in my paw, those fries were my little mouse.

We left Antwerpen on the road to Gent in the early evening, intending to look for a campsite along the way. Instead we suddenly found ourselves almost entering Brussels, a city we'd considered visiting anyway, but its sheer size overwhelmed us as we approached it in the early evening darkness, and we quickly decided to head straight on through and save that metropolis for another day and another trip.

Instead we headed for Waterloo, where, after our evening wine and sandwiches, we collapsed for the night.

We arose in the early dawn, before sunrise, at eight o'clock on Saturday and drove along small roads, some of which were paved with c-o-b-b-l-e-s-t-o-n-e-s, to Mons, where we each had a delectable *café au lait* and a croissant for breakfast, before traveling on to the relatively small and ancient town of Tournai, where we visited the cathedral and bought succulent apricot pastries at the marketplace in the central square. After that brief stop, we made another agonizingly stampless border crossing into France.

Our first stop in *La République* was Lille, a city of similar size to Malmö, where we admired the opera house and the fact that a city of such a modest size had such an impressive one. We exchanged our guilders (or was it florins?) to French francs at a hotel, then went shopping for bread, salami, juice, Beaujolais and candy. Everyone was most friendly and helpful. I'd heard that the French appreciated it when foreigners at least made an effort to speak French – a reasonable courtesy, it seemed to me. They are certainly every bit as proud of their language – *la belle language* – as anyone else is of their own. Fortunately, I still remembered enough French not to have to fall back on English all the time.

The pride Francophones take in their language, however, seems qualitatively different to me from the pride of Anglophones. Although French speakers apparently demand a competing place for their language as the *lingua franca* of the world, those I've encountered seem to retain a certain amount of surprise and pleasure when outsiders attempt it, and even more when they manage. English speakers simply seem to *expect* the rest of the world to speak English – an assumption more than a wish – as though other languages were not real, but mere suspicious tricks to encrypt their speech. Had this attitude not been rooted in ignorance, it might be interpreted as arrogance. But perhaps one doesn't exclude the other.

We'd noticed in Belgium, and now even more in France, that the restaurants were not limited to the cities and towns, but were also sprinkled along the roadsides in between. We found such a place after leaving Lille, and enjoyed a delicious and modestly priced lunch, before taking a quick look at St. Omer, a very small town with a very big cathedral. Then we continued along scenic routes to Calais, arriving just before nightfall, which meant the late afternoon. This was, after all, the time of the winter solstice, and our latitude was close to that of Vancouver and its similarly short winter days.

We'd stopped for gas once in Germany and again in Holland, and had no problem finding gas pumps with the four percent two-stroke motor oil blend our car required, although in Holland we had to try two gas stations before we found such a pump. We crossed Belgium without the need for a gas station, but in France we couldn't find a pump with the pre-blended mixture at any gas station. Instead, we had to buy the special two-stroke motor oil in cans, then calculate how many liters of gas we needed to add to obtain the four percent without making the gas tank overflow, which made it hard to get a full tank, which made it necessary to stop more often. And we wouldn't see another pre-blended pump on our trip until we returned to Germany on our way back home.

The tourist information office in Calais delivered the biggest shock of our trip so far: the round-trip ferry crossing to Dover cost about $80, many times more than the crossing of equal length between Malmö and Copenhagen, and hugely in excess of what we budgeted for. Faced with the dilemma of an exorbitant cost and a firm desire to make it to London, we repaired to a deserted campsite (who else would dream of camping in the dead of winter?) to drown our sorrows in the Beaujolais we purchased in Lille.

We awoke on Sunday, December 21st, the winter solstice, still feeling victimized by the lack of affordable options that required us to submit to the slings and arrows of an outrageous ferry fare or to forego Britain. We drove to the terminal and paid the price. Then Mike and I went to the men's room and shaved.

The ferry itself – the vessel – was nice enough, but the 90-minute ride was very choppy, stirring up unpleasant memories as well as moistening brows and palms that generated growing anxiety in Jeanette and me to reach solid ground fast. The *Stefan Batóry* had made deep impressions on our middle ears. On arrival in Merrie England, we were picked out for a perfunctory spot check in customs, and finally got stamps in our passports – oh, the joy!

Just five days before, England added itself to the growing list of countries whose progress along the arduous road towards civilization now included banning the barbarity of the death penalty. Capital punishment was officially abolished in Sweden in 1921 (nobody had been executed since 1910). Although executions in our native land were down to only about a quarter of what they were in the first half of the 20th century, they were still a quarter too many, in Jeanette's opinion and mine. We hoped that the US would someday take that next step along the road, but what our country was doing in Vietnam gave us little hope of seeing that happen in the foreseeable future. Indeed, some states in the US are still executing scores of people as I write this (2016). Jeanette will never see abolition; I remain hopeful, perhaps naively.

I was aware of my spontaneous fight reactions in the fight-or-flight adrenalin response, and could well imagine that in an adrenalin rush, I might attempt (and perchance succeed) to kill or seriously maim anyone attacking Jeanette. But how was that an excuse for cold-blooded murder by the state? Society must, of course, protect its members, but if it doesn't strive to do so in more civilized ways, it disqualifies itself from any claims of moral superiority. In my opinion.

But I digress again, and return to Dover and environs, where we enjoyed a few extra degrees in the direction of warmth, just enough to take a bit of the edge off the chill that had so far accompanied us everywhere. We marveled at the chalk-white cliffs. Jeanette and I had seen those famous cliffs from the deck of our ocean liner, but I'd never seen them this close up. We were awed and exuberant. I was also awed and daunted by having to drive as though in a mirror.

Allow me to digress again to an example of my circuitous thinking. "As though in a mirror" is the literal translation of the Swedish "*Såsom i en spegel*", the title of an Ingmar Bergman film that was a favorite of mine, taken from a Biblical quote that is rendered in English as "through a glass darkly" (I Corinthians 13:12). But deep down inside, most people know (I've been told) that the original Bible was written in King James English, and everything else is just an inferior rendering.

Nevertheless, driving on the left felt a bit like walking down a winding stairway while holding a full-length mirror in front of me. Driving in the dark without lights might be another way of looking at it, but darkness without lights doesn't lend itself to a lot of looking – or driving either.

That aside, it was my first time ever in left-hand traffic. Mike had a little experience, but our anxiety levels peaked at every intersection, particularly those where we wished to turn, and each of the many roundabouts along our way became a nightmare of stress. There were also patches of fog thick enough to make even right-hand traffic treacherous. Fortunately, it was Sunday, with no rabidly stressed commuters to compete with.

Wherever the fog lifted, the countryside was nothing short of splendid as we drove along, passing through Hastings and White Rock before stopping in Brighton. Some years before, when I began reading Graham Greene's *Brighton Rock*, I thought the title referred to some sort of cliff, like the Rock of Gibraltar, only to discover that it was a special kind of hard stick candy. I was curious to try it. I thought Greene was making it up – the notion that there could be a stick of candy with writing across the diameter at the flat end, and that wherever you broke off the stick along its length, the writing was still there. But that's exactly what Brighton Rock (the candy) was, even if *Brighton Rock* (the book) was much more.

We spent some time walking around Brighton, and had a dinner that merely took away our hunger without diminishing our appetites for good food. As we left Brighton in the evening darkness and headed north towards London, the fog evolved into a dull, constant, enervating rain that turned both the left- and right-hand sides of the road into a blur of puddles in a totally light-absorbing black abyss of pavement, exacerbated by our unfamiliarity with the surroundings.

We ended up stopping for the night at a layby between the highway and some train tracks. For once we were not alone in using it as a campsite; we shared it with a few other cars and a trailer, as well as a group of 10 or more men, women and children of all ages. Their stay seemed to be considerably longer than ours, judging by the fact that they had clothes hanging on lines outside their trailer, in the rain, probably getting even wetter than when they first hung them there. Jeanette and I strolled over to have a chat. They told us they were travelers. We said that we were also travelers. They looked at each other in some surprise, then began laughing. We laughed too, talked for a while, and said good night. Mike and I took sponge baths before retiring.

At that time, we had no idea that "travelers" in Britain referred to Gypsies. Nor did we realize that some people would one day consider "Gypsies" to be a pejorative term for the Romani people. Nor can I know whether "Romani" will someday come to be considered pejorative as well, to be replaced by something else. The people we met were, in any case and by any name, very nice people. And *words aren't mean, people are mean!*

When we got up at around eight o'clock the next morning, Monday, it was no longer raining. We cleaned out the car, shook the reindeer skins, rearranged all our belongings, waved goodbye to our friendly fellow travelers, and set off on our rather short hop to London. We stopped for a bite of breakfast in the village of Leatherhead (Surrey), before pressing on. We decided that we would only drive as far into London as was necessary to be within the range of the Tube. The first Tube station we spotted was called Tooting, so we stopped the car without tooting and began exploring the area on foot. We had the completely unexpected good fortune to find a bulletin board that listed a number of nearby bed-and-breakfast accommodations. We picked one and located it just up the street, at 43 Ritherdon Road, run by Mr and Mrs McIntyre. They had two small rooms available, clean enough and cheap enough. The only drawback was the heating – strange gas-fired units that had to be fed with tokens we could purchase from our landlords. They suggested only using them while we were in our rooms, but not at night. We were all settled in by noon.

Our first ride on the Tube took us to Piccadilly Circus, by way of Elephant and Castle. How strange it seemed to me to be in an English-speaking country, yet with many words and usages that were totally new for me. Jeanette and Mike had been to London once before, and Jeanette had briefed me; I was not to expect any flying trapezes or lions in Piccadilly. I was already marveling at all the fanciful names of pubs we'd been seeing ever since Dover, but I still felt a bit like a stranger in my own linguistic home. That names and signs would be different in Sweden, Denmark, Germany, Holland, Belgium and France was to be expected. But here in England? "Dual carriageway"? Really? Experience was continuing to chisel away at my multiple walls of naiveté.

None of us was prepared for the increasing crowds of commuters and Christmas shoppers we met as the Tube lurched towards Piccadilly Circus, nor that they would increase further when we emerged from the depths and made our way across the Circus towards Regent Street, then up to Oxford Street and over to Marble Arch. Unbelievable masses of people, last-minute Christmas shoppers, of course. My first impressions of the red double-deck buses and black boxy taxis were that I'd stepped into a storybook.

We walked and walked, taking in many of the traditional tourist sights on foot in the first few hours: Hyde Park, Buckingham Palace, Westminster Abbey, Big Ben and the Houses of Parliament. We had lunch in Haymarket Street, went to a play in Soho, had dinner at a cheap place near Piccadilly, and got back to very chilly rooms and icy beds in Tooting at around midnight. Fortunately, we'd already purchased a couple of tokens from our landlords, to dispel the worst of the clamminess as we undressed. And we were able to sleep.

We needed one more token just to be able to get our clothes on the next icy morning. The bathroom down the corridor had no shower, and the hot-water tap yielded only a lukewarm dribble that cooled off long before the tub could be filled with enough water in which to bathe. We decided not to bother. It wasn't as though we'd been warm enough to perspire at any point on the trip so far. The breakfast part of the B&B was my first encounter with what I would later learn to call (and avoid) a "full English": fried eggs, fried sausages, fried tomatoes, fried bread, fried mushrooms and baked beans. Well aware that *de gustibus non est disputandum*, I gagged at the sight of it, then ate the sausage, bread and tomatoes. The tea was excellent. It wasn't fried.

This time, we decided to take a double-decker into town in order to see where we were going and everything along the way. In those days, London had such a different feeling compared to every North American city I'd ever visited. There were only a handful of tall buildings, and they were spread out; one didn't feel dwarfed. There were countless small neighborhoods, each with its own small-town center and feeling, like tiny bubbles in lather, sticking together without merging, owing to nearly invisible membranes. There were relatively few long straight streets with sides that converged at the horizon. Instead, one could only see a few blocks ahead before the street curved or bent, further reinforcing the feeling of manageable size and nearness. It was only when trying to get from one end of London to the other, or to leave London, that the immensity of it became apparent as a sort of penalty for one's having the audacity not to stop at all the pubs along the way.

Anyway, we went back to Buckingham Palace to watch the pageantry of the Changing of the Guard. Neither Jeanette nor I could take any of it – the whole royalty business – seriously. It felt like Hallowe'en. I think Mike shared this view, although he wasn't given to the kind of running commentary on everything with which Jeanette and I were wont to fill silence. Besides, he had to leave us for a while to go to the American Embassy to apply for a new passport, as he hadn't realized that the five-year passport he acquired in early 1965 for his and Jeanette's trip to Europe was about to expire.

The Guard was still changing by the time he returned from making his application. From the Palace we headed to the Tate Gallery, where I'd been told we would find the biggest collection anywhere of the paintings of J.M.W. Turner, with their astoundingly layered (I was certain he never had to roll them up!) and diffuse skies and seas that defied simple visual focus. Jeanette and I spent the rest of the afternoon enthralled there, while Mike again left us to pick up his new passport. In the evening, we walked to Marble Arch, ate at a pub, then wandered around until about nine o'clock before taking the Tube back to Tooting. We were rather exhausted.

After an identical breakfast on Christmas Eve, we again took the bus into town, this time to Trafalgar Square. Our intention was to do a little shopping for clothes, but since the prices and our budget couldn't agree on the feasibility of that idea, we abandoned it. Instead we went to Charing Cross Road to visit the bookstores, then went to a pub for our evening meal. We ended the day in the West End, watching Dudley Moore in Woody Allen's *Play It Again Sam*, which made us laugh our cheeks wet.

On Christmas Day, London suddenly came to a standstill, and the streets were deserted, conditions that unleashed unprecedented levels of boldness in us to explore our unfamiliar surroundings by car. After the usual wholesome breakfast, during which we were able to use words to inform the McIntyres that we'd be leaving the following morning, we drove comfortably through the vacant streets past the Albert Hall and St Paul's, along Fleet Street and through Chelsea. Then, on a whim, we decided to find out what Oxford was all about, hoping unsuccessfully to find an open countryside restaurant along the way. In Oxford, we were too hungry to make an extensive search for eateries, and instead of a delectable establishment, we pounced on the first open place we chanced upon, only to find it detestable (in terms of both food and service). But Oxford itself was very impressive, fairly reeking of venerable learning and retching with hallowed traditions whose *raisons d'être* were lost in the mists of time, *raisons* hidden in a pudding, as it were. We had a great afternoon there. It was a Christmas like none other had been for any of us. We returned along blissfully empty roads to our abode in Tooting and spent the evening using our tokens, while packing, sitting around talking and laughing in our little corner of the McIntyre dwelling.

True to our promise to the landlords, we departed immediately after another full English, and headed eastward out of London towards Dover, again enjoying a remarkable lack of traffic, not having been aware of England's Boxing Day holiday. Along the way, we stopped for a couple of hours in Canterbury that I might better equip myself for the tales I would be telling. On the steps of the great cathedral, the seat of the Archbishop himself, I discovered too late that the architectural formations above the steps were a favorite hangout of the local pigeons, and on this damp and chilly morning I slipped in their shit and fell flat on my own seat, rather than the archbishop's, to the great mirth of Jeanette and Mike. I swore on those steps to a degree that might have led to my excommunication by Archie Himself (had I ever been communicated in the first place).

Once I'd wiped and scraped off the worst of it, and found a place to wash my hands, my equilibrium was largely restored (albeit with some growling), and we proceeded on to Dover, I with slightly greater distain for the Church (and for pigeons) than before. The small hamlets and patchwork hills calmed me further, and our late afternoon crossing at three was calmer than our previous one. The darkness was nearly total by the time we reached Calais.

We decided to head for someplace warmer; that would be "sunny Spain", wouldn't it? We studied a map and found a route through western France, where we could enter Spain near San Sebastián in the northeastern corner, then proceed onwards towards Madrid, and figure out where to go once we got there.

On the arrival of our ferry in France, we chose not to become embroiled in the traffic of Calais, but drove straight on to Boulogne. We spent a couple of hours walking around the old part of that fine city, along the castle wall and inside the cathedral. Before driving on, we bought provisions for our evening meal, then drove about 20 kilometers outside the city, in the direction of Abbeville, and camped in our car by the roadside.

It was Saturday again. We woke up with the daylight and drove on to the small town of Abbeville for our breakfast of croissants and *café au lait*. We liked Abbeville very much, despite the ruins that served as unsettling reminders of the devastation of World War II. Those reminders awoke in us some subconscious perceptions that began to emerge as soon as we entered France, perhaps even before, in Belgium, but were now ubiquitous: small shrines set up all along the roadsides, at just about every crossroads and curve.

These shrines contained an image of some saint or other religious celebrity or symbol, and sometimes flowers in varying degrees of freshness. We soon realized that the shrines were set up at the sites of fatal road accidents, presumably by the family members of the deceased. What I couldn't figure out was why they would set up a shrine to a saint who clearly failed miserably in his or her mission to safeguard and protect the person who'd died. If the shrines were at the sites of *near* accidents, there might be a case for appreciating protection, however coincidental, but at least there would have been no proof of a *lack* of protection.

I realized that this was largely a Catholic thing, but Jeanette and Mike were unable to provide any explanation to my musings about shrines to protectors who'd fucked up. Then I began to think more deeply about the eye-on-the-sparrow claims of God's watchfulness over His Own, how people prayed fervently for someone's life to be spared, yet proclaimed God's goodness whether they survived or perished. Does mere observation count as "watchfulness"? Isn't there any protective intervention involved in the definition? Doesn't the job description for a watchman include taking action to *prevent* devastation and destruction? Is he or she just supposed to *watch* intruders intrude or fires to break out and make a note of it while doing nothing else? Or what about the fervent eruption of gratitude to God when a lone survivor of an earthquake is pulled from the rubble – when hundreds in that same rubble have perished? And who's in control of the earthquake? In human behavior, having the ability to prevent a tragedy and failing to do so would probably be called criminal negligence.

The problems inherent in religious beliefs were beginning to emerge from the cracks in their pseudo-rationality. I wasn't yet prepared to think that Jesus was anything but good, but I was beginning to have serious doubts about his dad. I would have to think more about this someday soon.

When we looked at the map to see where we'd go after Abbeville, and also looked at the calendar, we saw how big France was and how the days were beginning to move more quickly, despite their having turned the corner to start getting longer again. We would have to be more selective if we were going to get to Madrid and back home before we risked jeopardizing our newly won residence permits. We had no factual grounds for that anxiety, but we felt it all the same. And then there was the risk of defaulting on our rent.

As a result, we simply drove on when we got to Rouen (except for a brief stop at a grocery store), and Le Mans (except for a pit stop), finally reaching Tours, where we moored briefly to enjoy a walkabout before settling down for the night at a layby a bit south of the city. Suddenly I made a connection to a jingle my high school history teacher had taught us: *"732, the battle of Tours, Charles Martel defeated the Moors."* Maybe I'd been paying more attention than either of us thought.

We got up in the dark, just after seven the next morning, and made a quick breakfast of the bread and juice we had with us. I seemed to have picked up a pretty bad cold in London, and all of us were becoming kind of weary from roughing it in the chill and darkness. Nevertheless, we traveled on, through Poitiers and Angoulême and into countryside dominated by mile after mile of vineyards, until we reached the town of Bordeaux, which we hadn't expected to be so modern.

Heading southward from Bordeaux, the landscape began changing considerably as we approached the border to Spain. It was becoming more mountainous and we were seeing more woodland and almost swamp-like vegetation. The streets in the towns and villages were wider now, for some reason nobody gave us, and the houses showed an influence we associated with Spanish. Mike even ventured to say that Bordeaux and the area around it reminded him of the merchant-filled streets of Saigon. He'd never mentioned visiting Saigon previously, at least not to us.

The next stop was Bayonne, which was nice, but we found the small towns nearby even nicer, particularly Saint-Jean-de-Luz, with its spectacular setting along the Atlantic coast just a few kilometers from the border. We took a long walk along the shore, among the rocks and sand and had some exquisite coffee at an oceanside café. Just beyond town, we found what looked like a suitable place to park for the night: a little unmarked gravel road or trail up a slight hill, about 50 meters from the main road, near an old concrete wartime bunker. It wasn't dark yet, and the view of the ocean was majestic, with the Pyrenees in Spain not far to the south. We decided to just spend the remaining daylight enjoying the view, our sandwiches and our wine. The grassy terrain around us was a bit windswept, almost like a heath, and the wind off the Bay of Biscay made the waves dramatically entertaining as day turned to dusk, then quickly to night. It was definitely our best layby spot yet, one of the best spots ever.

We woke up shortly after eight the next morning, feeling rested and ready for Spain. As we were stretching ourselves awake and cleaning out the car, we saw a lone light-blue car drive slowly past us along the road below. Mike was shaving when we saw the same car return the other way, again driving slowly past the turnoff for the dirt trail up to our parking place. A minute or two later, while we were still stretching our night-cramped joints and muscles, the same car appeared a third time. It passed the entrance to our little trail even more slowly than before. Suddenly it stopped and with a great roar backed up "our" trail at full speed. When it got about 10 meters from our car, the driver slammed on the brakes and three men jumped out with drawn pistols, shouting something at us in French, but I was unable to make it out. Then they demanded – in English – to see our passports and car insurance, which we somehow conjured up as if out of thin air. Our hearts were pounding. It was unreal; we were unable to grasp what was happening. Then we noticed that they were flashing badges – a welcome sight, under the circumstances.

I tried to explain that we were tourists on our way to Spain, and that we had no idea who they were or why they were interested in us. Their leader nodded, barked something to the others, and they all put their guns away. Then he explained to us, in a mixture of French and English, that they were part of a special unit looking for Basque separatists (he called them terrorists). We were, as it turned out, in the heart of Basque country, of which we'd been blithely unaware. We knew absolutely nothing about them, except that I remembered from my linguistics course that Basque is one of the only languages in Europe that is not part of the Indo-European family, and is not related to any other language in Europe. Then they drove off abruptly, leaving us to get our hearts back down into our chests. Jeanette and I clung to each other. I'm not sure what Mike clung to; I hoped it wasn't bad memories.

After that unexpected start to this gray day, we were very, very wide awake – shaken, not *störd* (the Swedish word for "disturbed, disrupted", pronounced almost like the English "stirred") – and proceeded cautiously the few kilometers to the Spanish frontier. Spain being under Franco's dictatorship and all (a fact we conveniently suppressed when coming up with our plan to add that country to our itinerary), we began to fear what was to come, but our border crossing was undramatic. They didn't even stamp our goddamn passports.

What made us nervous was that our smirks and chuckles might burst out into full-blown laughter at the sight of several members of the *Guardia Civil*, Franco's special national police force, who stood there sternly scrutinizing everyone around them, with guns ready, not funny at all. The funny part was their shiny patent-leather hats, *tricornio*, which looked like high-gloss lacquered black saucepans perched on top of their heads, and with a lacquered trapezoidal back brim folded vertically upwards, as if the saucepan had backed into an immovable object behind it. The closest thing we'd seen to such headgear were those worn by members of the Mickey Mouse Club. It was pretty clear that they wouldn't have joined in our laughter.

But the humor was black and the laughter sardonic; Franco's boys were no joke. He seized power following the Spanish Civil War, in which the Nationalists – a group comprising right-wingers, monarchists and Catholic conservatives – banded together to overthrow the democratically elected left-wing Republicans (How about *that*, America?) in a bloody and treacherous three-year struggle. A number of artists were involved on the side of the Republicans, including Hemingway, who fought with the Abraham Lincoln Battalion, the American part of the International Brigade that also included Picasso, whose painting *Guernica* came to symbolize the horrors of war and oppression; and Garcia

Lorca, one of my favorite poets, who was executed by the Nationalists. The Franco dictatorship was a reality, and these Guardia Civil were living proof that Franco was still calling all the shots.

We stopped briefly in a small border town, Irun, before heading on to San Sebastián, which was rather nice, but gloomy, poverty-stricken, and in need of freshening up. Or it might have been our awareness of the political and ethnic oppression that informed our perceptions more than what we actually saw. Most of the shops were closed – we were probably too early – but we managed to find some breakfast at a bar. When we walked across the bridge, we gasped at the horrible stench of pollution. The river looked like it also served as the municipal sewer. Our conclusion was that the Basques were not a high priority for the Spanish Government, and that if facts were obtainable, they might well support our impressions of oppression.

From San Sebastián we headed out and up, into the Pyrenees, on narrow winding roads with almost no car traffic, but quite a few donkey- and ox-drawn carts and myriad little flocks of sheep, all without hymnbooks. We intentionally chose a more scenic road (the one less traveled by) over a bigger highway, preferring to experience the Pyrenees rather than just get beyond them. Although the first "summit" was a mere 617 meters above sea level, the climb was steep and the view breathtaking. There was a timeless charm about the greens and browns of the vegetation and rocks, set off by the white patches of the flocks. We had to stop several times just to soak it in.

Although Jeanette was an excellent driver, she said she preferred Mike and me to share all of the driving on this trip. But I ended up with the lion's share (apart from England), since Mike seldom volunteered. If I asked who should drive, he deferred to me. If I really didn't want to drive, I would have to rephrase the question, and *ask* him to drive, to which he also invariably acquiesced. (Note to readers: When I mention that "we" thought or felt one thing or another on this trip, I'm referring to Jeanette and me, as Mike seldom related his thoughts or feelings, and we quickly began to feel awkward about the obvious awkwardness we were causing him by asking him all the time.)

After leaving the Pyrenees, we came to Pamplona (*Iruña* in Basque), primarily known to me through Hemingway and his (in my view) weird and morbid fascination with bullfighting in general, and in particular with Pamplona's annual "running of the bulls" festival, in which one or more people is inevitably gored or trampled severely or fatally along the narrowest streets. We were surprised to see the abundance of uniformed policemen, including those with the funny hats, as though they were expecting a riot. Maybe their numbers were simply to keep the face of oppression in the face of the oppressed? Anyway, our overall impression wasn't the best. The few people we met were not very friendly, but we *could* have met the only unfriendly ones for miles around, for all we knew. Or they could have been rightfully unhappy about their oppression and lost their ability to smile? We did manage to stock up on our usual grocery supply.

From Pamplona we continued south, down towards Madrid, which actually entailed *up*, into dry, hilly and sunnier countryside, liberally scattered with vineyards that our ignorance of Spanish wines kept us from benefiting from. With as little awareness that we were entering Basque country the day before, we left the heart of the Rioja wine district without so much as stopping for a bottle, instead taking a turnoff for Soria and continuing to climb slowly, as evidenced by the increasing frequency of patches of snow along the roadsides and on the surrounding hills. It was so beautiful that we longed to return even before we'd left it behind. Soria itself was very picturesque and offered a suitable campsite for the night. As the sun pretty much determined how much sleep we got, we were getting plenty of it – up to 12 hours a night – but that night we all woke up at midnight, gasping for breath. We'd forgotten to leave a window cracked and had nearly used up the oxygen (we were at our highest altitude for the trip, over 1,000 meters).

The next morning, instead of pistol-wielding secret police, we woke up to a burgeoning blanket of new snow. The frozen highway was crawling with trucks, trucks, and more crawling trucks. Ours was the only car in sight. The further we went, the more snow we met, both on the road and falling from the sky, and the slower the truck traffic. We had two good snow tires on our front-wheel-drive Saab, but since we felt it could be prudent to have greater protection under the circumstances, we stopped at a gas station to see about buying chains. They didn't have any new ones in our size, and right before our eyes the proprietor raised the price drastically on an old rusty pair. We bristled at that, and decided to rely solely our snow tires. We proceeded cautiously.

We hadn't driven far before we came to a roadblock. The police were checking that trucks and cars were properly equipped for driving in snow. The first officer duly noted our snow tires (albeit only two of four) and waved us on. A bit further on, however, we were stopped again by a crack young officer who flatly informed us that we would not be allowed to proceed unless we bought snow chains at the establishment behind him, where a sign with poorly crossed-out amendments indicated that the price was rising faster than the snow could fall. Besides, it would take hours to reach the front of the snaking line of unprepared truckers anxious to put on chains despite rip-off prices. My Spanish was worse than my French, and his English was somewhere in between. Somehow, among the three languages, I argued and pleaded and cajoled our case: that if snow tires were good enough for Arctic Sweden, surely they ought to be plenty good enough for Sunny Spain. He vacillated between irritation, amusement and growing impatience. I doubt that he was much swayed by my semi-lingual arguments themselves, but he couldn't contain a smile or two as I gesticulated histrionically. He eyed the growing line of trucks behind us and eventually waved us on through, shaking his finger at us as if to say we were on our own and had been given fair warning. (*"I warn, Señor, I warn!"*)

All this time, we'd been driving on a plateau, a fact we'd been unaware of until we left the snow behind us and began descending into Guadalajara, which bore evidence of both Roman and Moorish occupation, yet seemed relatively primitive to us – and very muddy. We strolled around in the center of town for a while, picked up some groceries. We were all dying for chocolate and found a bar of it in the supermarket. It turned out to be unsweetened baking chocolate and put us off Spanish chocolate for the rest of the trip. At last we headed onward to the bustling capitol city of Madrid.

We parked as close to the heart of things as possible and spent the afternoon at the Prado, fearing it might be closed the next day, New Year's Eve. Well into the evening on December 30th, there were large crowds of shoppers and others strolling and strutting about. We went into a huge department store – El Corte Inglés, I think there were seven storeys of it – where things seemed to be fairly cheap, except that everything is expensive if you have too little money. We made a few purchases, including a wineskin. We'd seen them in films, but had never used one. We felt it could be a good way to obviate the need for glasses at our roadside stops, and the subsequent washing of them every evening.

The shape of the wineskin was something like a large curved teardrop, with a valve at the upturned point. You filled it by unscrewing the valve and emptying a bottle into the wineskin. To help keep me warm, I bought a lined suede jacket at a bargain price. Unfortunately neither our budget nor our car had room for a Spanish guitar. When we got back to the car, we were very displeased to find a parking ticket on the windshield.

It was getting past our bedtime, and on a road out of town we had to settle for a campsite where we weren't entirely alone for a change. We sat and looked at our purchases while enjoying our evening meal – and we tried out our wineskin. To drink from it, you had to hold it up with the valve upwards, then open the valve, with the wineskin about 10 centimeters from and slightly higher than your open mouth. Then you had to tilt the valve towards you, keeping the distance and aiming carefully to get every drop of the wine down your throat and none down your clothes or splashing off your teeth or cheeks, all the while giving the skin a steady squeeze, and swallowing as fast as your squeeze dictated. Then you tilted the valve upwards again while relaxing your squeeze, all in one motion. We were remarkably successful, or had great beginner's luck. Or perhaps we just hated wasting wine.

On the morning of New Year's Eve we again awoke to a light snowfall. So much for the warmth of sunny Spain. We paid our modest camping fee, headed back into town and located the American Express office. We decided that we would indulge in a hotel for New Year's Eve, provided American Express could find us a cheap one in the heart of town. To our delight, they did. We asked what to do about the parking ticket, and they said we needn't bother about paying the fine. We moved the car near the Prado, which was also just a block or two from our hotel. It was easier to park there, since the museum was closed that day.

After we checked into our rooms, which were small but cozy and warm, we were thrilled to be able to take a decent hot bath and say goodbye to multiple thin layers of sweat and grime. We were prepared to spend a relaxing afternoon strolling around the town, do some more shopping, and perhaps get a delightful Spanish meal, whatever that might mean. None of us had eaten Spanish food before, and because of the language, we sort of assumed it would be like Mexican, but realized that an assumption like that was as absurd as assuming that Yorkshire pudding would be available anywhere in America because the language was roughly the same.

When we emerged from the hotel in the early afternoon, clean, refreshed, hungry, and full of expectations about what a city like Madrid might put on for New Year's Eve, we were stunned to find the streets deserted. Everything – shops, cafés, bars and restaurants – was dark, closed and shuttered. But we had to find something to eat! Our hotel was very small; it had only a breakfast room, and this was not the breakfast hour. Hardly a soul was out and about; we stopped several people to ask about a place to eat that was open, and someone finally directed us to the department store we'd visited the day before.

We found it easily enough, but it looked very different. Although the main entrance was open, it was dark inside. A signboard near the door announced that the cafeteria on the top floor was open, and there were decoratively uniformed attendants standing on either side of the entrance to a path cordoned off by velvet ropes, leading through the darkened store directly to the elevators. We figured that a cafeteria would be a great idea – we wouldn't have to figure out the Spanish and end up ordering *cojones* – and it would allow us to take whatever looked good. The elevator delivered us non-stop to the brightly lit and nearly deserted cafeteria on the top floor. We found some good food at reasonable prices, and took plenty of time; we had no other prospects for New Year's Eve in a city that shut down and went to bed, which would be all that awaited us.

When we finally finished our meal and lazed about over post-prandial coffee, we made our way back to the elevator, pushed the button for the ground floor and leaned back against the walls as we began to descend, still glowing from our meal. After just a few seconds of its downward journey, the elevator stopped – on the sixth floor. The doors opened. All the lights were on! It was *crowded* with shoppers! Same thing on the fifth, fourth, third, second and first floors. With our jaws hanging down to our collarbones, we exited the building to discover crowded, noisy streets. It was like we'd stepped into a time machine instead of an elevator, a parallel universe, a science fiction movie. The explanation came down to a single word: *siesta*!

The contrast was nearly indescribable. There were massive celebrations everywhere, bands and parades, fireworks and sparklers, Catholic processions with men in dresses, holding gilded statues of virgins and saints. Others wore even more outlandish costumes. Along one street, the crowd seemed especially excited, and our curiosity drove us to discover why. The cause was apparently a bullfighter in the full splendor of his bejeweled bullfighting gear, in the center of a tight ring of worshippers slowly making their way towards Puerta del Sol. He was strutting and swaggering regally to a degree that would make celebrities at the Oscars look like they were staggering and stumbling, relatively speaking. Of course *he* clearly knew who he was, enough to compensate for our and anyone else's lack of knowledge. We had the gall to ask someone in his entourage, who replied witheringly that El Cordobés was only the greatest bullfighter that ever lived, Señor, as if we were idiots.

We went to a bar and had wine and crab, then to a lovely restaurant and had paella, then ate the 12 grapes we'd been told that Spanish New Year's tradition dictated, then just wandered around watching all the dancing and merriment until well into the new year. Finally, exhausted, tipsy, and bubbling with joy, we went back to our hotel, only to find the street door locked. A kind policeman somehow managed to let us in for 10 pesetas, and we lay awake listening to the din of the celebrations until they finally began dwindling to a halt at around half past four.

On New Year's Day, we didn't get up until 10, then showered, had breakfast, checked out and headed off in our Saab in the welcome sunshine in the direction of Valencia. We were determined to do a little driving along the Mediterranean before heading for home. Jeanette bought a guide book and was reading about a few possibly interesting places along the way. The first and most spectacular of these was Toledo, about 75 kilometers south-southwest of Madrid, where we arrived shortly before noon. Perched high on a bluff in a bend in the Tagus River, the small, exquisite city dates back to the Roman times, with strong architectural and cultural influences from centuries of Moorish rule and a significant Jewish population – at least before the Inquisition and various other manifestations of the obstacles along the road to civilization contributed their chilling influences. The enchanting maze of narrow lanes, narrower alleys and even narrower paths, all of them uphill, made it easy to understand why El Greco was said to have done his finest work during the years he lived there.

From Toledo, we drove east and slightly north over very flat and arid red-soiled terrain to get a look at Aranjuez, which Jeanette's guidebook said was worth seeing and which I knew by name only, from a hauntingly beautiful eponymously titled Spanish guitar concerto by Joaquín Rodrigo; I had once been able to play a highly simplified version of it on my guitar. We were completely alone as we strolled around elegant fountains and through wistful gardens and grounds of the 16th century palace, apparently once the residence of some Spanish royalty, who like other members of such self-proclaimed exclusive bloodlines, could never accumulate quite enough wealth and opulence at the expense of the health and well-being of their subjects who, despite generations of subjugation, were never able to show quite enough groveling and subservience.

Soon after leaving Aranjuez, we noticed that our car was in rather acute need of a gas station. We finally found one out in the middle of the red-soiled super-flat nowhere, where the rain did by no means seem mainly to stay. There was of course no pump with the pre-blended mixture. A wizened and scrawny middle-aged man strolled out to see to our needs. He didn't speak a word of English. I pulled out my little English-Spanish dictionary to assure myself that "oil" was *óleo*. While he was grabbing the gas nozzle, I pointed at the gas tank and uttered that very word, smiling as I did so. He hesitated, looking puzzled. I repeated my gesture and word, and he put the nozzle back in its cradle, picked up a can of motor oil, and was just about to jam one of those spouts into the lid to open it when I stopped him, just in time, and searched feverishly in my dictionary for "two-stroke", in vain. I asked him to wait (*"¡Espere!"*), while I disappeared into the station to see if I could spot a can with a label that might possibly correspond to "*two-stroke* motor oil". There were plenty of dusty shelves, filled with dusty cans, and at last I spotted the magic words (in English) on a can on one of the higher shelves, which I couldn't reach. I went to the doorway and beckoned to him to come. I was very excited, and gestured at my find. He had a pole with a clamp on the end for retrieving cans from upper shelves. At last, after some error, I guided his reach to retrieve the very one I wanted. He took it down, wiped off some of the dust, looked at its English label uncomprehendingly, and led me back to the car, jammed the spout into the can, and attempted to raise the hood. *No, no, no!* I cried and pointed at the gas tank. His eyes went wide and he shook his head as if I'd just told him to pour whisky into a baby's bottle. I took the can from him, walked over to the gas tank and started pouring. He let out a loud guttural sound, a strange, strangled, muffled scream. Suddenly, out of nowhere, he was joined by several women spanning at least two generations, not counting a number of small children. After I'd emptied the two-stroke oil into the gas tank, I began pumping gas into the same tank. His strangled noises were no longer muffled. I just stood there, pumping gas, a big grin on my face, staring back and nodding at him and his friends or family. They seemed to be trying to figure out what planet I was from. Once I had the 24 liters of gas needed to achieve the right mixture, I returned the pump to its cradle and asked him how much. Once he regained control of his jaw, he was able to mumble a figure I understood. I counted out my pesetas and pressed them into his hand. I think I had to close his hand for him, around the money. He was paralyzed. As I took my seat in the car, all our spectators reacted instantly with a quick jerk backwards, as if on command or by reflex, perhaps fearing the car would explode when I turned the ignition key. Then we drove off, howling with laughter, me waving to them out my window. I could see them in the rearview mirror as they all moved out into the middle of the road, where they remained motionless until I could no longer see that far.

From there it was non-stop to Valencia. It was nearly 10 o'clock that evening before we had a tasty dinner at a cozy restaurant, but that late dining hour was not at all unusual in Spain, we understood. We didn't reach our campsite, just south of the city, until nearly midnight.

We spent the next morning walking around the Valencia city center, bought some food and had lunch by the sea – our first glimpse of the vast Mediterranean. My cold was still bothering me a lot, and the sight of the many orange groves and roadside stands we passed made a stop inevitable. We not only bought several dozen oranges, but also tangerines, almonds, figs and honey, all at astonishingly low prices. The oranges were sweet and juicy, and disappeared quickly as we continued on our way. I came to think of the vitamin C cures I'd been hearing about since I was a kid. It thought it couldn't hurt, and as we continued to observe the seemingly unending string of roadside fruit stands, with our orange supply rapidly dwindling, I stopped again, got out, told Jeanette and Mike I'd be right back, and returned with a long net containing around 10 kilos of lovely Valencia oranges, which I began wolfing down one after the other, as we headed northeast along the coast. Mike and Jeanette both had colds coming on too, and happily helped out on the oranges.

After some 150 kilometers we came to the remarkable ancient town of Peñíscola, a walled village built on a rock promontory that sticks out into the Mediterranean, joined to the mainland only by a sandbar. There was a 14th century castle on top for good measure. We simply had to stop and explore its steep, narrow cobblestone streets with spectacular lookout points over the sea and the mountains inland. The castle was certainly *grandissimo* in its day, for the rulers, at least. Now it was merely breathtaking.

On leaving the village, we stopped at a bakery and got some freshly baked bread, still hot, which Jeanette wrapped in a towel. Then we headed onwards another 150 km or so to a campsite along the coast in Alcanar, which meant that we were now in Catalonia, without having a clue that we were. The Catalans also had a language of their own (closely related to Spanish), but it was forbidden by the Franco regime.

We ate our still-warm bread with honey – a great break for me from oranges! – and wine from our wineskin, looking at the sea, reflecting on all we'd seen, heard, smelled, tasted, felt and thought on this somewhat wild and very wonderful trip that totally cleared our heads and hearts from all the anxieties of uncertain immigration issues. We hoped it might have cleared Mike's head of Asian issues as well....

We'd managed to do it all on a shoestring budget (it was that or no trip at all), but now that we'd reached the Mediterranean, we began to feel we'd reached our apogee, the final goal for the trip, a goal we hadn't been fully aware of ever having set. Our brains were switching to overload mode with all our impressions, and our financial reserves were becoming scarce indeed. It was time to head for home.

When I woke up the next morning, my cold was gone, or very nearly, but we all had splitting headaches. Jeanette's and Mike's tentative colds, unlike their noses, were now full-blown. Too many oranges for me and not enough for them? Bad wine? Weather not chilly enough? We took a walk along the sea, but got little relief. As we continued heading northeast, it began raining. We were now on bigger, faster highways, past Tarragona, and on towards Barcelona. The scenery along the way was sadly marred by all the billboards, commercial exploitation, and tourist traps. It stopped raining by the time we got to Barcelona, but it remained heavily overcast, rather like our moods, and we only made a perfunctory tour of the city (missing nearly every sight I would later come to love about the place), then drove out to the coast about 40 km beyond the city to a campsite. Just having the sea to look at meant a great deal.

On Sunday, January 4th, it was raining again when we woke up, late, and we headed for and crossed the French border without so much as a problem or a stamp. The weather soon cleared up, giving us sunshine for a while. That healed our strangely sour moods from the previous day. We stopped at the border town in France to exchange pesetas for francs and buy French pastries for our brunch.

We were reluctant to leave the sea behind, so we spent some time gathering seashells. Then we drove through the delightfully picturesque little town of Sète, our last stop along the Mediterranean, where we bought some local Muscat wine at roadside stands. We would now be steering pretty much due north across Europe. It was a bit foggy.

As we began heading inland, towards Nîmes, our car began acting up – losing power – forcing us to stop at a garage outside the city, in Uchaud, that Sunday afternoon. Jeanette's description is better than mine: "*Our mechanic was probably 15 years old and we were there 3 hours while he studied and practiced car mechanics. The car was worse off and finally another able worker came to advise jr. We needed spark plugs and must spend the night at this garage. It has been a trying night.*"

We woke up early at the gas station. The proprietor's wife (presumably the mother of yesterday's mechanic) went out to buy the spark plugs, and by 9:30 her mechanic husband had us rolling again, somewhat poorer. Now all we wanted was to get home.

We drove to Lyon mostly via the *autoroute*, which cost seven dollars, but it was fast. It was also quite scenic along the Rhône River Valley (no cowboys to love anyone so *truuue*) with mountains in the distance on either side. There were many fine laybys with stands selling delicious nougat, and when we left the *autoroute* to drive on smaller roads (we were making good time), we found them lined with stands selling fruit and wine as well.

We reached Lyon at around 1:30 and walked around the charming city center for most of the afternoon, before heading out for the small town of Mâcon, where we bought provisions for the evening meal. We ended up at a campsite about 20 km north of town.

In the morning we continued northward and stopped at a bakery in the first little town we came to. With a couple of huge (roughly 80 x 20 cm) loaves of warm, crisp French bread in tow, we found a spot to pull over and eat them with the lovely peach preserves we'd bought the day before at a market in Lyon.

Sometime after we passed Dijon, without stopping for mustard, we entered a no-man's land where we ran into a horror show. The temperature was dropping quickly as we proceeded north, and other aspects of the weather were changing too. Now we got the result: a thick freezing fog, combined with snowfall. Ice was forming rapidly, both on the outsides and the insides of every car window, despite our having the defroster and wipers running full blast. The fog continued to thicken and the snow to deepen incrementally, every minute. Mike was sitting beside me in the front seat, scraping furiously at the inside of the windshield, while Jeanette was doing her best on the side window on the passenger side. All this time, the road was becoming hillier and curvier and icier. Soon the sides of the road were no longer visible. I was creeping along, unable to see more than a meter or so ahead of us, even seconds after Mike scraped a section of the windshield right in front of me.

Time and space seemed to cease to exist, apart from the growing sense of panic inside our car. After an unknown amount of time, new layers of ice were building up on the outside of the windshield until I couldn't see a thing, yet I didn't dare to stop in case I was in the middle of the road and someone plowed into me from behind. But I had to go on, so I tried to drive close to the side of the road while avoiding the risk of driving off it. Mike rolled down his front passenger-side window, and Jeanette rolled down the rear driver's-side window, and as I crept along. They had to shout out when I was getting too close to anything dangerous on either side, like a rock, or a parked car, or an oncoming car, or a cliff with a 100-meter vertical drop.

The level of concentration required was horrific, yet we were all too focused to be terrified into chaos. I'm guessing that we'd passed Dijon at around 11 o'clock, hit the fog at around noon, some 70 km to the north, and began slowing down. The fog finally let up slightly in the late afternoon dusk as we were coming into Nancy, at about four o'clock, 150 km later, meaning an average speed of 30 km/h, and much of it around 10 km/h. The snow was deep and the fog was still there, although not as bad. We were all frozen stiff from driving with open windows, dying for toilets, starving and thirsty and big bundles of raw nerves.

We went into a small restaurant to use all of their facilities except the freezer. We picked a table that was closest to the biggest heater. We just sat there with food and coffee and emptied bladders and tried to stop shaking. When we were finally thawed out and calmed down, we had to decide how to proceed. We discovered that we could take a much bigger road out of Nancy, which meant it was more likely to be plowed and have better markings, and that it was a road that led to Luxembourg, only about 120 km due north, which we might as well visit.

Courageously or foolhardily, we set out once more in our Saab. As we passed Metz without stopping, we talked about how incredibly many fascinating places we were missing along the way, and how randomly we'd picked many of the places we stopped to visit, and how much we looked forward to being able to come back this way another time, when the weather was better and we had more time, more money, a better car and more security.

We reached Luxembourg at around 7.30 that evening. The wind was blowing and it was bitter, freeze-your-marrow cold. We looked for a small hotel, ready to pay almost all we had left to sleep in a warm bed and get a hot meal. We got lucky, very lucky. We found a small and inexpensive family hotel called the Beau Séjour. The owners, a Russian family, told us they had rooms for us, but that their restaurant was closed, because they were using it for their big family Christmas celebration; this was the big day – January 6th – when Russians celebrated Christmas. There must have been something in the look on our travel-worn, fog-frozen faces when they denied us access to their dining facilities, because the man and his wife – the proprietors – turned to each other and conversed briefly in Russian, then turned back to us and said that it would be bad luck for them to refuse to feed us at Christmas. (Sometimes traditions are *great*!)

So they let us into the restaurant, seated us at a table on the empty side of the dining room, and brought us a big tureen of hot potato soup and some fresh bread. Few meals have ever tasted so good or warmed us down to the bone like that one. The other side of the dining room was not empty: lots of family, extended family, maybe friends as well, filled the air with merriment – bursts of laughter, shouted toasts, squeals of delighted children, Russian folk songs increasingly vodka'ed off key. Their joy did nothing to detract from our feelings of purest pleasure to be there. The three of us finally went off upstairs to Jeanette's and my room to polish off the contents of our well-filled wineskin, before we kicked Mike out, climbed into our cozy bed, pulled the huge warm eiderdown comforter over us, and eventually drifted off to sleep.

What a pleasure it was to wake up in real beds, warm and comfortable, in Luxembourg! We went down to breakfast at nine o'clock, but having grown accustomed to good coffee since leaving England, we were disappointed by the diluted coffee-flavored fluid we found in the breakfast room. We had tea instead. After checking out and expressing our profound gratitude to our celebration-weary hosts, we walked around the center of town for a while and bought ourselves a big brown-glazed teapot and matching milk jug to bring home, a souvenir that filled a real practical need.

Home! For Jeanette and me, it was beginning to feel that way. We dared to hope that we'd crossed the first big hurdle towards making our new life together in Sweden. We somehow felt aware that we couldn't be aware of more than a fraction of the vastness it implied, and sometimes we would just stand there close to each other – in our room, in the street, in a restaurant, or by the sea – looking into each other's eyes, holding on to each other, living the feelings, lost in each other, blindsided by love, until Jeanette would start burrowing her chin into my breastbone, making me laugh uncontrollably.

The paralyzing cold of the evening before remained that morning, and we stopped at a café for some real coffee, before heading back to the car and on to the German border, which appeared quite suddenly, less than an hour later. Once again, no stamps in our passports. We decided to have a brief look around Bonn, about which we only knew that it was the capital of West Germany. Statues informed us that it was also the birthplace of Beethoven, but we didn't know a great deal about him yet either. Mike bought some clothes at a department store in the late afternoon, but since it was too cold to make further walking enjoyable, we drove off in the direction of Hannover and stopped at a deserted layby for the night.

We were rudely awakened at 2 AM by somebody pounding on our window. It was a truck driver who wanted access to the layby as well; my careless parking job at the empty layby the evening before was preventing that. Rather than starting the car (which would have required shifting a few bags), I got out and pushed it (with the aid of the trucker) a few meters forward to let him squeeze by. The pounding in the darkness really got our adrenalin pumping; it took some time before we could return to slumberland.

We were on our way again at 8:30, on Thursday, January 8th, and after stopping for coffee, we were relieved to enter the autobahn. The weather was still cold, snowy, and foggy, but the autobahn was clear, and despite the heavy traffic it felt like the safest alternative.

We were making excellent time as well. A few hours later, we passed Hannover and were heading for Hamburg, where we would close the loop of our journey in the late afternoon. What remained after Hamburg – Lübeck, the ferry at Puttgarden, the ride through Denmark, the ferry at Dragør – was all familiar territory to us now; we felt we knew what to expect and decided there'd be no more dillydallying, no unnecessary stops. Just go for it.

Luck was with us. And we made uncanny connections. We reached the ferry in Puttgarden in the early evening, five minutes before the ship sailed. We ate a welcome hot meal on board in the cafeteria, and took advantage of the duty-free alcohol prices in the big shop. On reaching Rødby, we made a beeline for Dragør, again reaching a ferry just in time – ours was one of the last cars to board before they shoved off. And we made it back to Ehrensvärdsgatan 14, to our cold apartment that no longer felt so cold and never so much like home, by 10 PM, after 26 days on the road (only six nights in beds for Jeanette and me), thousands of kilometers, truckloads of impressions and experiences, an unbroken average budget of less than $25 per day – for the three of us (excluding Mike's hotels and personal acquisitions) – and a great sense of satisfaction and accomplishment. We spent half the night drinking our wine, looking at our purchases, reflecting on all that had happened.

We also opened our accumulated mail. A letter from Mom contained newspaper clippings that announced to everyone in greater Chicago that I, Stanley Erisman of 1231 N. Euclid in Oak Park, had received *political asylum* in Sweden. But I put that aside for now; reality could wait until tomorrow.

CHAPTER 5

Settling in, up and down

In addition to the various Christmas cards and letters from the States, one of the pieces in the pile of mail waiting for us at the start of 1970 was a note in the Christmas card from Elsa, reminding us that the next term of Swedish lessons would begin on Monday, January 12th. Jeanette and I were eager to resume our studies, but Mike showed no interest and said he would drop out. It wasn't as though he had the slightest wish to make his future in Sweden, he explained. He also said he thought he might be doing a little traveling on his own now, before heading back to San Francisco.

Even though he seemed to have had a great time with us on the roadtrip, there was a restlessness and underlying anxiety he couldn't overcome on his own, and he wouldn't allow us or his parents or anyone else to help him. We felt sorry for him and at the same time frustrated over his apparent apathy. Our hopes – and perhaps his own, as well as those of the rest of Jeanette's family – that spending some extended time in the presence of our enterprising spirits would plant seeds of something even remotely like an enterprising spirit in him failed to germinate.

The prospect of him doing a little traveling on his own was nevertheless good news; we really needed some time on our own together, to start settling in to a new life in Sweden. Finding jobs was our number one priority. Without that, there could be no work permit, which in turn was the prerequisite for looking for a place of our own. Then we could think about continuing our education in one form or another – which would be free in Sweden – and I could at last return to painting.

On Friday, January 9th, the day after we arrived home, while we were at the laundromat doing our ton of laundry from the trip, I went out and bought a copy of the local daily newspaper (*Sydsvenska Dagbladet*, a.k.a. *Sydsvenskan*) to look for job ads. There were hardly any at all, and nothing the least bit relevant for us. We thought that maybe Swedish newspapers didn't run help-wanted ads. Perhaps we'd have to go back to *arbetsförmedlingen* and hope they didn't have two-year waiting lists there as well. What if we could get jobs "under the table" – would that mean cleaning restaurant and office floors? But a promissory letter for a black-market job?! Yet we refused to become disheartened; maybe the Saturday paper would have more.

I got up early the next day, went down to the newsstand at Värnhemstorget and bought the paper. Disappointed again, I flung the paper over to Jeanette to read. It wasn't as if there were no job ads at all; there were two of three pages of them, but nothing for which we were remotely qualified: nurses, welders, sales managers with at least 10 years' experience, forklift operators, math teachers, finance directors, etc. Not that I was unwilling to do any kind of job, but some actually required qualifications I didn't have. We'd been so focused on finding jobs in order to obtain permits that we hadn't been paying much attention to whether there were any jobs to be found.

Trying to read the Swedish newspaper was extremely challenging for us, but since it was need-driven, it was also very rewarding in terms of the development of our language skills. Moving beyond the job pages that day, Jeanette noticed an ad for English and other language courses at a language school called Demarets Språkskola. We thought it couldn't hurt if I got in touch with them and introduced myself. *You never know.*

I went down to the corner and phoned them that morning. The co-owner, Carmen Demaret, answered. I said I was new in Sweden, had a degree in English from San Francisco State, did a year of graduate school work at UBC in Canada, and was eager to apply my skills, in case they got an opening in the near future. She responded with much greater enthusiasm than I was expecting, and asked if I could come in for an interview next week, on Wednesday morning. Trying to keep my voice under control, I said I'd be there at nine.

When Jeanette and I went to our Swedish class that Monday morning, Elsa asked where Mike was, and was disappointed to hear that he'd dropped out. She asked about our Christmas holidays, and was visibly entertained by the brash adventure of our low-budget and rather bohemian roadtrip. Then we told her about my upcoming interview for a "teaching position" at a language school on Wednesday, and she seemed amazed at our ability to take initiatives. But she also cautioned us about getting our hopes up too high – good, steady jobs were pretty hard to find right now.

Demarets Språkskola was ensconced in a 5-storey building called Pilgården, on Sankt Johannesgatan, a block or two from the City Theater (which also served as Malmö's concert and opera venue). Pilgården was a peculiar, modern, very drab, beige-brick building, with a ground-floor restaurant that looked sterile and uninviting, like something I might have expected to see in East Germany.

Each of the other floors had a single, gray, very long, well-lit central corridor with numerous, rather closely spaced doors on either side. The building might have been suitable for small offices, student dormitories, a minimum-security prison, or a multitude of small studio apartments. Or perhaps the honorary consulates of all of Central America's nations. Most of them were apartments, except on the second floor, where perhaps 10-15 of the rooms were tiny classrooms. A couple of them had been knocked through to make one room out of two, for use by the school staff and as a place of refuge for the teachers. Each room had its own lavatory and kitchenette.

The administrative staff consisted of Carmen Demaret herself, a rather plump, flamboyant, fiery woman (like her namesake in Bizet's opera) of half-Catalonian, half-English extraction, in her late 40s, with dark curly hair that made her round face seem even rounder, big flashing eyes, and a fleshy mouth that frequently revealed prominent teeth and more saliva than she was always capable of containing when her speech became agitated. Her excessive crimson lipstick, which also dotted her teeth, brought out the fleshiness of her lips. Carmen ran the school with a hand of iron or of velvet, depending on her moods and whims. She could be disarmingly friendly and charming one second and smoldering in rage the next. She also filled in as a teacher in English, Spanish, French and whatever other language she felt she knew better than the particular pupil who wanted to learn it. Her English sounded more like it came from my native country than her father's, and her articulation sounded as though her mouth was constantly full of moist cake – Demosthenes gone soft.

At a safe distance sat the other co-owner: Carmen's diminutive husband Gaston, from Belgium, who was comfortably taciturn in several languages and strongly preferred to focus his efforts on providing the school's translation services. He might have been in his 50s – I found it hard to tell – and he was slender and bald, mild-mannered and impeccably dressed. He willingly answered any question with all the indirectness and convolutions he could muster, possibly in order to stave off the risk of receiving follow-up questions. If this was indeed his intention, he was generally successful. He occasionally took over some of the German and French lessons if the school were understaffed in those languages that day.

The third member of the administration staff was the school's salesman, Sven-Erik Hultén, a large, middle-aged, somewhat puffy man in tweed, with sandy hair, who contacted Swedish companies to sell language courses, and who also tried to compensate for his total lack of personal language skills by effusive salesmanship.

The three of them were present when I walked in. All three (including Gaston) greeted me with enthusiasm and made me feel very welcome. I told them I was looking for a job, but needed a work permit first, and was thus hoping they could offer me a job – in writing – to enable me to apply for that coveted permit. They nodded, and Carmen responded immediately, saying my situation with the authorities was one they often dealt with, and while she was speaking, she shoved paper and carbon paper into her typewriter and began typing my brief letter – even before she told me I could have a job.

Emboldened, I asked if there might also be some work for my wife, an American girl who was an experienced executive secretary, mind you, and Carmen typed out letter number two without blinking or slowing down. Only after she finished writing and signing both letters did she start to talk about the job.

The school was formerly part of the Berlitz chain, she explained, but was now independent. They still used Berlitz books, however, or rather books published by Berlitz, but with the publisher's identification ripped out. I was not mention that to the pupils, she pointed out, eyes flashing. The school, which was only for intensive, total-immersion courses, used *The Method*, which would take her less than an hour to teach me, she claimed. It entailed one teacher for each pupil, morning to evening, for one, two or three weeks at a time. No Swedish was to be used with the pupils, even if they were beginners. This was a strictly monolingual approach.

There were, however, breaks for the teachers, which usually involved rotation of teachers and pupils, so as not to become too boring for the pupil, she explained. The pay was 13 kronor per hour. I did the math: about $2.60 an hour, not much better than The Emporium. *How many hours per week?* That would depend on how many pupils there were. *But would there be work every week?* Probably. *Were there lots of teachers to compete with for hours?* No, she said, because several had visas that ran out at the end of the year, creating the vacancies that I (and possibly Jeanette) would now be helping to fill – perfect timing.

I thought to myself that this was pretty low pay for teaching, with no assurance of how many hours I'd get in any given month. It sounded awfully insecure. And yet, it meant getting the all-important letters to use for applying for work permits, so what the hell. "*Yes*," I said, "*Sounds good!*"

Carmen then informed me that it could take the authorities as long as six weeks to process work permit applications, a situation that she was no happier about than I was. Our money supply was getting dangerously close to the level at which we would no longer be able to afford a trip back to Canada if our application was rejected. Then Sven-Erik interjected, saying that there was an adult evening school called ABF nearby that offered evening courses for groups, and that he knew a guy who handled the courses. He could put me in touch, to see that I got some paid hours while I was waiting for the permit to come through. (Carmen had to translate most of the Swedish he was speaking to me.) Although it sounded strange, I really wanted it to be OK. So I took the information, thanked him, and said I would follow up on it.

Promissory letters in hand, I hurried home to Jeanette and told her the good news – for both of us. At first she seemed a little alarmed that I volunteered her services as a language teacher too, but she realized and agreed that the foot-in-the-door aspect of getting work permits outweighed everything else. And then we celebrated. (Little did I suspect at the time that the real reason Carmen was eager to hire me was that nearly half of her English teachers had suddenly *quit* just after New Year's, not because of expired visas, but because they were disgusted and furious with the haphazard and capricious way Carmen meted out working hours and ran the school.)

First thing the next morning, we took our letters and passports with us to the immigration police on Sallerupsvägen, filled in the application forms (this time, we needed only a little assistance on the Swedish), and the work permit wheels were set in motion. Now we just had to hope that the last of our savings wouldn't run out before we had some wages rolling in.

The next day, I phoned the man (whose name I unfortunately don't remember; I'll call him Mr Svensson) at ABF, a nationwide organization affiliated with Sweden's Social Democratic Party that provided a wide range of adult-education courses. He sounded kind and explained in carefully enunciated Swedish that the spring term was about to begin, and they were short one English teacher. If they couldn't find anyone, he would have to step in himself, something he *really* didn't want to do, so could I *please* take two evening "conversation classes" – meaning that they were already supposed to know the basics, and just wanted to practice speaking and improve their skills – one evening a week each? The pay would be 18 kronor per hour – some 40% more than at Demaret's hourly rate. I told him about my work permit situation, but he ignored it with a grunt, a nearly audible wave of his hand, as if his need to achieve a complete staff was of much greater national importance than immigration protocol. I said fine, and he said I could start the following evening.

At that time, just about everybody in Sweden in our parents' generation had studied German as their first foreign language. The switch to English as the first foreign language taught in Swedish schools came directly after World War II, during which Sweden and Switzerland were among the very few neutral countries in Europe. Swedes tended to be sensitive to criticism (especially from the German-occupied Danes and Norwegians) of their neutrality, given the abomination Hitler was. As far as I could determine, however, Sweden's and Switzerland's neutrality provided crucial safety valves – safe havens – for tens of thousands of Jews and other refugees who would otherwise have had no refuge, no escape at all. And it wasn't as though Sweden (or Switzerland, for that matter) would have been able to withstand the full force of the *Wehrmacht* and *Luftwaffe*, had Hitler been interested in hanging two more small countries on his belt of conquests.

After the War, English became a standard part of the Swedish school curriculum every year from the sixth grade on. As a result, Swedes of the younger generation were fairly good at English, while the older generation knew little. The younger generation – my generation – had the further advantage of the omnipresence of English and American popular songs, plus the fact that the Swedish and Danish TV channels broadcast numerous popular English-language programs every week, using the original soundtrack, in combination with subtitles, instead of dubbing, as was done nearly everywhere else in Europe. Besides, most of the movies shown at Swedish cinemas were in English – with Swedish subtitles. A significant generational language wedge was in place.

That evening I went to the ABF premises on Spångatan an hour before the class, to meet the elderly, white-haired Mr Svensson, to receive the course material (a book of 12 simplified English short stories called *A Light Dozen*), to see the classroom, and to get a list of the pupils, who'd been asked to write a short report about one of the English stories as homework over the Christmas break. He knew that, because he'd given them the assignment himself, having been obliged to take over the class late in the term; the ordinary teacher left suddenly, without notice. He told me all this in Swedish, most of which I understood, with a short time lag between hearing and comprehension. I was starting to feel a bit nervous – I'd hardly ever given a speech or made a presentation in front of a whole group, except when reciting the weekly Bible verse at Sunday School, which I hated. The nervousness was OK; it wasn't until the first lesson was about to begin and I had nearly 20 adults, ages 25-60, sitting there staring at me, waiting for me to begin, that I felt mildly terrified.

I started by introducing myself. I told them of my degree in English in order to instill confidence that my capability wasn't limited to the mere coincidence of having English as my mother tongue. They all stared at me. Then I told them that I'd come to Sweden due to Vietnam. They continued to stare. Two, perhaps three of them, nodded as I was speaking, and I would soon discover that they were probably the only ones in the English conversation group who actually had more than a vague gist of what I'd just said; my Swedish was already better than the English of most of my pupils in this "conversation" class.

In order to breathe life into my pupils, especially the silent ones, I then asked each one to tell me something about who he or she was, starting with the man seated closest to me on my right, who didn't respond. Then one of those two or three who'd understood what I'd said mumbled something in Swedish to the others (I couldn't catch it), and then the man on my right began answering my question – in Swedish. "*English, please,*" I interrupted with a smile, and he shut up again. I became very uncertain about how to proceed.

Then I said that I'd been told they were here for English conversation, which tends to be difficult to achieve without the English. No response, except that those who understood were squirming a little. I asked about their homework, whether they'd read the story. After a little Swedish mumbling, they nodded, and took out some papers. As I was collecting them, I was glancing at them. They were all written in Swedish; they'd *translated* the story – for an English conversation course, and utterly impossible for me to grasp, much less correct!

I took the bold step of asking them if they wanted to speak English with me, and was flooded with explanations, all in Swedish, that with two or three (guess who) exceptions, they weren't really all that interested in speaking English, the course just gave them a fun way to socialize, to get together for coffee and cakes once a week. They were essentially pleading with me not to make them speak English. They began lifting tins of cookies and cakes, thermoses of coffee out of the bags they'd parked on the floor, then on the tables, and shoving their notebooks aside. They were very lively now.

I understood enough of their Swedish to get a bit of the gist of it, and began using my Swedish in reply, which they found charming. At the same time, I didn't feel right about being paid to teach English and then just being on the receiving end of a real *kaffekalas* ("coffee party", a traditional Swedish form of get-together over coffee and at least seven different kinds of cookies and cakes). I asked them if they thought they should be teaching me Swedish instead, if they didn't want me to speak English at all. They protested effusively, they really wanted *me* to speak English with them. *"But this is a conversation course, and conversation means interaction! How am I to know whether you understand? How am I to help you understand?"* They chuckled and laughed at my literal interpretation of the stated purpose of the course, and the ice was broken. We found the beginnings of a platform for them to actually start learning something, without jeopardizing the *kaffekalas*, of course. I achieved similar results with the second group the next evening, and Mr Svensson came to tell me he'd had very positive feedback, and he was pleased.

At our Swedish class, we told Elsa the good news about Demaret's school and the letter and the work permit application having been filed. She was very happy for us, even though her face clouded up when I told her the hourly rate. It seemed this wasn't the first time she'd heard of cases of immigrant exploitation disguised as friendship. I also told her about the ABF work. She sighed and said it probably wouldn't cause any trouble.

The apartment on Ehrensvärdsgatan was never going to be a long-term solution, primarily because of the lack of a bathroom and a lease. A sponge bath in the kitchen was an emergency solution, and even though we'd found an alternative in the form of a public swimming hall, it was too far, too expensive and too inconvenient for maintaining daily personal hygiene. At the same time, we felt that we had to stay where we were until we had our work permits and jobs. My paintings remained stashed in their tube, easy to move on short notice. We came to terms with the realities of the local housing market situation – the assumption that we would have to wait at least two years to get our own lease on an affordable apartment, or pay a lot of money under the table to obtain a lease sooner. We didn't dare to use the last of our rainy-day funds – just under two thousand Canadian dollars still in our bank account in Vancouver – until we were absolutely certain we'd be staying in Sweden, with jobs and work permits. Even then, our funds wouldn't get us much, but maybe more than we had today. At least the lease would be ours.

Another week of waiting for work permits, learning Swedish, and teaching

English (sort of) went by. On Saturday morning, January 31st, I was intending to get to the post office first thing, to transfer the money for our next month's rent. Instead, we were awakened by loud knocking on the door. Thinking and fearing it might be Bruno or Margaretha, we rushed to open. It was Bror Landin. He apparently knew that we could manage some Swedish now, but like most monolinguals, he was unaware that knowledge of a language is always going to be a matter of degrees, not either-or, so he plunged into what seemed like a well-rehearsed speech, in Swedish. Although our visual and audible expressions of incomprehension and sign language were fairly screaming at him to slow the hell down, it took several re-runs before we finally got to the core of his business with us that day.

It wasn't good. He was moving back to *his* apartment – not ours, despite whatever illusions we might have entertained – and we had two weeks, until February 15th, to clear out. That's when he'd be moving back in, and that was that. To emphasize it, he had a "contract", more like a receipt, written down on a scrap of paper, that both confirmed our previous two months' of rent and indicated that it extended from December 1st to February 15th, with no extra charge for the first half of February, as if he were compensating for the overcharge in September. Or maybe the language barrier was hiding some intentions we never understood.

After he left, we stood there looking at each other. The timing couldn't have been worse: we'd heard nothing definite about our work permits; we thus had no possibility to invest our return-to-Canada savings in a new place; and there was clearly no chance of further help from Bruno. Yet we would need to find something – *have* to – and we didn't know where to begin. We were almost in shock.

The next day we again bought a newspaper to look through the classified ads for apartments to rent. Most of the listings indicated rents that were well out of our price range. We soon learned that the only rents cheap enough would be listed as "unmodern" apartments, and we began phoning only about those, hoping to get by on our primitive Swedish – or that people would be able to speak English. When I phoned one of them, the man who answered heard my thick English accent, of course, and asked where I was from. I told him I was from the US. "*Are you Black?*" he asked with an unmistakable tone of suspicion in his voice. I didn't reply; instead I slammed down the receiver. *Not here too!* I thought. *What the fuck difference might it make in any humane universe what the hell color my skin was?! Do we really have to face that crap here too?* Did I mention

I was furious?

When we arrived at our Swedish class on Monday, February 2nd, anxiety was written all over our faces, especially mine. I'd never been very good at hiding my feelings. Had I been English, I would probably have been run out of the country for treason for my utter lack of ability to maintain a stiff upper lip. When we told Elsa of our visit from Landin and our dismal failure to find new accommodations on such short notice, she was deeply concerned. Wheels were turning behind her kind eyes. Desperation seemed to be our perpetual and unwelcome guest. Day after day we bought papers and chased every possible lead, but there wasn't even the slightest sign of a breakthrough.

At Swedish class on the following Monday, six days before Landin would arrive to evict us onto the street, Elsa took us aside. It seemed that a lawyer friend of hers and Sven's had a 90-year-old aunt who'd just moved from her small condo into a home for the elderly, and their lawyer friend was willing to wait a bit before putting the condo on the market if we were willing to pay the rent until we could find a place of our own, with the understanding that it would have to be a question of weeks, not months.

Even if "home for the elderly" may turn out to be politically incorrect some day (the US seems the most likely bet), I don't give a flying fart, since I already qualify as elderly myself as I write this, and I reserve the right to "offend" myself. Also, I'll take this opportunity to announce my inability to take offence at "old people's home", and if anybody were to come up with "geezer gables" or "geriatric pastures" I'd be incapable of even the softest "harrumph". But I might manage a smile.

We just looked at Elsa. We tried to tell ourselves that she was no more a typical Swede than Bruno or Percy had been, which was in a way easier; her kindness was extraordinary. And there was no trace whatsoever that she was basking in her own altruism. To her it seemed to come naturally; it was just who she was. She wasn't looking for praise, nor even thanks (not that we didn't express our gratitude effusively). She had no agenda. Her kindness came from within her, without strings, without broadcasting. She had no religion to sell; in fact she had no religion at all. Her goodness had no ulterior motives; it was real, genuine, unique in our experience. Looking back as I write this many years down the line, I would have to conclude in all sincerity that without Elsa's extraordinarily kind help in so many ways, it is highly unlikely that we would have been able to remain in Sweden.

Settling in, up and down

The apartment to which we moved on Saturday, February 14th, Valentine's Day, was on Herrestadsgatan, just a block from Kronprinsen, Malmö's only skyscraper. The old lady's things were still all there, intact: tired clothing, hundreds of fragile porcelain figurines and ornaments, slightly yellowed lace tablecloths, doilies and runners, fringed lampshades, velvet cushions, teardrop crystal chandeliers, kitchen cupboards full of ancient spices and condiments, pots and pans of every variety, bathroom shelves sagging with colognes, powders, lotions and creams. In short, there was everything we needed, as well as incredibly many things we wished weren't there, but which we had to take all the greater care not to disrupt, damage or destroy. And my paintings still had to remain rolled up in the darkness of the tube.

Our new location put us on the opposite side of town, within walking distance of our laundromat, and no further from school or my presumed future place of work than we were before. We arranged at the post office to have our mail forwarded to us at our new, temporary address. Since it would probably be quite temporary, it wasn't worth notifying our families, friends and draft board of any change for the time being.

Just days after we settled in, more or less, at the old lady's apartment, we received two forwarded pieces of mail of the utmost importance. The first was a letter from my cousin Robert in Switzerland. He'd received our Christmas card and accompanying brief letter. His reply was very much longer than my letter, and was full of enthusiasm, although expressed in a way that was very different from how I usually expressed enthusiasm; I almost didn't recognize it as such. His style was markedly academic, like an article in a literary journal. He rejoiced to have contact with a kindred spirit, who also just happened to be a member of his extended family, a combination he'd long since given up hope in finding. He had lots of questions.

About himself, he revealed that he was working as an endocrinologist in one of the research departments at the pharmaceutical giant Hoffmann LaRoche (usually referred to simply as Roche, he said) in Basel, and lived in an apartment in the adjacent suburb of Binningen, in the canton of Basel Land. He mentioned that he'd left the Meeting many years before, had no current religious affiliation, and was still struggling with the basic tenets of religion. He was estranged from his wife and was not in terribly good health. He hated to be addressed as Robert by friends or anyone he felt close to; he asked me to be address him as Bob.

It appeared that we might find a great deal in common; in fact, even on the face of things, we had much more in common than would be possible for us to have with most other people anywhere in the world. After all, how many people had a background in the Meeting and escaped it? I frequently and invariably found it nearly impossible to explain successfully the ramifications of the Meeting to anyone who had no in-depth personal experience of it. Our respective escapes were achieved only through the greatest efforts of doubt (in my case) and systematic skepticism (in Bob's). Add to this the rarity (for me) of meeting another expatriate with whom I had a shared family history. We certainly had something to build on here. I sent my reply on February 20th.

(Bob saved nearly all the letters I wrote to him, as well as copies of most of those he wrote to me – an invaluable source for getting my facts straight while researching *Hindsights*!)

The second piece of life-changing mail to arrive at Herrestadsgatan was the notice that the decision about our work permits had arrived and could be picked up by bringing our passports to the immigration police on Sallerupsvägen which, although it hadn't moved, was now on the other side of town.

Trembling with excitement, we handed over our passports to the lady at the counter. She took them, retrieved some papers, scrutinized everything, and began thumping at the papers and our passports with her rubber stamps. Without further ado, it was now official: *we could stay and work in Sweden!!* We had a six-month residence and work permit which after the six months would almost automatically be extended by a full year provided we were still in Sweden, thereafter by two years, and then become permanent and on track to citizenship. We were already feeling the first signs of a sense of permanence, yet we marveled that any place could feel remotely like home despite our having no fixed abode.

We could hardly believe it had really happened. We were practically jumping up and down in the street. We kept shaking our heads, grinning and laughing, clutching our newly stamped passports, clutching each other, overflowing. The implications were huge and immediate: I could start working; we no longer needed a rainy day fund to enable us to return to Canada, but could use that money to find a place of our own; and I could start working and regain some equilibrium between income and expenditure. We'd had no income at all since Jeanette resigned from her job in Vancouver in July – seven months ago.

Yet we also felt it was of utmost importance to continue our Swedish studies. We could get by now, make ourselves understood, and could understand what we read if the text was simple enough and we took it slowly enough. But when Swedes spoke to each other in our presence, we understood almost nothing; we had a long way to go to achieve fluency. And Swedish radio programs remained frustratingly incomprehensible.

We decided that since the job offer from Demaret was primarily aimed at me, I would work, while Jeanette would continue in Elsa's class, then share with me what she'd learned, and I would join her whenever there was too little work at Demaret's, or she would join me when there was too much.

I phoned Carmen that afternoon to let her know that I now had a work permit, in case she had work for me any time soon. (I told her that Jeanette wanted to focus full-time on her Swedish studies at least until the end of the term.) Carmen told me I was to begin the very next afternoon, but she wanted me to come in during the morning, around nine, to run through The Method with me. We also sent a letter to our bank in Vancouver, requesting them to send without delay a cashier's check for the balance of our account, and to close that account. We realized it could take some time. We also opened an account at Skandinaviska Banken, cashing in our few remaining traveler's checks for the initial deposit in our new account.

Carmen showed me the total-immersion Method for beginners by giving me a German lesson (I knew no German at all), in much the same way Elsa began teaching us Swedish. She stood there in front of me, pointing at objects, stating their German names, repeating each one numerous times, getting me to repeat it after her each time. After we'd gone through the German for table, pen, book, window, floor, wall, ceiling, hand, foot and a few others, she began asking me, in German "*Is this a book?*" When I didn't get it immediately, she would answer her own question, nodding vigorously, "*Yes, this is a book!*" in German, of course. Over and over, with the different objects, getting me to supply the German answers. And repeating.

Then she went through the questions again, this time holding up or pointing to different objects than the ones she'd asked about, eventually getting me to say, "*No, it's <u>not</u> a book.*" The next step would be to ask those same questions, this time cutting me off as soon as I'd said "*Nein*", going through three or four objects before landing on "<u>What</u> *is this?*" to which the answer would be "*It's a book.*" I now had the yes and no answer formulations as well as the "what" questions, plus some nouns and their indefinite articles. Then we went on to colors and "*What <u>color</u> is this book?*" Then a variety of visually demonstrable adjectives and their opposites – long, short, high, low, thick, thin etc. At first it seemed crazy to me, absolute madness. But within half an hour, I had to admit that if this be madness, there's Method in it.

By the time she finished the demonstration, I was sold. Then she explained briefly that the courses were structured in such a way that the pupil was obliged to invite his or her teacher to lunch (during which the lessons would continue, of course) at a restaurant of the pupil's choice, within walking distance. Both the walk to and from the restaurant and the mealtime itself were all to be a continuation of the lessons; no other language was allowed. Nearly all of the pupils were sent to these courses by their employers (unless the pupils *were* the employers). Most of them were well-heeled executives and managers, as well as some technicians and a few secretaries. And they all tended to select some of the best restaurants in Malmö, a city with a surprisingly excellent selection.

During this time, I began meeting the other teachers, mostly the English teachers, as they came out of their respective classrooms for a break, at which time we would generally switch pupils, after having given the pupils short reading assignments. Miss Buhre – Enid Buhre – was a strikingly affectatious and haughty figure, in her late 50s, with a long cigarette holder constantly dangling from one corner of her perpetually sneering mouth. She didn't *walk* into rooms, she swept. She seemed to have crash-landed from some *fin-de-siècle* artsy ideal, which was remarkable in view of the fact that she hadn't been born at the *fin* of any *siècle*, and lacked anything resembling artistic talent. She took the sound of American English as a personal affront to her ears, also remarkable given the fact that she was Swedish and her English was horrible ("the brown book" came out as "duh bwown boook"). But she was, as it turned out, one of Carmen's inner circle, a handful of loyal old-timers who lived in a curiously symbiotic long-term relationship that had helped keep the school afloat for years.

Another of these was an Englishwoman named Juliana Fredin, who seemed well past retirement age, and whose English – not only what she spoke but what she taught – had little to do with the needs of pupils wishing to conduct business or life in the modern world. Although (or perhaps because) she had no teaching qualifications beyond it being her native language and, presumably, Carmen's Method instruction, she was anachronistically pedantic; proper English could not be spoken without liberal use of "shan't". Another favorite of hers was teaching pupils that in proper English, the male equivalent of "Miss Brown" should be "Master Brown". (I was still too unsure of myself to have asked her if that also applied if one's name were Cecil Bates.) She married late in life a man she presumed was Swedish, and towards whom she displayed perpetual resentment for the fact that she'd ended up residing in Sweden. Unfortunately, her husband, though he lived in Sweden, was Danish, spoke Danish and probably taught her Danish words and phrases that she presumed were Swedish. I have no idea how many years it took for Mrs Fredin to discover this little aberration.

The other English teachers, whom I met over the course of time, included two from Australia: John Bramble, a friendly fellow my age, with a bushy red beard; and a woman about my age (Alice somebody) who was insufferably snobbish. She considered herself far more English than the English, which is to say that she seemed to wish to hide her Australian origins by deriding anything she deemed less British than the queen, despite the fact that those who were English could immediately hear that she was not. Later, during that summer, when Carmen needed Jeanette to fill in for some hours, Alice ran a campaign to make my darling wife feel totally incompetent, even at speaking her own language. I only wish I'd found out about those attacks before the Aussie bitch left the school in the early autumn. Jeanette tended neither to let me know such things nor to stand up for herself.

There was also another American guy, Guy Morrill, who came to Sweden by way of Finland and whose name appeared in the same Chicago newspaper article as mine because he was also from Illinois (Carbondale). He flatly refused any discussion of it or of his personal life (rumor had it that he'd robbed a bank). He always wore a trenchcoat and had a cigarette dangling from his mouth, pathetically fancying himself an incarnation of Humphry Bogart.

Then there was a Scottish girl, Joan Potts, from Edinburgh, who was very sweet and kind-hearted, the object of the bridled ardor of a very nice German teacher in his late 20s named Arno Kirsch, from Karlsruhe. Her efforts to introduce Jeanette and me to haggis after one of her trips home to Scotland were highly successful. Her aspirations that we would find it delightful, or even edible were, however, a total failure, as were Arno's of ever getting inside her virgin-till-the-altar pants. I felt his pain.

It wouldn't take many months before the high turnover of teachers vaulted me into the ranks of the senior staffers. As far as my workload was concerned, I really had to hit the ground running. After the first week or two, I could hardly handle all the work Carmen was throwing my way. Together with my two evening classes at ABF, I was working 50-55 hours a week.

Jeanette and I felt we could afford a maximum outlay of 7,000 kronor for "buying" an apartment. There weren't many apartments available in that lowly price range, but we didn't need more than one. Elsa was trying to coach us on how to avoid swindlers in a market rife with extremely dubious credentials to start with. Day after day we looked, scrutinized and scoured. We had plenty of patience; it was the waiting part that was difficult. We saw a couple of places that turned out to cost many times more than what was advertised in the paper. One or two were cheap enough but uninhabitable. One place would have been a deal if our money transfer had been ready.

Then on March 1st, we saw an ad, contacted a realtor named Åke Olin, and went to see a place just one block beyond Värnhemstorget, on a street called Vårgatan. It was a 5th-storey walk-up, but our legs were young. It was kind of dreary and shabby, but our spirits were indomitable. It was terribly chilly and damp, but there was a heater that hadn't been on for a while. We reluctantly found the price acceptable: 5,200 kronor "for the furniture". But the rent was a mere 158 kronor per month (around $30 at the time), excluding heating and utilities! It was *very* tempting, but we hesitated owing to how monumentally great this piddling investment was to us. We said we needed a little time to think about it. Later that day, we phoned to request a second look, and arranged to meet Mr Olin there the next day, after I finished work.

The agent was eager for us to sign the contract then and there, but we had to inform him that we were still waiting for a money transfer from Canada, which should come any day now; for a 200 kronor deposit he was willing to wait. We paid the 200 and assured him that we'd phone him the moment the rest of the money came through. There was another reason for wanting to wait: we couldn't understand more than isolated words in the lease. Elsa cautioned us about signing a contract, and said she'd help us if we found a place. We contacted her that day and she promised to join us and the seller at the apartment when it was time to sign. We were biting our nails hoping that the seller meant what he said – that he'd wait for our money to come through.

Tuesday's mail delivery included a slip informing us that there was a registered letter from our bank in Vancouver, to be picked up at the post office at Värnhemstorget; our check had arrived! We'd been fearing the worst, that it would take weeks more and that the deal would be scuttled. Instead, we were able to phone the agent and tell him we now had the money. We agreed to meet him and the seller at the apartment the next day at five o'clock, after work. Then we phoned Elsa, (whom we probably should have phoned first!), and fortunately it was convenient for her as well. But the seller didn't look too happy to see her there.

Elsa read through the sales contract carefully; the 5,200 kronor was indeed "for the furniture", which consisted of a moisture-damaged sofa, a couple of rickety chairs, a disgusting-looking bed and old wall-to-wall carpeting that was dirty, but hid an even dirtier floor beneath it. Elsa sighed, shook her head in disbelief, but said that if this was what we wanted, the contract would be OK to sign, so we did. The seller then showed us (and Elsa) how to work the old kerosene heater.

The metal housing of the unit was about 60 cm wide, 35 cm deep, and 75 cm high. The top was hinged at the back and could be lifted to reveal two chambers of almost equal size. The one on the left consisted of a thick-walled iron drum (A), a pressure vessel into which a trickle of kerosene could flow from the right-hand side, a metal canister (B) into which the contents of a 25-liter jeep can of kerosene could be poured, once we'd procured the kerosene by phoning a certain Herr Delén in Limhamn, who would drive his small tank truck to the door of our building to fill our waiting and empty jeep can. Then I would have to haul the 25 liters up the 89 steps, and fill up B without spilling the flammable fluid. (25 liters = 25 kilos. Do that conversion from gallons to pounds in your head, why don't you?) For safety reasons, the heater would have to be off and reasonably cool before doing this. Then I had to lift the heavy lid off A, and (if it was empty at the bottom) press down a lever at the base of B, then set the small valve on top of B to 6, wait for kerosene to trickle into A until it covered the bottom, then turn off the valve on top of B, causing a valve at the base of A to open. Then I would add 1-2 teaspoons of denatured alcohol into A, throw in a lighted match, and hope to retain my eyebrows. After waiting some seconds for the burning kerosene to build up enough heat to achieve an updraft in the chimney, it was time to close the heavy lid on A, and hope that the fire didn't go out. If it did, I'd have to wait for everything to cool again, then start the whole thing over. Once it got going, I could turn up the flow via the valve on B to the setting 1-2, depending on how much heat we needed, according to how cold it was outdoors. Ideally, we'd get the heat we needed. (As it turned out, it wasn't always ideal, and we ended up having to get a couple of electric heaters as complements for the studio and bedroom when the weather turned really cold the following winter.)

After the agent, the seller and Elsa left, we stood there with the lease in our hands, trying to make it all real. The next day, we went to a telegraph office and notified the Johnson Line in Vancouver that they should without delay ship our four trunks and 67 cartons of books to our new address. I seem to remember that the fee was around $125 Canadian.

Elsa told us she had a table and a couple of chairs that were cluttering up her basement storage area, and that we'd be welcome to take them off her hands. There seemed to be no limit to her kindness. We moved on Saturday, March 14th, and picked up Elsa's furniture that same day (I don't remember how; it may have fit into the Saab). When we did, Elsa handed us an envelope with a little money, one-tenth of a month's unused rent for the place at Herrestadsgatan. Our occupancy was one day shy of a full month, and February had just 28 days, which meant three and one-tenth days. We were renting from a lawyer, who was obviously on our side. The unreal details of our reality just kept piling up.

I feel I need to keep pointing out that I'm not making any of this up. It all really happened to Jeanette and me, however strange it may seem, and it still seems strange to me too. Also strange was that we never met that lawyer.

Our apartment on Ehrensvärdsgatan was one block from Värnhemstorget, towards town. Our new apartment on Vårgatan ("Vår" means both "spring" – the season, not the coil – and "our") was also one block from Värnhemstorget, but in this case away from town. Both Ehrensvärdsgatan and Vårgatan are rather short streets, only about three blocks long. Vårgatan is perpendicular to Lundavägen, which is the same street as Föreningsgatan would have been if it hadn't changed names after Värnhemstorget. Our address was Vårgatan 4a: no more "c/o". It was ours. We immediately sent letters to notify our parents of our new address. And I sent one to my draft board.

Our red-brick building was one of four conjoined L-shaped buildings comprising the entire perimeter of the block, making a square donut, with a large square central courtyard that was divided into four sections, one for each building. Our building had three roughly identical entrances (three stairwells), two of which were from Vårgatan (4a and 4b), and the third from around the corner on Mellangatan, where there was also a portal to our building's section of the courtyard. (Our block lay between Lundavägen and Mellangatan. When I gave directions in Swedish to our place, I expressed them untranslatably thus:

"*Vår gata heter Vårgatan och ligger mellan Mellangatan och Lundavägen.*") The 89-step stairway, from the sidewalk to our level, led to two apartments – a two-room apartment to the left and a three-room to the right – on each floor. Ours was on the top floor, to the right. The doors to the apartments were tall, about 220 cm, divided vertically into two narrow halves, with fairly large, mostly frosted glass windows in the upper half of each. There was a small landing outside the doors on each floor. The stairway wound around in such a way that there were no vertiginous views down to the street level.

Our entry, through the right-hand half of the pair of doors (the left-hand part also could be opened for moving furniture in and out), comprised a tiny hallway from which there was a narrow door to the kitchen, straight ahead; a doorway to the living room, to the right; and double doors to the room we would use as our bedroom, along the same wall as the entrance. The ceilings throughout the apartment were three meters high, making it seem more spacious than it was. The whole apartment was about 72 square meters.[5]

The kitchen was galley-style, with a gas stove along the wall to the left, but no fridge. We would soon be adding a countertop supported by two drawer cabinets along the same wall, and then as big a fridge as possible. The far wall became diagonal at the far end, with a door leading out to a spiral stairwell and down to the courtyard, a door we never used. Along the wall to the right were more cabinets, a countertop and wall-cabinets, followed by a doorway to the living room, and beyond it, partly tucked into a niche, was a small stainless steel sink with cold water only.)

The kerosene-fired heater was just inside the doorway to the living room, along the wall that included the chimney. Further along that wall was a door to what would eventually be my studio. In the far corner, opposite the doorway from the entry, was a narrow door to a small lavatory, with a small sink and a toilet with the water tank mounted on the wall two meters above the seat. It was flushed by pulling a chain. To the left in the lavatory was a wall with a tiny door leading to a small storage area, perhaps better called a broom closet. One of the first things I noticed about the lavatory was that if we were to move back the wall to the broom closet, we might have room for a bathtub and a wall-mounted water heater, thus turning the lavatory into a bathroom. The far corner of the small living room was also diagonal, which made furnishing a bit tricky. The far

---

5   See apartment floor plan, Appendix 1

wall had a large window overlooking a corner of the courtyard. We eventually placed a dining table there. Along the wall to the left was the doorway to the kitchen.

The bedroom also had a large window overlooking the balcony, which in turn overlooked the street (Vårgatan) and beyond. If there'd been a Manhattan skyline, we'd have had a good view of it from there. As it was, we overlooked the Malmö skyline. Access to the bedroom was via two pairs of doors: one from the entry, the other from the studio. There was room for a queen-size bed (160 x 200 cm), the size we had more or less randomly chosen in San Francisco, and for which all our Emporium sheets were dimensioned.

The studio, finally, was by far the brightest room, nearly square, with a very large window, and a pair of half French doors that opened onto the small, rather shabby but adequate balcony. The one unbroken wall, to the left on entering from the living room, struck me immediately as the ideal place to build bookshelves for all the books that would soon be arriving. Before we left Vancouver, I measured how many meters of shelves we needed. Thus I knew how many meters of shelves to build when we found a new place, which meant now. Some quick measuring and calculating revealed that the wall in the studio was the absolutely perfect place, with enough space for all our books and one or two meters of shelf space to spare.

I made it my top priority to build those shelves. We could expect the arrival of our 67 cartons of books in about six weeks. The cartons were numbered, and the contents were more or less in the order I wanted them. If I could just get the shelves ready in time, we wouldn't have 67 cartons in our way for weeks and months, but could put the contents directly into place. The four trunks would serve as ideal end tables and coffee tables while providing extra storage space. We knew we had a sort of open locker area in the attic above us, but it didn't feel like a terribly safe or weatherproof solution.

As soon as the deal was done on our apartment, we had to rush out and buy a bed for ourselves. For Mike's remaining weeks in Europe, at least when he was in Malmö, he would have to make do with the hugely expensive old sofa that came with the apartment. The studio became my workshop for building bookshelves, kitchen cabinets, storage closets for the bedroom etc. And at last, I could remove my paintings from their temporary home in the tube, re-stretch them and hang them on the walls. Jeanette was overjoyed by the feeling of home they imparted to her as soon as they were up. I was pretty thrilled myself.

Unfortunately, I remember very little about how Mike spent his time after our grand European roadtrip, during all the milestone events that were unfolding in Jeanette's life and mine. I seem to remember him taking a couple of short train trips on his own, but not whether they were to Berlin or Stockholm or both or elsewhere. The gap between his interests and ours began growing rapidly once he dropped out of the Swedish class, and he stood outside of our preoccupations and aspirations concerning permits, jobs and apartments. Once I started working, the gap became enormous; perhaps my initiative to find work was a painful reminder to him of his own lack of such ambition – and the abiding pressure from the elder Mike back in San Francisco.

In late March he made an extensive train trip to Greece via Germany, Austria and Yugoslavia. He was gone for several weeks. We received at most a postcard or two from him during his absence. Before he left, he announced that he would be returning to the States on May 3rd, a couple of weeks after getting back to Malmö. Although we never expected him to stay with us for such a long time, his announcement still came as a bit of a surprise. We'd had many moments of fun together, but our hopes that he would open up and/or begin to structure his life in some way remained unfulfilled. And our own lack of privacy was something we never could get used to.

In April, we decided to buy a TV, not so much because we were suffering from a lack of entertainment, but because on the few occasions we'd tried watching Swedish TV programs at someone else's place, we understood almost nothing. We were doing pretty well on reading the Swedish subtitles when they broadcast English-language programs, but even the most well-enunciated Swedish news programs were a great strain to grasp, and the challenge of following Swedish entertainment programs completely overwhelmed us.

Since our experience of teaching Swedes English by speaking only English to them showed the amazing potential of mere exposure, we thought we'd give it a try; just watch, listen, let the visual content reinforce the audio, pick up nouns, verbs, adjectives, expletives, phrases, sentences, contexts. When we first started watching TV, we understood less than 10 percent. Within half a year we understood well over 50 percent, just by watching and listening. But listening to the radio as a way of increasing comprehension was no help at all at this stage – there was no visual reinforcement of the spoken word.

Contact with my parents remained strained, like the strain of having to develop new muscles because the two separate rails on which your roller-skate-shod feet are whizzing along are gradually widening. In early March, they sent us the second Bible since our arrival in Malmö. This was in addition to the one I still had since I was about 10, the next when I graduated from high school, then a Catholic one for Jeanette's benefit, then a Swedish Bible during the autumn. And now another.

Perhaps they thought that Bibles had best-before dates, and that ours had gone bad. And they had, in a way; I was finding far too much disturbing stuff in them, stuff that I thought should have been deeply embarrassing and troubling to anyone who felt that the Bible should or could be used as a foundation of morality. It wasn't that they dwelled on the dark sides of the God their Bible explicitly portrayed, it was that by not editing them out, while still holding onto the notion that every word of the Bible was the Word of God – a good God – they were accepting and worshipping a horrifying deity. But we thanked Mom and Dad anyway, believing that they meant well, because we believed that they believed that they meant well.

About the only times I'd read anything in the Bible since leaving Oak Park were when my brothers sent me the works of their flavor-of-the-year Christian apologists, notably Francis Schaeffer and C.S. Lewis. My brothers challenged me to read and comment upon the books, which I always did. In reading them, and analyzing their arguments, I was frequently obliged to consult the Bible extensively to substantiate my refutations of their claims, and to be able to play their game by their rules. In so doing, I was becoming increasingly aware of the extensive cherry-picking going on, and the spongiform nature of the arguments of the apologists, of my brothers, and of the Bible itself. As I read – reading what the Bible actually said rather than being mesmerized by how I'd been told to hear it before I understood it – it scared me to realize that I once believed what others believed to be "the gospel truth".

Another thing that was gradually working its way into my consciousness was that I'd been accepting – as axioms – many of the premises on which their faith and their arguments were based. I knew that the logical validity of an argument was whether conclusions could be drawn from a set of premises, not whether the premises themselves were valid. So by accepting the premises of any ideology (including faiths), you were already conceding as unquestionable nearly everything on which the argument rested. Maybe it was time to question those first premises even more.

As this was happening, I was increasingly convinced that I would be able to air these thoughts and doubts in future correspondence with Bob, whose own skepticism seemed to be developing along very similar lines. Had my brothers not given me these "assignments", I've often wondered whether I might have simply let the whole religion thing fade away to the periphery of my life like most normal people seemed to do (at least in Sweden), instead of actively developing rational foundations for why I did *not* believe what my brothers still did. But the chaos of juggling and balancing many crucial and practical matters during that spring of 1970 was too great to allow me to explore all these doubts in as great depth as I might have liked.

I was aching to paint again. My paints and brushes were among the greatest treasures in the trunks that were on their way from Canada. I'd seen an artists' supply store in town, but before I bought some canvas and stretchers, I had to finish thinking of something that had been slowly forming in my mind for well over half a year. It was an area of anxiety, especially for Jeanette, one we talked about many a late evening, a frustration she couldn't resolve. It was about Mike, his strict and self-imposed isolation, the way he looked without seeing and listened without hearing, probably what made Simon & Garfunkle's *The Sounds of Silence* appealing to him, his sanctuary from the world and from life. I also thought of Fred Neil's *"Everybody's talking at me..."* with the characters surrounding him.

The visual expression came to me all at once. I saw the finished painting in my mind. All I had to do was buy a canvas and stretchers to fit, a few brushes and paints to work with until our things arrived, then find some way of propping the canvas up on a table to enable me to paint it.

I call it *Sanctuary*.[6] Jeanette was thrilled beyond words that I was painting again, and told me the painting went straight into the heart of her – that I precisely captured and resolved the conflict about Mike that was raging within her as well, both during his time in the Army and during the nearly eight months he'd spent with us. Mike was away in Greece when I painted it, and we decided it wouldn't be prudent to show it to him when he got back (he'd never expressed any interest in my painting anyway). We kept it in our bedroom and only hung it up after he'd gone back to the States. The work on it exhausted me mentally; there was just too much else going on in our lives, but I felt I had to get that one out. It would take a while before I was ready to start painting in earnest.

---

6   Painting #13 – see Appendix 2

The intensity of my work at Demaret's was by no means constant. There were weeks of very heavy workloads and long days, then perhaps a week with little to do. But I could see that I was getting just about all the work I could handle, more than most of the other English teachers. (Not until mid-June, when Elsa's class was over for the summer, did Jeanette begin working part-time at Demaret's as well.) I could tell that Carmen was making sure that I spent more time with the pupils she deemed "important", and she told me that some were asking for me. While it was very flattering, I didn't feel I deserved it. I was teaching what I already knew, but not what I already knew how to teach – a big difference. I was learning how to teach as I taught, as I went along, making up rules if I couldn't find any that made sense, then testing my own rules over and over to see if they worked.

Teaching my own language to others was teaching *me* incredibly much about English. Even simple things like when to use "a" or "an" was always just automatic for me, a thing I sensed without understanding. If I'd ever learned a rule, I'd long ago forgotten it – not how to use it, but how to express the rule itself or explain it to others – I had to figure that out for my pupils. I had no access to grammar books, and Google hadn't been invented yet. I also had a strong aversion to giving my pupils incorrect answers. Instead, I tried to avoid guessing, and when needed I would admit I didn't know, but would find out and get back to them. The more advanced my pupils were, the more complicated the grammar I had to teach them, and the more I had to learn about it myself – often for the first time, unless I'd already learned the corresponding Swedish grammar from Elsa. I was becoming highly language-conscious.

When we studied grammar and diagrammed sentences in 7th grade, it had just been a silly game to me. I did well enough to get a good grade, but since the possible value of learning about grammar in terms of relevance outside the classroom had never been adequately explained and impressed upon me, the things I learned quickly back then equally quickly receded into the far corners of my brain, there to remain idle and dormant.

"*What good is grammar?*" I thought as a child. As children, we learn to speak our native language without learning the meanings of "*conjugation, participle, past perfect tense, infinitive, preposition, subjunctive, demonstrative pronoun,*" and the whole vocabulary of grammar that sounds like it comes from a parallel universe. As young children, we just learn to speak. On the other hand, it takes several years for a child to learn to speak even simple sentences and express anything abstract, even though a child has the advantage of being free from the massive interference of a pre-existing language. Learning to express complex thoughts takes many more years. Is it only because children haven't developed the cognitive skills to think complex thoughts? Could at least part of the reason be that children don't have the *language* skills with which to first think such thoughts, then express them?

I began to see grammar as a set of shortcuts. For adults who can grasp and apply abstract working principles, grammar enables the learner to skip years of trial-and-error with thousands of examples and repetition. If I could explain a point of grammar clearly, in the form of a principle or rule, perhaps I could speed up the learning process for my pupils, but first I would have to learn how to clarify such shortcuts myself. And once having understood them more clearly than ever myself, I could apply them, in principle at least, to learning Swedish.

It's not as though my first couple of decades of life had inured me to follow rules strictly and blindly! Language is a living thing, an evolving thing, while grammar books are static. Nobody speaks 18th century English today (and modern English could never give Meeting people the kind of sanctimoniousness they required for their prayers). I felt that grammar should be seen as a tool, not a weapon, that it should be more descriptive than proscriptive, just like dictionary definitions. Silly and archaic rules like not ending a sentence with a preposition could simply be ignored or thrown out. I love Churchill's alleged comeback on being upbraided for having done so: "*There are some rules of grammar up with which I will not put!*" But I was up against an entrenched cadre of archaic teachers who felt otherwise. Enid Buhre huffed. Mrs Fredin puffed. And then I collected evidence of contemporary usage from their own respected contemporary sources to meet their challenges, which soon ceased, at least within earshot of me.

Among the "VIP" pupils that spring was a man named Henry Carlsson. One Friday, Carmen informed the teachers that he would be among the next week's pupils for a one-week intensive course, as a beginner. His extra-special VIP status was largely due to his being the head of Malmö's most prestigious building construction and administration company, Hugo Åberg, named after its eponymous founder, who'd been killed in a car crash in November 1969, whereupon Henry took the helm. The company's properties included Malmö's only skyscraper (Kronprinsen), as well as Pilgården, making Henry in a sense Carmen's landlord.

Henry reminded me quite a bit of the famous Swedish actor Max von Sydow, whom I'd seen in several Bergman films. He was tall and slender, in his late 40s, but seemed much older, with graying, immaculately groomed hair, and deportment that was formal, extremely cautious and timid, yet quietly authoritative – a kind of father-figure quite unlike my father. He seemed eager to learn, although his eagerness only occasionally showed up in his eyes. Surprisingly (to me at least), my combination of a cajoling, ebullient manner and professional earnestness apparently agreed with him, even though he seemed to find it highly unusual. After the one-week course, he told Carmen that it was his intention to continue, but only two or three hours per week, and only if I could be his teacher, nobody else.

Henry also wanted to get to know me as a person, not just for English. After two or three of our "private" lessons at Pilgården, he said that he and his wife Elsa would like to have me and Jeanette over to their place for dinner. They lived in a lovely yet modest, very traditional modern home near Jägersro. Every detail was perfect without being outlandish or extravagant. The four of us spoke mostly Swedish that evening. Elsa didn't seem terribly comfortable with English (although hers was much better than our Swedish then), while Jeanette and I were eager to practice our Swedish. We told them about our adventures in winding up in Sweden, and when I mentioned my ongoing carpentry projects, Henry said he might be able to get us some deals on building materials. We had no idea what an impact Henry would turn out to have on our lives.

After we moved back to the area around Värnhemstorget, we began getting more frequent visits from Boris, especially when Mike was out travelling. It could also have been that it was because Mike wasn't around; Boris didn't seemed to hit it off very well with him, for some reason. Boris was a born tinkerer, meticulous, the kind who would take radios and other electronic devices apart and put them together again just for the fun of learning about them. My own contact with electricity was limited to changing light bulbs; in view of my fear of wiring since some presumably shocking yet forgotten experience in my childhood, Boris began doing some rewiring jobs for us, showing me how, and my fear gradually dwindled down to a healthy respect.

Boris also liked to practice his English, and he helped explain to us some of the trickier things in Swedish we'd encountered. His proficiency in Swedish was soaring, and he was already looking beyond it to Danish. He looked a bit like a young, less self-confident Burt Reynolds.

He and his mother, Mrs Borisova, were living an apartment on Ehrensvärdsgatan (of all places), in a relatively new building practically next door to Bruno's office. For a while, Boris was coming to see us almost every evening. One evening he explained that we would have to come to his place instead, as his mother was both jealous and suspicious of us, and of all the time he spent with "strangers". People often seem to become suspicious of anything unknown.

Mrs Borisova hardly looked old enough to be the mother of a 17-year-old – she was probably in her mid-30s – and might have once been as pretty as she still thought she was. She made sure we understood that most people told her they thought she was her son's sister. She was very protective of and affectionate towards Boris, constantly caressing and fondling him, to his considerable embarrassment. Sometime later, Boris told us that his mother still always insisted on scrubbing him when he was in the bathtub. It seemed to us that he really needed to tell someone about it. Fortunately, we didn't need to pay many further visits to Mrs Borisova, and Boris continued spending lots of evenings with us. He was inquisitive, friendly and kind-hearted, and seemed to have an exceptional capacity for learning that was not limited to his demonstrably phenomenal ability to learn languages.

In mid-April, we got notice in the mail from the Malmö agent of the Johnson Lines that our things had arrived from Canada. We phoned and arranged for delivery the next day (they would only deliver to the sidewalk, not to our door five stories up!). That evening, when Boris paid us his usual visit, I asked whether he could come around after school and help, and he enthusiastically agreed.

The next afternoon, while Jeanette was up in our apartment making snacks and dinner, Boris and I were scurrying up and down the 89 steps with the 67 cartons of books, setting them down on the floor in the studio, where the new bookshelves were ready and waiting. Jeanette saw to getting the cartons in numerical order. Finally, Boris and I struggled with the four big trunks. The ones containing china were the worst. Since both Boris and I were in pretty good shape, and young, it all went rather quickly, but we were very glad to get the last of the trunks inside our door. We'd tramped nearly 13,000 stairway steps in total, including the trips back downstairs.

One evening when I came to my ABF class, I was told there would be a new pupil joining the group in mid-term. I was a bit skeptical about the advisability of letting pupils just drop in like that, but given the lack of seriousness of the course in other respects, I just shrugged. The new pupil, however, made my eyes bulge:

a truly drop-dead gorgeous knockout bombshell blonde with long flowing hair, bright blue eyes, a demure smile and a shapely figure that could cause traffic accidents (picture a 20-year-old Claudia Schiffer). I was totally unprepared for that sight and simply couldn't take my eyes off her for more than a few seconds, which made me extremely flustered, then embarrassed that I was flustered, then ashamed that marriage failed to make me immune, then uncertain where I was or what to do. Every step in this deterioration of my self-respect and self-control was obvious to the group (except that she herself didn't seem to notice, or was probably all too familiar with having to pretend not to notice such things). The whole thing was also clearly to my group's considerable, if muted, amusement. She only showed up two or three more times, to my relief.

Somewhere around this time, possibly close to Easter, Carmen threw a party for all staff members at the Demaret family home, a huge and fabulous old ground-floor apartment on Kungsgatan. Jeanette and I drove there for some reason (it might have been cold or raining or both), instead of making the 20-minute walk. Jeanette got to meet most of the people there, including future colleagues as well as the Aussie. Since I hadn't mentioned much about them in advance, Jeanette could draw her own unbiased conclusions, but she did wonder who the hell that Australian bitch thought she was. Most of the people were reasonably nice, however, and there was plenty of good food, and all kinds of beverages. A lot of people were getting really tipsy. A couple of them were already well beyond that stage.

When we felt it was time for us to go, Arno (the German teacher from Karlsruhe) asked if we could possibly give him and Joan (the Scottish lass from Edinburgh) a lift back to his place. Answering the unspoken question written all over my face, he took me aside to explain that he and Joan often shared a bed, but that she kept her clothes on below the waist. He had no trouble reading my equally unspoken response of deepest sympathy, although I had no idea why he felt he had to explain anything to me.

Arno was renting a room in someone's home out at the end of Sallerupsvägen, near the Malmö airport. I said sure, we'll drive you out there. I felt completely sober. Jeanette was a bit tipsy. We all got into the car and headed out to Föreningsgatan, turned right into Sallerupsvägen at Värnhemstorget. It was late at night, there was very little traffic, and we were laughing all the way.

Along Sallerupsvägen in the direction of Bulltofta, there was a spot just after Danska Vägen where the street made a slight, sweeping left-hand curve, before straightening out again. You couldn't see what was around the bend before you entered it, but once you did, there were no side streets, no places to turn off or around. Just as I was entering that curve, a car passed me. I had not a care in the world. Half a second later I did. The traffic police were out making spot checks for drunk driving. In a split second, the following happened: I made a mental inventory of my evening's alcohol consumption: two strong beers, two snapses, three large glasses of wine and a small glass or two of liqueur. *Shit!!* I realized that I'd be *way* over the limit; I had visions of deportation and broken dreams; I felt my pulse rate jump out my throat and through the roof of the car.

Two police officers out in the street had already waved cars over and were conducting breath analyses on the drivers of each. The third policeman had just pulled over the car that passed me moments before. I could thus drive right on through, slowly, there being no unoccupied officer left to wave me in. My heart was clogging up my throat. I hadn't been that nervous since my encounter with Slim and Burly two years earlier. A few blocks later, we dropped Arno and Joan off, but I had to sit there for a while, till my nerves settled. Then we had to drive home via a maze of side streets. Before entering each new one, I stopped, Jeanette jumped out to check that the coast was clear – no police cars in sight – and gradually, street by street, we got home. It would be the last time I ever got behind the wheel after drinking more than half a glass of wine.

On April 29th, Nixon began a new escalation of the war in Vietnam by invading Cambodia, taking the hopelessness of my draft situation down to a record low level, and making Sweden feel more like home than ever. Mike left to go back to his chosen home in the States on Sunday, May 3rd, as scheduled, with no ceremony or fuss. We felt genuine melancholy waving him off, but I was keenly aware of the sea change that took place in Jeanette's relationship to him during the course of his stay. Where she anguished over him while he was in Vietnam and afterwards, those protective feelings began disappearing during the autumn and were now either gone or below the radar. The day after his departure, four anti-war protesters at Kent State University were shot and killed by the National Guard, intensifying student protests throughout most of the US. And we hung up *Sanctuary* on our living room wall.

To my knowledge, Jeanette and Mike never corresponded again. And with the very limited information provided by Rose or Marilyn (Rosanne hardly ever wrote, and the elder Mike not at all), Jeanette found herself with very little insight into any news from her family, apart from a few vital statistics. Jeanette told me it felt like her family regarded her move to Sweden as something on par with treason towards them – that she'd forfeited her right to be included in the inner family circle. I told her I thought she might be making an unnecessarily melodramatic interpretation, that they probably never wrote regularly to *anybody*. She admitted that, but remained unconvinced.

One huge and joyful change that seemed to be causally related to Mike's departure and our suddenly nearly unlimited privacy was a bursting into bloom of our sex life. We'd begun our relationship with Catholic taboos on premarital sex, got off to a very fumbling conjugal beginning tethered by inhibitions in San Francisco, then moved on to a less-than-soundproof basement suite in Vancouver, and since arriving in Sweden had very few nights that involved both a bed and privacy. Now, at last, we could let go, and we did.

When Jeanette came home from Swedish class one day during the week after Mike's departure, she told me that Elsa had invited us, and Boris, to join her and her daughter to visit the Braun's summer cottage in the woods up near a tiny village called Hästveda, near an even tinier hamlet called Glimminge, in northernmost Skåne. She wanted to get a little help from us to open the place up for the summer, and thought we might enjoy seeing how very many Swedes spent their summer vacations.

With four weeks of paid vacation every year for all Swedes, guaranteed by law, plus quite a few holiday weekends in the spring and at year-end, rather many Swedes enjoyed getting away from it all ("all" meaning the already relatively low-key city bustle) by investing in little cottages, sometimes in "villages" of such cottages that were largely uninhabited during the winter, sometimes completely isolated, but preferably close to water, whether at one of Sweden's thousands of small lakes, along Sweden's extensive coastline, or on one of almost innumerable small islands in several Swedish archipelagos. It was at these cottages that the normally rather formal Swedes would let their hair down, wear comfortable old clothing, not worry too much about shaving or makeup, show their feelings, laugh out loud, drink without shame, forget all about prestige and hierarchy, socialize with their neighbors if and when they felt like it, and generally enjoy life.

When Elsa and Moisan picked us up, Jeanette, Boris and I filled the back seat as Elsa's car traversed Sweden's southernmost province. The cottage was, as we would eventually learn, very similar to thousands of others in southern

Sweden: dark horizontal exterior wood paneling that could have used a fresh coat of stain, and white trim around windows, doors, house corners and other trim. Elsa's cottage was very low and small, even cramped. There were a couple of out-buildings: one was for storing garden tools, fishing rods, boards and other necessities; another had room for two extra single beds and not a toothpick more. There was also a small pier that extended out into the small adjacent lake. On the grassy shore near the pier was a small rowboat.

The place badly needed airing. It had been shut up all winter and smelled like old unwashed socks. We opened doors and windows, brought bedding and small carpets outdoors into the sunlight and hung them over benches and branches. After everything that could reasonably be brought outdoors was outdoors, we all took a walk, first out on the pier, dragging the rowboat from its winter resting place several meters from the shore into the water parallel with the pier and tied it up, ready for use.

Elsa told us there was a big grassy recreational area just through the woods ahead. Boris and I found a football (European, not American) that we kicked along as we all walked that way. The tomboyish Moisan joined in the kicking. Jeanette wasn't much for sports and walked with Elsa. After a while, Moisan, who was quite a bit taller than me, suddenly jumped up on my back from behind, and we laughed our heads off. But after a while Moisan stopped laughing and was holding me much tighter, and things suddenly became a bit awkward. I didn't want to hurt her feelings by telling her that I had none of the interest in her that she clearly did in me. I didn't want to arouse Jeanette's green-eyed monster either. Nor did I want to upset Elsa. But then Moisan just slid off my back and it all faded away as suddenly as it had arisen.

By this time, I'd eaten lunches at most of the best restaurants in Malmö, and my deep-pocketed pupils seemed eager to get me to try the finest delicacies. There were some Swedish specialties I loved right from the start, such as nearly all of the dozens of varieties of pickled herring available to me when the restaurant of their choice included a *smörgåsbord*. I'd never in my life eaten herring before coming to Sweden, but I soon came to select almost only herring from the huge spreads that a real *smörgåsbord* should entail. (There were also a few Swedish specialties I had no problem leaving alone.)

One day, a pupil of mine decided we should have a real steak. He took me to the Falstaff Steakhouse restaurant on Baltzarsgatan. He also thought we should have real French *escargots* for our first course. They were delicious. That evening, when I came home to Jeanette and said what felt to her like "Hhhhi hhhhoney!" she looked like I'd punched her. I totally forgot about all the garlic in the butter with the snails. Then we both roared with laughter.

One of my pupils was an executive at Bolinder-Munktell, Volvo's tractor-producing subsidiary in Eskilstuna. His wife joined him for the trip down to Malmö, and she spent her time sightseeing and shopping in Copenhagen while he studied English. At the end of the week, my pupil wanted to invite both Jeanette and me to join him and his wife for a nice dinner on the Friday evening, at Kockska Krogen, in the cellar of a building from the early 1500s in the northwestern corner of Stortorget. It had low, vaulted brick ceilings, a candlelit atmosphere and a menu to quiver at the sight of. The cellar restaurant sort of meandered around corners and pillars, and my jaw was dropping at the architecture, more than a century older than the first English colony in the New World.

My seat gave me a view across the restaurant in the direction from which we entered. As we were finishing our fabulous meal, I saw a man who, when he emerged from around the corner, I instantly recognized as someone I'd met before. I couldn't place him at first. His reaction was obviously identical to mine; he stopped in his tracks and stared long and hard right at me. It hit me who he was just a second before it hit him: Bruno Nyman. Perhaps it was the recognition in my expression that triggered his own. He remained stunned for a moment, closed his mouth grimly, did an about-face, and was off like a shot. We never saw him ever again. Jeanette caught only a glimpse of him, but we said nothing until we'd parted from our hosts.

The party we'd enjoyed (apart from the trauma of the drive home) with my colleagues at Demaret's inspired a number of the teachers we liked best to hold a series of smaller parties. A few of these were at Vårgatan. Everybody brought wine, in the best tradition of the Precarious Vision, and some brought food. Our place soon became a favorite venue, largely thanks to Jeanette's delectable and plentiful nibbles, and the low risk of disturbing the neighbors. None of us had any money; we always bought the cheapest bottles that *Systembolaget* had to offer, such as a Spanish wine called Parador (the parties came to be called "Parador parties"), a Portuguese wine called Estremadura, a Hungarian wine called Egri Bikavér ("bull's blood") and four or five others. They weren't wild parties, just a lot of drinking, eating, talking, and laughing.

In late May, Carmen announced that as from June 1st, the school would be moving from Pilgården to new premises, on the third floor of an early 20th century building on the corner of Exercisgatan and Östra Förstadsgatan. The locale was originally a rather luxurious apartment for a prominent family. It had seven large rooms, all with beautiful parquet floors and high ornamental plaster ceilings. The big kitchen was equipped with an old servants' call system that enabled the gentry to push a button in any room, and the staff in the kitchen could see which room the call came from. There was a bathroom and a separate lavatory, as well as a small room that would serve as the teachers' room. I now had a nine-block walk to work – one block over to Värnhemstorget, then eight blocks along Östra Förstadsgatan to the school. On Saturday, May 30th, Carmen threw a staff party to inaugurate the new premises.

I had a miserable time. My rectum hurt like hell, and I couldn't understand why. It felt swollen, like my intestine was turning inside-out, and the pain was becoming excruciating. It felt like I was morphing into a pain-in-the-ass baboon. Carmen spotted my anguished face and hurried to take me aside. "*I used to be a nurse*," she hissed at me when we were alone. (Carmen had reportedly worked at St Mary's Hospital in London in the early 1940s, first as a nurse and then as a research assistant to Alexander Fleming, who won the Nobel Prize in 1945 for the discovery of penicillin.) "*You can tell me what the matter is!*" I felt incredibly embarrassed, but told her of my rectal swelling. "*It's hemorrhoids!*" she exclaimed in an aspirated whisper. "*You've got to reach round with your finger and just shove them back in!*" Then she saw the look of disgust all over my face. "*Just shove them back in, and keep shoving them in. That's the only way the swelling will go down! And then wash your hands!!*" And she was right. Thorns in lion's paws again.

Perhaps Carmen's kindness towards me in this helped Jeanette overcome her reluctance to try her hand as a teacher, particularly since Elsa's class was on a summer break. In any case, she began taking a few hours in mid-June. I could tell she didn't like it much, and when I asked her about it, she said she felt unqualified (I knew nothing about what the Aussie bitch was up to), but she said she was sure she'd get used to it. Anyway, she only saw it as a temporary thing, a way to make some money over the summer. She ended up working at Demaret's through October, averaging 25 hours a week. The pupils seemed to like her too.

Sometime in early June, Jeanette and I were walking home from town one day and heard a lot of horns blaring and young people screaming and cheering.

Then we saw a couple of flatbed trucks decked out with balloons, birch branches, streamers, and kids in their late teens clearly celebrating something they considered quite fantastic. There were some old classic cars as well as luxury cars decked out the same way and containing similar celebrants. One thing the kids had in common, apart from the wild cheering, was white caps, mostly with black patent-leather brims – almost identical to the ones the milkmen of my childhood wore. Being told that this was a Swedish rite of passage, the way of marking the completion of high school – graduation – didn't stop us from finding it considerably amusing: pomp and circumstance, Swedish style.

The time for one of Sweden's biggest holidays was rapidly approaching, the Friday before the summer solstice. *Midsommarafton* was one of only two of Sweden's somewhat surprising collection of holidays *not* based directly on religious traditions, the other being New Year's, the surprise being that Sweden had any religious holidays at all. Despite being such a secular society, with few people who attended church and even fewer who actually believed, Sweden had an official state religion, a variant of Lutheranism, to which everyone born in Sweden more or less automatically belonged – and paid church tax to support.

Anyone not wishing to remain a member of the Swedish Church had to actively file for resignation (a very simple procedure). At least that was a significant improvement over the situation that prevailed in Europe throughout the Middle Ages, when apostasy was a capital crime punished by burning, beheading, confiscation of all property, and other pleasant repercussions (similar punishments for apostasy remain in a number of Islamic countries as of 2016, where "freedom of religion" only means freedom to *become* a Muslim, not freedom to leave it). The Church, for most Swedes, was where you christened your children, got them confirmed at the age of 14 or 15, got married, had your funeral, and maybe sometimes went to an actual church service at Christmas for the ambiance of the music and candlelight. The difference compared to many other countries was that for most Swedes, the Church and the holidays were for religious *traditions*, not religious *observance*.

Good Friday, Easter Monday, Whit Monday (I had to look it up), Pentecost, Ascension Day – these were all public holidays in Sweden, yet none of them were holidays in the very religious USA. The deist Thomas Jefferson insisted on both freedom of religion and the complete separation of Church and State in the drafting of the US Constitution. He explained and emphasized that the latter was contingent on the former, but his concerns found only very limited success in practice, as it would turn out.

In Sweden, all religions that were not the Swedish Church were referred to as "free churches", taking some liberties with the definition of "free" by applying it to people who voluntarily bind and even enslave themselves emotionally and mentally by refusing to question dogma unsupported by evidence. Yet the "free churches" in Sweden tended to be the most enslaved to dogma, while the Swedish church was most enslaved to tradition. As long as you were enslaved to *something*, it was OK.

Midsommar, however, was special, Elsa explained, and with the days becoming incredibly long, and the full life force of all the greenery and flowery and birdery having returned, the gloom of winter darkness was nowhere to be seen. It was a time when Swedes celebrated Midsommar Eve – if possible at their summer cottages, preferably outdoors – with lots of herring and new potatoes and meatballs and beer and *snaps* and strawberries and cheese. And singing, particularly if the intake of *snaps* was sufficient. The celebrations might go on until the sun set in the northwest (that's where it sets in the south of Sweden; the farther north you go, the farther north the sun sets, until it doesn't set at all), and the residual twilight simply shifts to the north and northeast; dusk glides straight into dawn, and only the brightness of returning daylight and the pain it can cause to the eyes of those who've enjoyed too much liquid refreshment is the signal to retire.

If the celebrations take place in some kind of community, whether in town or in any of numerous small country villages and hamlets primarily composed of summer cottages, there will invariably be a Midsommar pole around which children and their parents gather in the afternoon to dance to Swedish folk songs played on fiddles and/or accordions (or portable stereos).

About a week before Midsommar, after our last Swedish class for the term was over, Elsa asked Jeanette, me and Boris to wait around a bit. When the four of us were alone, she said that she and her family were going up to central Sweden for the Midsommar weekend to celebrate with old friends, and if we'd like, the three of us were welcome to spend our Midsommar at the Braun's country cottage. She handed me the key. We were stunned and thrilled – and overwhelmed yet again by Elsa's generosity.

We drove up on Midsommar Eve, June 19th, in the late morning, having bought a few groceries the day before and a few perishables along the way. It was a beautiful clear day, and we unloaded the car, looking at how green and lush everything had become in the month or so since we'd been there. There wasn't another person or house in sight. The rowboat was tied to the little pier, and Boris and I found the oars in one of the small sheds, where we also found a fishing rod, with a lure already attached. The three of us decided that in the late afternoon we'd go on a little fishing expedition out on the lake.

Boris had some fishing experience, but not from Sweden. I'd fished a couple of times in my life, in a small fishing pond in Thatcher Woods with Johnny K. when I was about 10, but my "success" was limited to finding a dead bluegill floating in the pond, then stabbing it with my hook and displaying it as a "catch". My patience leaked badly and had run out. In spite of my total absence of expertise, impressions I'd gleaned from descriptions in various novels gave me the totally unfounded confidence to declare that the reeds growing in the water on the far side of the lake would be a likely spot to catch perch or pike. (I already knew that those two species were common in Swedish lakes.) We rowed and rowed. Boris and I took turns, Jeanette cheered us on, all three of us laughed until a reverent, don't-disturb-the-fish silence fell upon us as we neared the reeds.

Jeanette handed me the rod. The lure at the end of the line was hooked into the reel. I freed it and was preparing to wind it in a bit, in preparation for my first cast, but the reel was jammed. The line was hopelessly tangled. It was impossible to reel the line in or let more out. The only free line we had was the meter or so from the end of the rod back to the reel. What a letdown!

While Boris was trying unsuccessfully to unjam or untangle it, I was looking into the water over the side of the boat. It was clear and beautiful, probably only about a meter and a half deep. And suddenly I saw a fairly big pike swimming around, hunting for food. My heart leapt. I whispered to Boris to hand me the rod, and I dangled the lure over the side, gently moving it back and forth, round and round in the clear water, jerking it a couple of times. Within 30 seconds, the pike struck and I jerked on the rod to get it securely hooked. Without thinking, I reflexively tried to start reeling it in, but the jammed reel made that impossible. I pulled it as hard as I could towards the boat, then relaxed a second and let it furiously swim a meter away, then jerked it back towards the boat. I repeated this a couple of times, and the next time the pike started swimming away from the boat, I hissed "Get ready!" When it had almost reached the boat again, I leaned back hard, jerking it upwards and into the boat, flapping and flipping (the pike, not me) for all it was worth, while Boris wrestled it to the floor of the boat and delivered a hard blow to its head with the heel of his clog.

Practically squealing with triumph, Boris and I took the oars and began paddling furiously to get back to the cottage, while Jeanette was already figuring out how she would prepare it as soon as we got back. Boris knew how to clean a fish, and Jeanette prepared a stuffing of fresh dill, parsley, salt and lemon. She found some breadcrumbs in the cupboard and breaded it, then fried it in butter to a crispy golden brown, and served it with potatoes and melted butter. I remember the pike as 50 cm long; it might have been 40, allowing for a possible fish tale. But the objective truth is that three hungry young people enjoyed and filled up on an especially tasty dinner in the 9 PM sunshine and wondered if night would ever fall. It was our very first Midsommar in Sweden, and we couldn't have dreamed of a better venue.

In late June I received my long-awaited and long-dreaded induction order from the Selective Service, dated June 19th, addressed to me at Vårgatan. The letter began with the draft board's infamous and customary salutation: "*Greeting*". It tersely informed me that I was to report to an address in Forest Park, Illinois, on July 15th at 6:15 AM. I immediately wrote the following short reply: "*Greeting: In reply to your 'Order to Report for Induction' of 19 June 1970, I am unable to comply because I cannot afford such a great move. Sincerely*," and my signature. Thus, as from July 15th, 1970 I would officially become a fugitive from US justice, a peril to the public safety of all true Americans. There was no legal precedent to indicate that I would ever again be allowed to visit my native land without facing arrest and incarceration; there was no statute of limitations for a crime as heinous as mine. The bridges behind me were blazing.

On June 30th, Jeanette and I visited the public swimming pool, as we often did, having no other alternative to the sponge baths in our kitchen, where we used the stove to heat a pot of water. After swimming for a while, taking a sauna, scrubbing and being scrubbed, and showering, I returned to the locker room to get dressed. To my gasp of bone-chilling horror, I saw that my locker had been broken into. My trousers had been thrown into the next locker, but my wallet was gone. And so was my *passport*!

At that point in my life, I was convinced that it was a CIA job, that they knew (thanks to the *Chicago Tribune*) that I'd been dodging the draft, and that they actively and purposefully targeted my passport, thinking I'd have to go to the Embassy to get a new one (US Embassies are legally American territory) – and they would nab me there. It seriously rattled our peace of mind. But I was more afraid of being nabbed by the US at the Embassy than of getting into trouble with the Swedish authorities for not having a valid passport into which they could stamp my extended work permit when that came due in late August.

Since my draft notice was so fresh that I hadn't yet had time to become a delinquent (or an outlaw), we almost immediately went to the Embassy in Copenhagen to see about a new passport. They told us we'd have to wait a month to see if the stolen passport turned up, which it didn't. By the time the month was up, my date to report for military service had passed, officially making me a fugitive from justice. Jeanette went back to the Embassy on her own to enquire whether I'd be able to get a new passport under the circumstances. They told her it was unlikely. Then I went to the immigration police to see about getting an alien's passport, but was told that I could only get one if I had a letter from the Embassy stating that they refused to issue me a passport. Jeanette went back to the Embassy again to make inquiries about getting such a letter, and was told that I could, in fact, get a new passport, since my name didn't yet appear on any of their blacklists. So we went back again, and got a temporary three-month passport, during which time an investigation would supposedly be carried out in Washington DC, which would either end in rejection or in issuance of a new five-year passport. Apparently the State Department didn't communicate a lot with the Selective Service (the age of computers hadn't yet arrived in anything like full force); I was able to pick up my new passport in mid-September.

Apart from the passport trauma, it was pretty much a summer of being. Jeanette was getting quite a few hours at Demaret's, which she didn't mind now that Swedish classes were over till the autumn. The Aussie bitch left Demaret's and was presumably trying to lord it over others elsewhere. My working hours were not excessive, and I was glad I no longer had the ultimately unsatisfying work of the ABF *kaffekalas*.

Boris and I occasionally went fishing, first for bony fish in the canals, then – fearing a possibly high mercury content – we (I use the term loosely) fished for cod in the sea. Boris was good at it; "we" ended up filling our small freezer with five or six fish, all caught by him. As usual, I had too little patience.

Our correspondence with Bob that summer was continuing and blossoming into areas of extreme interest to all three of us. We'd mentioned that we might like to travel down to see him in the autumn, but the passport problems threatened to spoil those plans. Bob, however, mentioned the possibility of visiting us in early September, if he could get himself invited to present a paper at a scientific convention in Hamburg, and could manage to get a couple of extra days off to head north.

Our correspondence with Krzysztof began flourishing that summer too. He wondered if I could help him acquire certain books on advanced mathematics. He sent me a list, which I forwarded to my mathematician brother Al, who kindly sent me all of them. I paid Al, and Krzysztof promised to reimburse me some day in the form of cheap Polish canvas. I was eager to resume my painting, and we were beginning to talk about how we could arrange for Krzysztof to visit us in Malmö in the not-too-distant future. Al also sent me additional books in his ongoing campaign to align our religious beliefs with his. And again, by challenging me further to examine what I did and didn't believe, and compelling me to think deeply about it, Al inadvertently widened the gap between our beliefs into a chasm.

I was told, innumerable times throughout my childhood and youth, that the Bible was the *only* source of Truth, of Happiness, of the way to Eternal Life. I had lived and breathed it – and nearly suffocated from it. When I began to have doubts, I was pretty much alone with them. Those whose differing, dissenting ideas and skepticism I encountered weren't people I'd ever met or would ever be likely to meet: authors, scientists, philosophers, from different eras and distant parts of the world. Bob, however, sounded real. He'd been where I'd been, was where I was, and we were pretty sure we were struggling in the same direction.

Why was it a struggle? If we didn't like it, didn't believe it, why not just walk away from it? Jeanette seemed to be able to do this without a problem. There were reasons of great importance to Bob and me: just because we both found it intellectually unsatisfactory to hold a belief without good reasons – factual reasons – for doing so, we *also* found it unsatisfactory to abandon a formerly held belief without similarly having examined it to the ground and pinpointed its fallacies. Then there was the highly significant matter of the emotions: close family bonds that I'd been explicitly warned that I'd be jeopardizing and possibly destroying. It was implicit emotional blackmail. The familial pressure remained long after I left Oak Park. I was *still* breaking free.

There was also the psychological need to overcome group pressure (although much less for me now that I was in Sweden). Nearly everyone in the world believed in one god or another, and many of them were constantly fighting about whose god was the Only True God, without ever having established that the whole idea of a god – any god or gods at all – had any validity in the first place. Just a few hundred years before, most people on earth believed the earth was flat. Arguing about the shape of its flatness wasn't going to make it any flatter, although many seemed to flatter themselves that it would. Facts aren't determined by majority (*or* minority) rule. Not even unanimously.

Once Bob, Jeanette and I had each other's close friendship, we were no longer alone in our struggle. Just as Norm and I had helped each other achieve escape velocity from the Oak Park Meeting in 1964, Bob and I had were now about ready for ignition of the second-stage rocket that would convey us out of the gravity of religion of every stripe and brand of malarkey that would try to cross our paths thereafter.

In mid-July, mounting protests in the US may have influenced Nixon to begin withdrawing troops from Cambodia, completing the withdrawal on Jeanette's 26th birthday. But by this time, it felt too late; I'd already been drafted and become a fugitive, and was likely to remain one forever, in the eyes of the authorities in the USA.

In early August, Bob wrote to say that he would be presenting a paper at the World Congress on Hormonal Steroids in Hamburg in early September, and was cautiously hopeful that he could get two extra days off to come up and see us. We were fairly seething with excitement, and rushed out to purchase a sofa-bed to replace the somewhat raunchy sofa we'd been saddled with when we bought the lease to our apartment. We were going to give Bob a decent place to sleep. We also bought a simple pine dining table, with a pull-out leaf on each end, and four pine chairs. As the details of Bob's trip began to fall into place, we agreed to meet him at the Central Station in Copenhagen on Wednesday, September 9th, our first meeting ever, the first time we'd even hear each other's voices.

CHAPTER 6

Cleaning up the mess

On Monday, September 7th, we received word from the US Embassy in Copenhagen that my new passport – the five-year version – was ready to be picked up. Since we would be making the crossing on Wednesday anyway (to pick up Bob at the central station in the afternoon), we decided to take care of our business at the Embassy that same morning. It was a great relief, and in a way it put us in a more desirable position than if I hadn't lost my passport when I did, because there seemed to be a chance for me to gain Swedish citizenship within five years after the issuance of our work permits, which meant that I'd still have a valid US passport until that time, and wouldn't have to bother about filling the gap with an alien's passport.

Although we were excited about picking up my passport, I was not a little nervous about being back inside the US Embassy. Ever since my dawning childhood understanding of my country's savage mistreatment of the Indians had nullified the proposition of "my country right or wrong", I began finding myself on the opposite side of patriotism. And then I found myself facing induction into a war that I could in no way conceive as "defending my country". Nobody was attacking us. We just wanted to be the top dog, to exercise colonial powers over people and peoples practically everywhere – in the name of defending "democracy" and "liberty"?! Was I to kill and die for that?!

But on this particular day, we were even more excited about meeting Bob for the very first time. We'd exchanged photos through the mail a couple of months before, and I'd commented on the family resemblance I saw to his father Harold, but Bob didn't comment on that comment.

The tone of his letters was so different from anyone else I'd ever corresponded with, that I didn't really know what to expect him to be like in person. His vocabulary and ability to construct complex yet lucid sentences made it obvious to me that he was very intelligent, but some of his comments were difficult to assess in terms of whether they were sarcastic, ironic, bursting with subtle humor, smoldering with rage, weary with depression, smug, insecure or contented – or any combination of the aforesaid.

When Jeanette and I arrived at Copenhagen's busy central station, we were not totally certain which train Bob would be on. The station was shaped like (and was as cavernous as) an airplane hangar, and the track numbers were listed along one long wall, with escalators and stairs leading down to and up from the various tracks on the level below. We decided to wait upstairs and watch everyone coming up from the platforms, to see if we could spot him, based on a single photo. We arrived rather early, and I paced up and down for quite a while. Jeanette understood and let me pace.

At last I saw Harold Krause coming wearily up the stairs clutching a suitcase and a briefcase, and I knew instantly it was Bob. We ran over to greet him the second he got to the top step, with warm handshakes instead of embraces – there was something about him that exuded more formality than either Jeanette or I normally possessed, and we didn't want to overdo things at our first meeting. I told him I'd recognized him immediately because of his father, and he winced visibly. I tried to cover my glaring error by adding that I only meant the physical similarity, nothing at all to do with the kind of person he was. Bob relaxed a bit and let me off the hook with a wan smile.

It was immediately apparent that Bob had little practice (or perhaps interest) in casual, getting-to-know-you small talk. Every response to my cascade of questions was delayed to allow for reflection and careful formulation, as though he felt he were on trial. In my usual jovial manner, I started making a few quips, telling a few jokes, laughing at them, laughing at myself, making sarcastic comments about the signs around us, verbally flitting around like a fly on amphetamines, trying to get him to relax and enjoy himself. We had a bit of a walk from the central station to the ferry terminal at Havnegade. In our exuberant youth, it never occurred to us that Bob might be hard of walking. First we passed Tivoli, walked across the main square, then continued along the entire length of Strøget, a pedestrian street stuffed with small shops and boutiques and cafés that ran all the way to the square called Kongens Nytorv. This square was the location of Copenhagen's opera house, as well as a very grand, ritzy establishment called the Hotel d'Angleterre. When Bob saw it, he took great pleasure in stopping, to inform us that some very important summit meeting took place at that very hotel a few years before, what was or wasn't decided then, what wine they drank at the banquet, what part of France that wine came from. On and on the knowledge flowed from him, like a crossword puzzle unravelling multilevel facts upon which we could feast.

When we at last boarded the ferry to Malmö, we sat at a table in the cafeteria. I asked Bob if he'd like a beer and his eyes lit up. The crossing took two beers and five minutes. From the ferry terminal in Malmö, we walked across to the train station and took a bus to Värnhemstorget, then walked a block and a half to Vårgatan and up the four flights of stairs to our apartment. Bob was visibly weary by the time we sat down.

He first opened his briefcase and took out a liter bottle of Glenfiddich he'd bought in the duty-free shop on the ferry from Germany to Denmark, and Jeanette brought three glasses from the kitchen. I was clearly not as accustomed to drinking hard liquor straight as he was; I had to refill his glass before I'd had more than a sip of mine. Nor was I accustomed to whisky that good; it was my first-ever taste of a single malt. (No wonder. Single-malts were virtually unknown outside Scotland before the 1960s. The first commercially available Glenfiddich single-malt was released in 1963.) Meanwhile, Jeanette was already busy preparing one of her wonderful meals in between some sipping of her own.

Jeanette's prowess in the kitchen started in her mother's; her Italian ground-beef meat sauce was amazingly rich in flavor, cooked in plenty of red wine and crushed tomatoes, and packed with large quantities of garlic, basil, oregano, rosemary, marjoram, to which she usually also added tarragon and sage. She would make the meat sauce in the biggest pot we had, to use with spaghetti, or as the base for her mouth-watering lasagne, for which her liberal use of cheese obviated the need for béchamel. From there she moved on to things like veal cacciatore and dozens of other great Italian dishes, including desserts like *zabaione*.

Jeanette had already introduced herself and me to French cooking when we lived in Vancouver, and was working her way through the recipes in a Chinese cookbook she got for her birthday from her friend Elsie. She baked delicious breads and intoxicating pies – both fruit and meat – and quickly mastered my childhood birthday favorite: Treasure Chest Cake. Only my youthful high metabolism stood between her seductive cooking and my out-of-control obesity.

After several whiskies, Bob began to relax and mellow, all the while railing at the ruthlessness of Nixon and Kissinger. I began to become a little concerned about how much whisky he seemed to need to loosen up. But what the hell, he'd had a rough week at the congress, a long trip from Hamburg to Vårgatan, and was pretty far out of his comfort zone. *Let him find his way there however he wants.*

As the roughest of the edges began to soften, Bob began to look around at his unfamiliar surroundings and caught his breath when he caught sight of *Hurry up with the Lumber, for Christ's Sake*, then again when he saw *Sanctuary*, and again at *Man with Guitar* and *Self-Portrait*. He literally froze, with his whisky glass in mid-air, put it back down on the table, and struggled to get up and take closer looks. There was no need to ask whether my paintings spoke to him; he and they were already far too deep in conversation.

Bob turned 42 just over a week before our first meeting; I would turn 25 in just a few days. But Bob seemed *very* much older than 42, particularly in his physical agility (I probably acted much younger than 25 in his eyes). As the evening wore on, with a delightful meal and some cheap wine over which to converse, we found ourselves tripping over each other in our efforts to cover topics so wide-ranging, and with so much potential for depth that we knew neither how to make the evening last nor how to bring it to an end. We'd never before met anyone with whom we could speak as freely and as intelligently on *any* topic.

After dinner we remained at the table, and I inquired about his health. The question opened yet another floodgate. After a deep sigh, he began by explaining that he and his ex-wife Sigrid had tried repeatedly and unsuccessfully to have children. A barrage of tests in 1965 revealed that Bob was sterile – which he thought was what triggered the demise of the marriage – and that his sterility was due to congenital and hereditary kidney problems (his severely diabetic mother died of nephritis), and that Bob was born with only one kidney which didn't work satisfactorily either, and that (according to the doctor) Bob had just two years to live. (He'd already been told that the year before, in 1964, i.e. five years before he told me.) Besides, he had angina, chronic bronchitis and hypertension. As far as he knew, everything was now on borrowed time and there was nothing to be done about it, and it was all very depressing and Sigrid treated him like shit, like the big disappointment and utter failure he was, and there was no point to anything, as he had sort of given up and was just waiting for it all to be over, and all the crap he'd been force-fed as a child wasn't worth a pile of steaming turds, and how can people do that kind of thing to their children, feeding them lies and not letting them develop their minds and actually think and find out for themselves whether any given thing has anything at all that merits the label of Truth, and that meeting me, meeting us, was such an unexpected breath of pure oxygen in the atmosphere of carbon monoxide he was living in, and were we really for real and did we really want to meet and develop something along the lines of something that could turn into something like friendship with the likes of him?

All the while he went rambling on, he was sipping his whisky between gulps, but it took quite a while before any of the customary signs of drunkenness appeared, long after he revealed to us all these innermost, darkest thoughts, full of agony, self-pity and scathing nihilism, as well as a cry for help with no trace of willingness to surrender his intellectual integrity to some snake-oil merchant or peddler of dogma promising simplistic solutions to the enormous complexity of life in the real world.

He awed me. His pain went to my marrow, his nihilism froze my blood. I suddenly found myself in a totally unexpected role: not so much a catcher in the rye, but more like a trapeze catcher, and Bob – the one I was to catch – had already let go of his trapeze and was hurtling towards me with no safety net below. There was no way I would allow myself to let him fall. But I didn't have a clue how to catch him.

I have no memory of the hour or Bob's condition when he finally flopped into bed, mumbling about my needing to go on painting, whatever it took, nor at what hour we met the next morning, if indeed it was still the early side of noon. A lot – but not all – of his inhibitions returned with his relative sobriety the next day. But it was more like two steps forward, one step back. It took the entire day and evening until our discussions gradually returned to full force that Thursday, this time without requiring the catalyst of excessive alcohol.

I mentioned that I inferred a look of pain or disapproval or offense or something negative when I mentioned the family resemblance to his father. He gave a grunting sort of serious chuckle; he was a bit surprised, either that it showed, or that I was perceptive enough to pick it up. But it was true; he *hated* his father, everything about him, including the fact that his father called Bob "Bud", as did his brother Charles. This was why he wanted me to call him Bob.

Every Saturday evening from the time Bob was about 12, until he was off to college, Harold Krause took him down to the basement (or out to the garage or somewhere) to beat him. This was not punishment for any particular wrongdoing; it was a matter of principle, following the Biblical injunction, "*He that spareth his rod hateth his son.*" Apparently, Harold got it backwards: he hated his son and spared not the rod. And Bob felt all the more hated for it. Bob's great sin was apparently to have become so immersed in his own indoctrination that he wanted to go as deeply into it as possible. While I rebelled against the Meeting and most of what it stood for, Bob fought to understand it in greater depth than Harold was capable of, by avidly reading the writings of its initialed founders, JND, CHM, CHB, CIA, LMNO goldfish, whatever, and Harold felt first challenged, then threatened, then furious, then sadistic. This went on for years. Bob was beaten systematically in spite of the fact that he wasn't "naughty" in any of the ways I was naughty, much less in any of the ways I wanted to be naughty. Since Bob was *self*-disciplined, it must have taken a great deal of blindness on his father's part not to see that further discipline would be entirely superfluous. I turned pale as Bob related what happened, occasionally gritting his teeth, occasionally adding a splash or two to his glass.

I was almost equally surprised about Bob's former great interest in probing the Meeting to its depths, but this was before I discovered that there was very little that Bob took any interest in at all without taking exceptionally great interest in getting to the bottom of it, and beyond. When he began his studies at the University of Michigan in 1946, having just turned 18, his original academic pursuit was the somewhat arcane study of Classical Greek, for the primary if not sole purpose of being able to read the New Testament in the original language – at least those parts originally written in Greek. This too was a pursuit frowned upon and only reluctantly accepted by his father, again because Harold felt challenged.

I should point out that although all the details of Bob's history provided here are true to the best of my ability to record them, having been told and/or written to me by Bob himself, and supported by numerous original documents kept by Bob, the facts came to my knowledge much more piecemeal and over a much longer time than told here. It took me years of confusion to put together the sequence of events, and I am more interested in recounting the correct sequence relative to Bob's life than portraying my confusion relative to Bob's scattered accounts.

Bob's knowledge was encyclopedic and his thirst for knowledge was unquenchable. While studying Greek, Bob was obliged to find a part-time job to help cover his living expenses; he found a job as an orderly in the local hospital. This fostered an interest – a *deep* interest, of course – in what he was actually doing as an orderly, in what nurses were doing, doctors, even medical science as a whole. Within a couple of years, he decided to abandon Classical Greek in favor of pre-med. His fights with Harold continued. After taking his Bachelor of Science degree from Michigan in 1950, he continued his studies at Michigan's medical school for another year. Then, having heard that the University of Rochester (NY) medical school offered a more exciting challenge, as well as the opportunity to put extra miles between him and his father in Detroit, Bob transferred to Rochester, taking his Doctor of Medicine degree with honors in 1954, the same year Bob officially broke with the Meeting.

Harold made it clear that a break with the Meeting would automatically result in a break between Bob and his parents, assuming for some strange reason that Bob would mind breaking with his father. The rupture was comprehensive. But Bob had no desire to break with his mother Edna, and he felt rather lost. He developed a few friendships in Rochester, but the gaps were many and wide, and friendship in depth was hard to find; none of them shared anything remotely like his background and experience. I knew that feeling quite well.

In combination with Bob's exceptional intelligence, all his knowledge and desire to know would eventually lead him to start questioning the foundations – the first premises and the previously unquestionable axioms – of his childhood indoctrination. His increasing exposure to and interest in science (not limited to medical science) was providing him with the tools to test not only the reasoning but the premises.

He found it scary on many levels, as I had also come to do. Indoctrination invariably has a powerful emotional foundation, and the tools of reason are not necessarily more adequate in dealing with runaway feelings than screwdrivers are at sawing boards. Norm and I had had the decisive advantage of each other's support in escaping the influence of the Meeting, with all its emotional and family-related chains. Bob and I now began to feel that we could provide each other that kind of mutual support in cleaning up the mess, getting over the last hurdles of ingrained superstition and becoming truly free. He told me he thought my paintings were like road signs for finding the way, and he pumped me for information about them, what I'd been thinking and feeling when I painted them, why I painted, where I wanted to go with it – the latter of which I didn't know at all.

Bob had to get the train back to Basel on Saturday morning, something he dreaded for reasons our conversations hadn't yet covered, but after Jeanette prepared another wonderful meal on Thursday evening, Bob was determined to return the favor by taking us out to dinner on Friday evening, preferably at the very best restaurant Malmö had to offer. Since my wealthier pupils at Demaret's made a habit of finding and taking me to Malmö's finest, I suggested Kockska Krogen. Right from his first impression, Bob was delighted with our choice. We had an absolutely superb meal in an unbeatable atmosphere, followed by a brandy snifter of Grand Marnier Cordon Rouge, at Bob's recommendation.

As we mellowed during the meal, Bob told me of his surprisingly clear memory of our first meeting – in Des Moines when he was 20 and I was just three. He was quite clear about his first impression of me, and that he had commented to himself, "*This one is going to be different!*" I said he must have been right, at least where our other cousins were concerned; Bob and I were the only ones who managed to "escape". Then we laughed.

Bob's depression, as well as its causes, were real and deeply troubling to me and to Jeanette as well. All three of us were terribly eager not to allow this first meeting to be anything other than the start of a beautiful friendship, and we racked our brains to come up with a plan for our next meeting. Jeanette and I had our fourth anniversary coming up in less than a month. Thus far we'd managed to celebrate each one in a different country. Now that I had a new passport, maybe we could take a week for a car trip down to see Bob in Binningen, leaving on Friday afternoon, October 2nd, and arriving the next day? Bob responded with hesitant enthusiasm; he was very enthused about our coming, but very hesitant because he saw innumerable practical obstacles, theoretical hurdles, and geopolitical quandaries, but Jeanette and I resolved them faster than he could mention them. He was probably a bit bowled over by our youthful alacrity and spontaneity, and just chuckled, waved his hand in delighted resignation, and joined us in drafting the plan.

One potential snag was the fact that he had no telephone (no wonder my parents had been unable to give me his number!), meaning there was no way for us to contact him on short notice regarding possible last-minute changes, delays, further instructions and the like. Bob had a strong and largely irrational aversion to phones, fearing that Sigrid would hound him constantly if he had one.

We already knew quite a lot about orienting ourselves on German autobahns, in strange cities, and foreign countries. Thus we felt that all we needed were some simple instructions for how to find Gorenmattstrasse 41 once we arrived at the Swiss border, presumably in the late afternoon on the Saturday. But Bob felt it was too complicated to explain, that we'd never be able to find it on our own; instead we acquiesced to his insistence to meet us at the train station in Freiburg, Germany, a couple of hours' drive north of Basel, at about 3 PM that Saturday. The plan was therefore that he would take the train to Freiburg, and we'd ride together in our car to his home in Binningen.

Shortly after Bob's departure, Jeanette resumed her Swedish lessons at *Kursverksamheten*. I occasionally joined her if my work schedule allowed, which wasn't often. The idea was that Jeanette and I would together go through what she'd learned, thus enabling me to benefit as well. Elsa wasn't conducting the new class, since her focus was on beginners. Instead, the teacher was a young woman, not more than a year or two older than us, also named Margareta. Jeanette said she was nice, but was no Elsa. When I finally had a chance to attend one of the lessons, I was rather surprised to find that the new teacher looked like a cross between Bruno's Margareta and Raquel Welch. I scrutinized her to discover what it was about her that contributed to that overall impression. It might have been her excessive makeup (borderline vulgar for my taste), frosted lipstick and exaggerated mascara. Jeanette mistook my scrutiny for ogling and instantly became disturbingly jealous. The fact that I didn't find Margareta the least bit attractive had no mitigating effect, while Margareta's flirtatious behavior towards me exacerbated Jeanette's jealousy intolerably. I avoided accompanying Jeanette to any more of those lessons.

In the couple of weeks before Bob's visit, and increasingly in the weeks that followed, there was trouble brewing at Demaret's. Many of the teachers were upset about being treated like serfs, only getting work when Carmen felt like it, getting wages that were difficult to live on for anyone with a "normal" apartment (cheap "unmodern" places like ours were not for everybody, nor were they plentiful), and the complaints were at last reaching Carmen's ears.

Her response was *not* to sit down and try to work out a satisfactory solution, but to bare her claws and fangs. She drafted contracts that she wanted every teacher to sign, contracts that would entrench the feudal conditions, contracts that all but those few in Carmen's inner circle – who, incidentally, had no other employment options – were very reluctant to sign.

Those of us who were unwilling to write our names in blood got together over some bottles of Egri Bikavér (still among the cheapest wines in Sweden in 1970) to discuss how to respond, what possible counteractions we could take, how much was at stake, and what we were willing to risk. Arno, the German teacher who'd been living in Sweden for several years, meaning several years longer than most of the rest of us, knew quite a lot more than anyone else about what Swedish employers may or may not legally do. He felt we ought to agree to fight this thing together, in solidarity, and to find out about possible membership in a trade union, one that would be willing to stand in our corner, maybe even fight for us.

We agreed unanimously that this was the way to go (Miss Burhe and Mrs Fredin weren't present at this subversive meeting), and Arno said he had a few union contacts he could get in touch with; all we could do was see if any of them would back us. That was how we left matters when Jeanette and I took off for Basel.

Perhaps because it wasn't the dead of winter when we were driving on the autobahn this time, or because our Saab was more road-weary than it was nine months earlier, but the traffic that Friday seemed far more intense than we remembered. Pulling out into the left-hand lane to pass a slow truck in the right-hand lane required checking the rearview mirror for *anything* in the left-hand lane, as far back as the horizon. Failure to do so could result in the very sudden sight of a powerful Mercedes, BMW or Porsche doing more than 200 km/h, 10 cm behind us, furiously flashing its high beams as if the driver of that high-powered vehicle rightfully expected us to pull over into the side of the truck we were in the process of passing. It could be kind of scary at times. Just south of Hannover we found a layby for our overnight stop, and were glad we didn't have the bitter cold of winter to deal with.

On Saturday morning we set off early. We were making good progress, and were well ahead of our projections for reaching Freiburg by 3 PM. We hoped, in fact, to have a couple of hours to look around the town before Bob arrived. On we drove, past Kassel and Frankfurt, towards Heidelberg, but by about 2 o'clock, well past Frankfurt and still on schedule, we began experiencing car trouble. I noticed on the temperature gauge that the engine was suddenly very hot. I pulled over to have a look (not that I'd ever had a clue about what goes on beneath the hood of a car), and was able to determine that there was very little water in the radiator. We stopped at the next gas station and filled it up, then headed out again.

The temperature gauge returned to normal, but we hadn't travelled very many kilometers, limping along much slower this time, before it began creeping up again, getting close to the red zone, meaning danger. Again I stopped by the side of the road and checked the radiator again. The water level was very low. Then I looked under the car, and saw water dripping from the area of the radiator. We stopped at the next service stop, hoping to get service, not considering that this was Saturday afternoon in Germany, which meant no service till Monday. Realizing we might have trouble keeping our three o'clock appointment, we tried to page Bob at the Freiburg station. A few minutes later, we were told that no Herr Doktor Krause had presented himself. We had no way of knowing whether they really tried to page him or not. We bought a jeep can, filled it with water, filled up the radiator, and headed out into the southbound autobahn traffic again.

Since I didn't dare to try to keep the pace of the slow lane, we drove along the shoulder at about 50 km/h, stopping to add water every time the needle hit the red zone, which was more and more frequently. And we stopped at every service station to see if we could get help, to fill up the jeep can, and to try once again to phone the train station in Freiburg to page Bob. They said they'd posted a message on their bulletin board.

I made one of our increasingly frequent roadside stops at one of the many places where there were emergency telephones for highway service. We were told to wait there. After 10-15 minutes, a mechanic arrived, looked at our car, and told us we had a broken water pump, and we could follow him to a repair shop some 20 km further south. We were thrilled, until he roared out, doing 120 km/h, never looking back. He simply left us in the dust with dashed hopes.

When we finally limped into the Freiburg station at nearly 11 PM, frantic and exhausted, we rushed in to look for Bob. He was nowhere to be seen. We asked at the information desk. They knew nothing about any Dr Krause. We were nearly distraught, a feeling not alleviated by our discovery of an obscure bulletin board tucked away somewhere in a corner of the waiting room – with a note for Dr Krause. He obviously hadn't seen it, which meant that the question of whether the German message was correct or not was now moot. Throughout Germany, language was a great barrier. Our communications at gas stations, with mechanics and at the station were a combination of sign language, individual English words and a few German words we recognized through their similarity to Swedish.

What could we do? We couldn't drive anywhere because our car was broken. Nor could we sleep in it, because our nerves had also broken down. We walked a few blocks up into the town – the very name of which we'd come to hate (totally unfairly; Freiburg is actually a very charming town) – and found a reasonably cheap hotel. Before we checked in, we asked if we could send a telegram to Switzerland. They said of course. We wrote to tell Bob the name and phone number of the hotel, said that we'd had car trouble, asked him to contact us immediately at the hotel so we could decide how to proceed, and then we went straight to bed, exhausted.

The first thing we did on getting up at 7.30 the next morning was to check whether there was a reply. There was none. Since it was Sunday, we wouldn't be able to see about getting our car repaired until Monday anyway. We waited in the lobby. We waited and waited until the 11.30 checkout time, then decided to take the next train to Basel anyway, try to find Bob's apartment, and ring his doorbell. When we checked out of the hotel, we left a message in case Bob phoned in response to our telegram, telling him to stay put, we were on our way to Binningen. When we arrived at the central station in Basel at 2 PM, we first checked for possible messages at the information center in the station. Nothing. Then we found a tram to Binningen – on a line with a stop right on the corner of Gorenmattstrasse. As soon as we found ourselves on Bob's street, just before 3 PM, I recognized the building where he lived from the slide my parents showed us in Oak Park when we stopped there on our way to Sweden more than 13 months earlier.

It was a 13-storey building, very modern, with a long balcony for each of the four apartments on every floor. A few steps up from the sidewalk was an open area paved with concrete, and on to a glassed-in outer entrance hall with modern mailboxes in burnished stainless steel. Inside, there was another locked door leading to an inner hall where the elevators were. Next to that door was a list of all tenants, with a button to push next to each name. Our pulses quickened when we saw the name Dr R Krause on the top floor, and we pushed the button. We were bursting with excitement. Nothing happened; no response. *Maybe he's out on an errand*, we thought. *What if he's gone to Freiburg*, we thought. *We can't go back, because then we might miss each other and be back to square one. He lives here. Sooner or later he'll have to come back. We'll just have to wait.*

After about an hour of trying his bell every 10 minutes, we happened to spot his mailbox among the 50 or so others in the outer lobby. Affixed to it was a red notice telling him that a telegram had arrived – and thereby telling us that he hadn't seen the notice. A couple of impatient and anxious hours went by. There were no seats in the lobby, we had nothing to read or do but lean against the wall. Other tenants, especially those whose comings and goings we'd now observed several times, were beginning to eye us suspiciously.

Shortly after six o'clock, with evening approaching, we decided to head back to Freiburg, spend the night at the same hotel, try to get our car repaired on the Monday morning, then return to Binningen. Before leaving, I rang the bell for the umpteenth time. Just as I was turning away to go back to Jeanette in resignation, there was a scratching noise in the loudspeaker and a very weak male voice said *"Krause...?"* (Bob always pronounced his Germanic surname in the German two-syllable manner with a tonal *s* [*KRAU-zeh*], having abandoned the Americanized monosyllabic pronunciation). I rushed back to the microphone and told him we'd arrived. He buzzed the door to let us in. We took the elevator to the top floor, where he stood waiting by his open apartment door, looking alarmingly disheveled and hung over.

After we overcame our initial shock at the state of his apartment and he overcame his at seeing us alive, he told us that he'd arrived in Freiburg in plenty of time, waited until seven PM (nobody paged him), then decided we simply weren't coming (how well did we know each other after one meeting, after all?), took the train home, and drowned his sorrows. I told him all about our water-pump woes, and pointed out to him that none of the aforementioned misunderstandings would have needed to happen, if only he had a phone. (The telegram delivery guys just ring the bell once, Bob explained, and if there is no response, they put the telegram in the mailbox with a red note on the outside. Bob was already well past hearing by the time the telegram arrived.) He said he'd never before felt the need for a phone, or felt that the benefits might outweigh the drawbacks, but in the light of recent occurrences, that position might be worth reconsidering, and that he felt that once having done so, he might investigate what steps would have to be taken to introduce such a novelty into the sanctity of his residence – a process of reconsideration, investigation and introduction that would take more than a year and a half to realize.

We then drew up a plan of action for the next day, Monday. (Fortunately, Bob had also taken the week off work to spend with us.). Late the next morning, the three of us took the train back to Freiburg. Bob, who spoke German, found a garage that could undertake to repair our car. The problem was that water pumps for Saabs were not to be found in Freiburg, and they couldn't get a replacement until the next day. So we all took the train back to Basel for the rest of Monday and Monnight, then back to Freiburg on Tuesday to pick up the car and at last return to Binningen in our Saab. At that point, we were all well and truly fed up with the entire concept of Freiburg.

Bob's apartment, although certainly of the high structural and architectural standard found in modern Swiss buildings, was even more of a hovel than my apartment in Daly City when I first saw it, more than any other dwelling I'd ever visited. Jeanette and I were both convinced that it was not only an *expression* of Bob's rather severe depression and nihilism, but quite possibly had become a contributing *cause* of it, and certainly a major exacerbating factor. The smell that pervaded everything was stale, musky, moldy and pungent – a penetrating smell capable of annihilating any trace of freshness.

The small entrance hall, about three meters long and two meters wide, had piles of old cartons, cardboard, newspapers, crumpled wads of paper, bags, an umbrella or two, and items of clothing leaning against the walls and lying on the floor. Immediately to the left was a narrow door to a narrow passageway, full of more cartons, never-used and old clothing, laundry, mail, old lamps and light bulbs and anything else that would fit, or could be made to. The very small kitchen, straight through the entrance hall from the front door, was piled full of dirty dishes on every flat surface and overflowing the sink. The only accessible surface was one of the burners on the stove, upon which a saucepan was parked, caked inside with layer upon layer of lime deposits from the archeological history of Basel's supply of very hard water. The small fridge contained life forms that were unfamiliar to me – over a dozen different kinds of mold on the interior walls and on the surfaces of opened containers of food, as well as a number of tiny black, white and dark-red insects the size of ground pepper, crawling slowly from one source of food to the next. The odor in the fridge was staggering. The floor was home to significant layers of grease and grime; there was a high risk of slipping, and the smell was rancid. At the far end of the kitchen there was a large dirty window and an entrance to a balcony piled high with refuse and chairs, some of them broken.

To the left from the entrance hall, between the doors to the kitchen and the passageway, was the door to a dark living room. The darkness was due to metal shutters outside the windows. These were principally for keeping out excessive radiant heat during the summer, and could easily be rolled up from inside, although Bob seldom did. Suddenly we understood why Bob had the lights on in the kitchen in daytime; the shutters were down there too. He simply couldn't be bothered to raise them. I asked Bob if I might let some light in, and he smiled, and showed me how to operate the crank for raising and lowering them. They creaked and groaned from years of disuse. On the lower floors of the building, the shutters could conceivably have provided some privacy from people in buildings in the next block (if they had powerful binoculars), but there were no buildings facing Bob's side of the building.

The living room contained several pieces of furniture that Bob built himself once upon a time before leaving the US: a couple of large bookcases crammed with books, a low wooden bench, and an imposing set of cubicle-type cabinets for his stereo, as well as his vast and eclectic collection of LPs. The books reflected Bob's extremely catholic taste: science, fiction, science fiction, philosophy, history, travel, poetry, music, science, biography, and more genres than I'd heard of. He'd picked up an interest in Nietzsche from the nihilistic Sigrid, but had moved on to Popper and recently to Bertrand Russell, from whom he was gaining great help in his struggle against the darkness. In fiction, his clear favorite for years was Aldous Huxley, but even here his taste spanned an incredibly broad range. He was always open to suggestions, and devoured new books with a passion and a desire to glean whatever could be gleaned from them.

The only obvious seat in the room was a low wicker chair, as the low Bob-built bench was burdened with 30-40 cm-high stacks of newspapers, magazines, ads and envelopes. The floor was similarly filled; only tiny patches of bare space were visible anywhere. There were windows and a second door to the balcony, with shutters but no curtains. We realized that we'd have to undertake quite a lot of clearing of floor space just to have a place to sleep, something that Bob also suddenly realized. I asked if it was OK for us to move the papers around at all, if they were in any special order, or if he were saving them for any special purpose. He smiled sheepishly and said we had *carte blanche*; they actually needed throwing out, unless there was any first-class mail in among them, in which case he'd need to see it first. Newspapers for disposal had to be tied with twine in bundles not higher than 30 cm and left in a certain place in the basement that he would show me later.

At the far end of the living room, there was a door to a small hall that was the extension of the passageway from the entrance hall. Opposite the door to the living room was the bathroom, and to the right, Bob's bedroom. We hesitated to open the bathroom door to take a look – with good reason, as it turned out. The toilet and the sink were, to put it euphemistically, vile. The bathtub was merely nauseating. Jeanette and I both began looking around for cleanser, and there turned out to be plenty of it, as well as all manner of other mostly unused cleaning aids, fortunately including rubber gloves. I took upon myself the first round with the sink and toilet, before I could stomach using either myself; then Jeanette took a finishing round, at least as well as we could manage for the time being, until we found some razor blades to penetrate the most stubborn stains and deposits.

There were multiple rock-hard, caked layers of things we preferred not to know too much about, but within about 30 vigorous minutes of razorblades, scouring pads and heavy-duty cleansers, we managed to make enough of an improvement to live with.

The bedroom door couldn't be budged from its halfway open position due to a 30 cm thick, motley "carpet" on both sides, consisting of clean and dirty laundry, newspapers, magazines, beer bottles, other bottles, scraps of cookies and nuts, personal papers, ads, cartons and other things that would take roughly a year for us to get to the bottom of – and close the door. The small bedroom also housed two pieces of furniture that Bob had made: an odd-sized bed (about 105 by 220 cm) and a small nightstand. The sheets on his bed looked like they hadn't been washed since he moved in five years before. A huge and totally cluttered roll-top desk (Bob bought it before he left the US) dominated the room. There were full ashtrays everywhere.

Bob had plenty of Feldschlösschen or Warteck beer in the fridge, as well as in crates on the kitchen floor, and in more crates on the balcony. The kitchen turned out to contain a tiny table. A couple of stools out on the balcony could be used to supplement the lone rickety chair in the kitchen. The three of us sat down there in the bright fluorescent lighting and had a beer, while Bob showed us some cans of ravioli he'd bought at the Migros grocery store next door, which we were to have for dinner. Then he showed us how to cook it. He filled the small pot on the stove halfway with water, made a couple of holes in the lid of the can – it suddenly occurred to him then that he was cooking for three for the first time, and that the small pot wouldn't hold more than one can at a time. Each can had to stand there in the boiling water, label and all, for twelve minutes; then it could be opened the rest of the way and the contents eaten, except that he had no bowls; we had to eat from our respective cans, at 12-minute intervals.

We insisted on letting Bob have the first one, while Jeanette and I energetically tackled the living room floor, to free up enough space for us to sleep on. When Bob saw his living room again, he seemed very relieved that we'd managed to clear away enough space to lie down on, and although there were no clean sheets, with the help of some of his extra blankets and quilts, we had ourselves a futon-style bed of sorts – a straw mat without the straw. We were very happy to be able to help him, but there was *so* much to be done, far more than we could ever have imagined. Yet we were driven by the belief that getting his house in order would help him into a frame of mind to get his life in order.

There were two reasons for not vacuuming at least the part of the floor we were going to be lying on that first evening. The first was that Bob didn't have a vacuum cleaner. The second, he told us, was that even if he'd had one, the "house rules" forbade any noise-making of any kind at any time on Sundays or after 10 PM on any of the other days. Bob lived in holy terror of Mrs Theinert, an elderly widow living in the apartment directly beneath his, who would complain immediately and fiercely about any breaches of said house rules. Although Jeanette and I could hear plenty of noise emanating from other apartments – families with small children weren't exactly silent, nor did people seem to refrain from watching TV (although Bob had none at this time) – he was totally unwilling to jeopardize his already very bad relationship with the fearsome Mrs Theinert.

Apart from the excursion to see to the car in Freiburg on Monday, it was pretty much more of the same work at Gorenmattstrasse. As soon as Jeanette and I began sorting the papers covering Bob's living room floor, it became apparent why Bob feared any kind of wholesale clean-up. Among the hundreds of newspapers and flyers, we separated out a pile of first-class mail for Bob to go through, along with a number of unpaid bills, overdue bills, dollar bills, 100-Swiss-franc bills and personal letters he wished to keep. We made stacks of the newspapers, magazines and ads to be eliminated, and tied them with twine from a ball Bob fortunately had on hand. The number of stacks grew quickly, as did the visibility of the underlying floor. I asked Bob if we could go have a look at that disposal place in the basement, since merely moving the stacks from one part of the living room floor to another didn't really seem to solve the problem. Bob took me down to the big and spotlessly clean garbage room. There was a special bin for newspaper bundles. Then I began making trip after trip to the basement while Bob smiled broader and broader.

In the meantime, Jeanette was working wonders in the kitchen, washing and scrubbing and scouring the dirty dishes (including the "clean" ones in the cabinets and the cabinets themselves), the flat surfaces everywhere and the greasy floor. We agreed that tackling the fridge was something we'd have to do as soon as Bob went to bed, when we could close the door to the hallway and open the one to the balcony, then remove everything from the fridge, most of which had to be thrown out, and temporarily place the rest on the now-free worktop while we scrubbed and disinfected the walls of the fridge.

On Tuesday morning, since replenishment of supplies in the nearly empty fridge was necessary, we told Bob we'd be going next door to Migros to stock up on things for breakfasts and other staples. Bob said there was a better place than Migros, called Co-op, and that he would drive us there. We soon discovered that that the concept of a simple errand was an oxymoron when Bob was involved. First, we and our breakfast had to wait well over an hour for him to get ready for this excursion. Then we all took the elevator down to the ground floor, slowly walked half an uphill block to a parking lot (Migros was half a downhill block away) to get his Deux Chevaux, then drove down Gorenmattstrasse, past number 41, past Migros, turned right three blocks, turned right again, back two blocks, made a left turn and entered the parking lot for Co-op, a grocery store with far less to offer than Migros, with one exception: Migros sold no alcohol, Co-op did. After buying what was needed, plus a few duplicate and triplicate bottles that weren't needed, we had to repeat the procedure to get home, but by a different route, due to many of the streets being one-way. It wasn't until we got back to Bob's apartment and Jeanette and I were standing on his balcony for a breath of fresh air, that we saw that the Co-op store we'd just been to was a block and a half away. A simple 10-minute walking errand (for Jeanette and me) that would have provided a little much-needed exercise – and breakfast – took 45 minutes and gave almost no exercise.

After that highly complex errand, it was high time to get the train to Freiburg to pick up our Saab. Bob, who was visibly overjoyed with the transformation that was beginning to take place in his apartment, announced he was taking us to dinner in the basement of the train station that evening, at an excellent French restaurant called L'Escargot. During the delicious meal, he further announced that the next day, the three of us would be heading off to the Alps, first to Luzerne, then to Lauterbrunnen, from where we would take a cog-wheel train up into the high Alps, to a place called Kleine Scheidegg, at the foot of the Eiger (3970 m), Mönch (4099 m) and Jungfrau (4158 m). We would be spending the night at a venerable old hotel in Kleine Scheidegg, over 2000 meters above sea level.

All this had been carefully planned. Bob presumably started making the plans as soon as we agreed on the trip back in Malmö. There was very little Bob did spontaneously; his approach was to plan, then go through "the proper channels", often taking unnecessarily circuitous and convoluted paths to do so in order to avoid real and imagined obstacles that only he could see, in stark contrast to his messy world in other respects. It was as though he desperately *needed* order around him, and yet he *couldn't* give it enough priority to create or maintain.

Rather early the next morning the three of us took off in our Saab for Luzerne, an amazingly beautiful town, where Bob took us through Kapellbrücke, a covered wooden footbridge from 1365, with hand-painted medieval panels along the entire ceiling, and with views of snow-covered mountains that took me back to my childhood thrills of the first glimpses of the Rockies. (The bridge was extensively damaged by fire in 1993, but restored the following year.)

By the time we got to Lauterbrunnen, we were in the heart of the Alps, or in the depths of them, with glimpses of Jungfrau towering over the village that lay at the bottom of a deep, steep valley. The cog-wheel train that took us up the steep slope on one side yielded views whose beauty made me feel faint – emerald grass pastures for grazing cows whose bells rang up and down the valley, waterfalls everywhere, the peaks more and more majestic as we climbed. Until we got to Wengen, the best views were down, into the valley. When we got to the top, by which I mean to Kleine Scheidegg, the view of the mountain peaks rising almost straight up from the treeless Alpine meadow took away our words and our breath. Perhaps the most stunning was the clear view we had of the north face of the Eiger, with its 1300 m sheer vertical rise above the meadow (it's said to be one of the most difficult climbs in the world). Everything petty and banal simply vanished. I stood there with my mouth open, slowly turning around to see the snow-covered peaks surrounding us in this rocky dish of Alpine paradise to which a little green and yellow train managed to bring us.

We checked into the hotel and had a quick light lunch – a sausage and a beer. Then Bob said we had to take advantage of the clear weather to take another train ride all the way up to Jungfraujoch, some 1,500 meters almost straight up from Kleine Scheidegg (i.e. around 3,500 meters above sea level). Another, steeper, cog-wheel train took us there, mostly through a tunnel in the rock. But by the time we reached our destination, everything was enveloped in thick freezing fog. Visibility was about three meters and we were not dressed for the extreme cold and high winds that were waiting for us. We remained there for a while, hoping for a break in the clouds, then took another train back down.

The hotel was a very large, five-storey timber construction that appeared to have a lot of history. The beautiful old parquet floors were as creaky as the graceful wooden stairways. It was quietly opulent, possibly a resort for the wealthy wishing to appear to be roughing it. There were only a handful of other overnight guests at this time of year. The rooms were comfortable but Spartan (or perhaps Spartan but comfortable), as if it were assumed that nobody would look at anything but the views from their windows. After an hour of freshening up, and a quick hike for Jeanette and me, we met Bob in the restaurant where we spent most of the evening. We'd learned that Bob wasn't much for walks.

Over dinner and wine and beyond, Bob began unravelling further details of how he came to be residing in Switzerland. On moving to Rochester in 1951, his suddenly broadening horizons led him to look at the world – not with new eyes exactly, because he never really looked at or was allowed to look at the world at all before, so perhaps with virgin eyes. His taste in music began to develop from hymns to jazz and classical, plunging into each genre (except hymns) in characteristic depth. He could play the piano. He told me how difficult it was to play Rachmaninov, and from that I suspected that he was no novice, yet I never, ever heard him play. I often saw him fingering a piece on the table or his trouser leg while listening to it. I believe he was so demanding of himself that he would rather not play at all than play poorly, and he denied himself (and probably others) the joy of just playing for fun. (I suspect that if he'd had access to the next generation's technology, in the form of a good digital piano he could play while wearing headphones so as not to disturb Mrs Theinert, it might have been a different story.) While at Rochester, he sang in one or more productions of Gilbert and Sullivan operettas, which he loved.

He soon became enamored of everything European, having developed a love for many European composers, authors, philosophers and scientific pioneers. In 1954, the summer after getting his medical degree, he took a steamship from New York to Tilbury and spent some time exploring London, beginning his lifelong love affair with that city and its many booksellers, theaters and museums. Then he flew to on Paris (his first flight ever). On returning to the States after nearly ten months, couldn't wait to get back to Europe. He had a new dream: to find a way, somehow, someday, to *live* in Europe.

He continued his medical studies, now as a resident in pathology, first in Rochester, then in Charleston, West Virginia, before joining the Armed Forces Institute of Pathology in Washington, DC in 1957. One reason for enlisting in the Army, he explained, was that it gave him the opportunity to pursue his interest in pathology while getting pretty decent pay and amenities as an officer. But the main reason was that they promised him that after a time in DC, he would be stationed in Europe for several years – his dream come true. During his time in DC, he lived for a year (1957-58) in a cabin near a place called Cabin John, Maryland, around 10 miles up the Potomac from Washington DC (the DC population was then around 1.6 million). He frequently spoke of it as the happiest time of his life. It was certainly the least complicated, but it was also the time when the seeds of all his later problems began to grow.

Also in 1957, he lost his virginity to a Swedish girl he'd met in New York, and whom he would often refer to as "the one who got away" – a road-not-taken relationship that he felt he should perhaps have taken. Among the other friendships he made in Washington were a German colleague at the Army hospital, Erich Theiss, and his wife Sigrid. Bob described them as "two brilliant, sensitive human beings living in utter cynicism." The three of them began to meet regularly as their friendship developed – and so did a powerful attraction between Bob and Sigrid. By 1958, Bob realized he'd fallen in love with Sigrid, and something occurred that Bob described only vaguely as an "impropriety" (nothing more than kissing), but it enraged Erich and led to the Theisses' estrangement from Bob.

Shortly afterward, Bob shipped out to the US Army's Medical Lab in Kaiserslautern, Germany, where he began to learn German and thrive on the plethora of opportunities to visit all kinds of places in Europe, within a radius roughly related to the lengths of his furloughs. He remained in Kaiserslautern for about a year, and was then transferred to a US Army base near Orléans, France, as Assistant Chief of Lab Service. He was apparently not required to live on the base, but could live and dress as a civilian, except for certain formal military events; a lab coat over civvies or over a uniform makes little difference.

In mid-February 1959, Bob was summoned by his CO, who informed him that his mother Edna, my aunt, had died (she was just 53 years old), and that Bob was entitled to fly home for the funeral on a free military flight. Although he hated his father, he'd always felt a strong emotional bond with his mother. But he had very mixed feelings about attending her funeral, especially one held under the auspices of the Meeting, where his father would of course be in attendance. He was pleased that the flight didn't get him to Detroit in time for the funeral service itself; still in uniform, he caught up with the funeral party at the graveside. He braced himself for some sort of confrontation and browbeating, assuming it would most likely come from his father. Instead, it came from our Aunt Shirley, the most liberal of the Larson sisters and thus the least likely source. She strode right up to him and began screaming and beating on his chest with her fists, castigating him for all the grief he caused Edna by "turning away from the Lord". Not wanting to make a scene at his mother's funeral, Bob held his tongue, but seethed inside, and vowed never to return.

In France, Bob found himself a house to rent near La Chapelle-St Mesmin, just west of Orléans, an old two-storey dwelling with a walled garden, very high ceilings, and somewhat primitive in terms of modern conveniences. But it was a place he said he loved "unspeakably".

From here he travelled to Athens, Istanbul and Jerusalem, London, Vienna and Stockholm, and of course all through the countryside in different parts of France. It was at this house that he developed passions for photography and pipes, always accompanied by wine, whiskies, Cognacs and Armagnacs, as well as music and books. He took great advantage of the dirt-cheap prices of goods from the PX on the base. He didn't mind the primitive aspects of his living quarters a bit – they only seemed to add to his rustic and charmed enjoyment.

After more than a year of this bliss, and with the end of his military tour of duty in Europe in dreaded sight, Bob received a totally unexpected letter from Erich Theiss. He and Sigrid now had a daughter, Karin, born in 1959. They'd moved back to Europe for Erich to begin a high-flying research position at Roche in Basel. Erich begged Bob to meet them in the late summer of 1961 in Frankfurt (where Sigrid's mother lived). Bob readily accepted the invitation.

At a restaurant in Frankfurt, with Sigrid present, Erich revealed his ongoing affair with a mistress from DC, and told of his desire to bring her to Europe to set up a *ménage á trois* in Basel. This was the first time Sigrid had heard a word of such plans, and Erich's news caused her so much distress that she fainted, right there in the restaurant. On reviving, Sigrid asked Bob if she could visit him in France. Bob agreed "heartily" and Erich "grudgingly". Eventually, Sigrid and Karin both visited Bob in France in November, a month before Erich's mistress arrived in Basel.

During the spring of 1962, Bob kept in touch (presumably figuratively more than literally) with the Theisses. At some point around this time, Erich told Bob he needed to see him about an important matter: Erich wanted to marry his mistress, but he didn't want to divorce Sigrid because then he'd have to pay her too much of his considerable salary in alimony; but if Sigrid were to remarry, then Erich would no longer face the burden of alimony (both Erich and Sigrid were independently wealthy, but that didn't stop either of them from wanting whatever they could get and more). Since Bob harbored strong feelings for Sigrid, and she for him, apparently, Erich wondered whether Bob couldn't do everybody a favor by marrying Sigrid? And if he agreed to do so, Erich was in a position to offer Bob a position in endocrinology research at Roche.

Bob's tour of duty in the Army would soon be coming to an end. He was thinking of re-enlisting for another three years, but was told that it was no longer certain or even likely that he would be able to remain stationed in Orléans, or even in Europe. Thus Erich's offer turned out to be Bob's ticket to stay in Europe. Consequently, Sigrid divorced Erich on grounds of infidelity and married Bob on August 2nd. Bob was jubilant. He claimed they had a great sex life, and enjoyed each other's company and deep philosophical discussions, despite Bob's misgivings about her underlying cynicism. Both she and Bob were, however, totally looking forward to having children, lots of children, as soon as possible.

They were expecting to remain in France for the rest of 1962, since Bob's tour of duty didn't officially end until December, despite Erich's wish to have Bob start at Roche as soon as possible, and to have Karin (and Sigrid) nearby in the Basel area. But in the early autumn, Bob discovered that he was due quite a lot of furlough time, a couple of months' worth, and after discussing it with his CO, it was agreed that Bob could leave the Army in late October, prior to his official discharge date on December 10th. Bob formally and legally adopted Karin in the local French court on October 24th, and the three of them moved to Arlesheim, a suburb of Basel, the next day. Bob started his new job at Roche on Monday, October 29th, under his new boss, none other than Erich Theiss, the ex-husband of Bob's bride. For some reason I've never quite understood, Bob also made Erich the executor of his new will.

Bob told Jeanette and me, with tears welling up in his eyes and his face twitching, that the move to Basel was a disaster for their marriage. It wasn't just the discovery of his sterility and the dashed hopes of a large family. Over the next three years, another, much more subtle and profound change was taking place in Sigrid and in the precarious balance (or imbalance) of their relationship. Bob was convinced that it was because in France, where neither of them spoke French with anything like fluency, they were pretty much on an equal footing, dependent on each other. But in German-speaking Basel, Sigrid was back in the territory of her native language, while Bob was no better off linguistically than he'd been in France. (Another factor may have been money. While Bob, with his first non-military salary ever, was making more than he'd ever made, it was far below Erich's level; Sigrid thus suddenly had access to far less than she was accustomed to.) For whatever reason, Sigrid began treating Bob with increasing condescension, then with constant (yet possibly unconscious) scorn and sarcasm, gradually progressing through disdain and derision to loathing. Bob's mounting desperation was in a race with his slide into depression, a race that would determine whether the depression would make him unable to take any action at all before the level of despair made action necessary to save his life.

Despair won that race by a nose, so to speak, and one day Bob heard of an available apartment in Binningen, a Basel suburb closer to town (and to work) than Arlesheim. He signed the lease and fled to Gorenmattstrasse on Friday, October 1st, 1965. He never saw it as a new home for himself, he explained. It was nothing but a *Flüchtort*, a place of refuge, a hiding place, a sanctuary. And for the past five years, he'd been in deep depression, drinking heavily, hating his work because Theiss was making his life miserable because Sigrid was hounding him. And Sigrid withdrew nearly all Bob's money from their joint account.

Bob regarded Erich Theiss as a person

> "...who lives by exploiting the weaknesses of others. [...] He can be (and usually is) perfectly charming (that is the secret of his success, since his abilities are modest). His first unconscious act on making your acquaintance is to estimate your degree of exploitability as well as the size of the dagger needed to penetrate between your ribs from behind."

The misery Bob experienced as Theiss's subordinate would color Bob's entire career at Roche.

In his state of emotional paralysis, Bob agreed to a financially crippling (for him) separation settlement with Sigrid, one which Bob's own lawyer called idiotic. Bob agreed to this out of almost fawning deference to Sigrid's aunt, Lore von Lom, a highly intelligent and fabulously wealthy heiress whom Bob met in 1968, when he was completely and unpleasantly alone. Her family's fortune in the cement industry had undoubtedly been enhanced by the construction of the Autobahn system, concrete runways, and bunkers, at the behest of a certain notorious Austrian in the late 1930s.

Hans von Lom, Sigrid's mother's brother, was in charge of one of his wife's family's factories, enabling him to make his fortune supplying Germany's thirsty demand for cement during the War. It also enabled him and his family to live in a mansion in Garmisch-Partenkirchen. Apparently Sigrid was requesting money from her miserly uncle Hans, which Lore forwarded to Bob, along with a terse command to Bob: "*Fix this*".

Bob's respect, deference, obeisance, subservience to the lady he always referred to as "Tante Lore" was one of several such relationships Bob had with people he stood in awe of, yet whose actions threatened Bob's financial (and ultimately emotional) stability. Apparently Bob had visited Garmisch several times with Sigrid, and after their separation Lore treated him respectfully, at least in contrast to Sigrid's growing disdain towards him, thus making Tante Lore's lack of outright loathing seem like friendship by comparison. It elicited Bob's uncritical deference towards her, bordering on obsequiousness. Bob would obey her every command, which I suppose suited her very well. It didn't seem to matter to her that what would have been pocket change for the von Loms – to placate Sigrid's appetite for maintaining whatever station in life to which she felt entitled – was enough to put Bob on the brink of ruin. It was just "*fix this*", like "*pay the driver, will you, Jeeves?*" in the manner of those members of the wealthy class who never carry cash and allow their "inferiors" to besmirch their hands with such lowly and mundane transactions. It infuriated and exasperated me that Bob was unwilling to recognize how badly he was being exploited.

It got worse. Bob was also paying costly child support for Karin, whom he was not allowed to see, yet Erich, her father, was paying nothing at all, while seeing all he wanted to of her in his super-expensive Basel penthouse, when he wasn't tooling around in his new Ferrari. No wonder Bob was depressed when Jeanette and I met him. No wonder he didn't care about his "home" or very much else, but effectively sequestered himself in misery, driving his flimsy Deux Chevaux, drinking himself to sleep, letting his health deteriorate. It wasn't until early 1970 that Bob, on the insistence of his lawyer, actually filed for divorce, a process that he was told could take as long as eight years in Switzerland if Sigrid contested, which she did.

Jeanette and I were overwhelmed by Bob's story, the soap opera that was all too real, the slings and arrows he'd endured and was still struggling to endure with the little strength to struggle he had left in him. We didn't give him our pity – he had more than enough self-pity to need ours. But we could give him love, we could be there for him, we could turn his *Flüchtort* into a home, we could try to make him see what a fantastic person he was. We thought him wonderful; he didn't. On that we would disagree for quite a while.

On Thursday, October 8th, our anniversary, we had a somewhat lazy breakfast, took the cog-wheel train back down to Lauterbrunnen, then drove back to Binningen by way of Thun (where we had lunch) and Bern (where we didn't stop). On Thursday evening, Friday and Saturday, Jeanette and I worked intensely to get as much of our clean-up done as possible before our return journey on Sunday. In this we had Bob's full support and encouragement, and to his amazement, his place was taking on the feel of what might possibly become a home someday. We managed to clear and clean pretty much of the kitchen, bathroom and living room. But we didn't have time to touch the hallway, the balcony or his bedroom, nor his basement storage room. We'd seen them; we felt we'd scarcely begun.

We took great care not to overstep any invisible boundaries, not to cause him undue embarrassment about the state of things, not to stumble over his integrity. He only expressed how thrilled he was, and his face lit up and his mood lightened up in ways we hadn't seen before.

We began early and worked the whole day on the Friday. That evening, Bob took us to dinner for our first-ever cheese fondue at a cozy restaurant in the heart of Basel. We were thrilled, and Jeanette was eager to find a recipe. After another nearly full day of work on the Saturday, Jeanette managed to put together an amazing meal in Bob's kitchen that evening, making enough to give Bob leftovers he could enjoy for several days after our departure. We spoke of when we could meet again, and we invited him to our place for Christmas, when he would be getting some time off. He was eager to see us again, as soon as possible, but his brow wrinkled as he felt he had to inform us that for the past few years he felt sort of obliged to spend Christmas in Garmisch with Tante Lore, and with her children and grandchildren who mostly tolerated Bob as some sort of Christmas fixture. Bob's presence gave Onkel Hans the opportunity to show off the contents of his wine cellar: *well over* 10,000 bottles, most of which Bob felt certain had already turned to vinegar. In short: if Tante Lore summoned, Bob would have to go.

Jeanette's and my trip home was filled with plans for how to help Bob on every level we were capable of, and with reflections on what a unique and rewarding experience it was knowing him. However, our trip home was marred by a blowout of our muffler on Sunday morning, and there was nothing to do about it but roar our way through northern Germany, Denmark and back to Vårgatan by Monday evening. Our Saab was beginning to be much more of a burden than an asset.

Cleaning up the mess

A week or so before we left for Switzerland, Arno said he'd talked to an ombudsman from HTF, a union that mainly represented employees in the retail industry, but what the hell. Arno and I were to meet him a couple of days later to discuss whether they could and/or would take us on. They could *and* would. We passed the news along to the other teachers, and we informed Carmen of our rather modest demands. On our return on Monday evening, I phoned Arno to see if there'd been any developments with the union and Carmen in my absence. Carmen said our demands put her back to the wall, that the great number of teachers at the school would make it impossible to meet our demands, yet to our surprise she went and hired two more. We gave her an equal surprise by promptly recruiting them both into the union as well, before she had a chance to get them to sign her slave contract.

A couple of days later, Arno and I had another meeting with our ombudsman. We went through a few reasonable demands that the teachers agreed on – 18 kronor an hour, minimum 2,500 kronor per month – which the union guy thought were perfectly reasonable, if a bit too modest. We just wanted to be able to make a living, not to be punitive. The union rep said he would draft a formal proposal and send it to the school. Union membership and representation had long been a self-evident civil right in Sweden, and no employer was legally entitled to dismiss any employee seeking the protection of union membership and collective bargaining.

Carmen' first impulse was to find a way to quash or circumvent this right. Instead, she found herself obliged to join the Federation of Swedish Employers (SAF) in order to have a legal counterpart at the negotiating table, an obligation that made her squirm with rage. Even worse in her eyes was that SAF also found our demands most reasonable and sought no compromise whatsoever. We stuck together (but Jeanette threw in the towel on the whole language-school racket), and by mid-November we had signed contracts – the union's, not Carmen's – giving us what we'd modestly asked for. We were glad to have one less mess to think about. The new contract would go into effect on January 1st.

On November 13th, while I was away at the union negotiations, Jeanette had an uninvited visitor at our home, a man called Gullens. My parents said such a person might come to see us (we hadn't invited him; my parents had – to *our* home). It seems he was a preacher from Halmstad (a town a couple of hours' drive north of Malmö) whom my parents contacted by virtue (or vice) of a gospel tract he'd written. My parents apparently felt his having written a tract entitled them to invite him to visit us! He spent two hours waiting in vain for me and browbeating Jeanette, who steadfastly refused to speak English with him. Her view was that if she had to put up with his preaching, she could at least get some Swedish practice out of it, plus the hope that his fanaticism might lose something in translation. During the course of his stay, he rudely helped himself to what must have been an eye-opening inspection tour of our apartment, including the entire contents of our library and magazine basket, as well as my pipe collection and our bedroom. It turned out he was an American citizen with Swedish roots. He'd already given up on waiting for me by the time I got home, and after hearing what Jeanette had to say about his visit and manners, I almost hoped he would return; there were a few things I might have liked to mention.

Jeanette and I told Bob of our intentions not to have children, which he initially found appalling, given his opposite intentions until the sterility was discovered and ended up crushing him. He claimed that we would make ideal parents. We told him we couldn't see the necessity of reproducing in an already overcrowded, overcomplicated and overaggressive world, and that we couldn't see ourselves as ideal in any other way than in relation to each other.

Another thing we decided to do something about on returning from Switzerland was our lack of hot water and facilities for having a bath or shower at home. We found a cheap bathtub through an ad in *Sydsvenskan* and Henry gave us the name and phone number of a reliable plumber. We then set about converting our lavatory into a full-fledged bathroom, enabling us to get clean without facing the choice of a kitchen sponge bath or a trip to the swimming hall across town. And we asked the plumber (through whom we bought a wall-mounted water heater) to run a hot-water pipe through to the kitchen as well. Our standard of living was soaring.

On November 4th, news from Chile stunned the world: Salvador Allende was elected president, in one of the first peaceful democratic elections in the whole of South America, which should have been fantastic news to supporters of democracy everywhere, except for the fact that Allende openly held Marxist views, which made him knee-jerk anathema to the American Government and to a sizeable share of its voters, who felt that democracy was great as long as other countries stuck to electing people Americans approved of. After all, we were the ones who counted, we were the ones who decided, weren't we? On reading and hearing such opinions, I guessed and feared it would just be a matter of time before Allende was out on his ear.

At my urging, Bob finally began putting a little pressure on his lawyer, to speed up the formal divorce proceedings that would bring to an end at least some of the financial hemorrhaging Sigrid was wreaking. We also continued urging him to get a phone, to avoid any future Freiburg-style incidents. He said he was still considering it.

A letter from Bob in late November brought bad news. Tante Lore had summoned; Bob would be spending Christmas in Garmisch. He sounded disappointed too. But having observed our love of the cheese fondue in Basel, he sent us not one but three fondue sets for Christmas, so we could make it ourselves. We found a good old cheese shop on Skomakaregatan where they sold the required Emmentaler and Gruyère cheeses.

Our project to convert the lavatory into a proper bathroom was completed just before Christmas, although the revamping of the kitchen was still underway. And we got a surprise visit from Dave Henderson (Norm's cousin from Oak Park) for five days. It was very odd to see him again, or anyone from Oak Park. Dave spent many years as a professional student before finally getting a job with the State Department, and was working at the US Consulate in Palermo, Sicily. I tried to pump him for information about Norm, of course, but he claimed he didn't have much contact, no address, no direct information nor much indirect either. Dave seemed to have left the whole Meeting business behind him as well; we didn't engage in any conversations of substance. I had no idea what he thought of our new way of life.

To assure the year would end on a sweet note, just before Christmas, another package arrived from Bob, this time a large-shoebox-size tin full of Basler Läckerli, a kind of chewy, almond-honey-spicy cookie that was a local specialty, particularly at Christmastime. It just made us miss him more.

CHAPTER 7

Inside and out

Before the Christmas holidays, Jeanette applied for a government-run secretarial course in Furulund, starting in late January 1971. It took a bit more than an hour to commute each way. She felt it was high time to be getting out into working life in her own field, but in order to do so, there was a lot she needed to learn about Swedish business practice: business letters, the Swedish shorthand system, typing with a Swedish keyboard configuration, Swedish business vocabulary, etc. She knew it would be very challenging: it wasn't a course for immigrants either, but a program – conducted in Swedish only – for Swedish secretarial aspirants. It was like jumping off the deep end. Jeanette would be the only non-Swede in the class, but she seemed to love the challenge.

After the first couple of days, however, her head was absolutely swimming, spinning, tumbling and whirling. First the feeling of *almost* understanding; then actually understanding, but after a time lag, during which new things to understand had already been said, and replied to, and commented on again by the others. It was wearing her down. Part of the problem was plunging into this Swedish-language environment by day, then coming home to our largely English-speaking environment every evening. I also felt that the development of my Swedish had stagnated, after the great boost it got from watching Swedish TV programs. We therefore took a radical decision: we would henceforth speak Swedish at home to each other, only Swedish, our own self-imposed, self-inflicted immersion course.

We were remarkably self-disciplined. We forced ourselves (and each other) to use only other Swedish words to explain any new words one of us didn't already know. Gestures and pictures were allowed, but no English whatsoever. The amount of frustration and irritation during the first couple of weeks was almost frightening, but there came a point, a threshold, like reaching the crest after a long and strenuous uphill climb, and suddenly we felt as if we were coasting, finding words instantly where we'd had to search the far corners of our brains for them the week before. And we found ourselves actually thinking in Swedish for the first time. The feeling was remarkable. Suddenly Jeanette was whizzing through her program with ease; she was already a damn good secretary, it was just the language that had been difficult. Now she no longer felt like the outsider among her classmates, and spoke of them as friends. She was, in short, enjoying it.

My work was another story. The new year brought a new mood of thinly veiled hostility to the school, and a few new faces to the teaching faculty. There was Simon, a very sincere young philosophy student from Oxford, a sort of upper-class rebel who came to Sweden for the experience of it, and to Demaret's for the hell of it. There was Bob Jolly, a middle-aged, red-faced giggly man with an ill-disguised toupee, an equally ill-disguised gay orientation, and a big heart. There was Paul from London, a young man taking a break from his advanced studies in the budding new field of electronic data processing. He was a whiz at organizing time sheets, and had a good sense of humor.

And then there was Melvin Smith from Edinburgh. He, like so many other non-English citizens of the British Empire who chose to teach English, strove ruthlessly to be more English than the English. Mel had worked for Demaret's for many years, and was the crown prince of Carmen's inner cadre until, like Lucifer, he fell from grace, and was only mentioned in hushed whispers during my first year at the school. His sin was never spoken of directly, but there were various rumors: of drunk and disorderly behavior, of piracy in being part of the launching of a competing school, and of debauchery. Any or all of these things might have made him an interesting person had he also been a nice person.

Mel was short, slim, middle-aged, with curly blond (possibly bleached) hair, vaguely resembling a short, raunchy version of the English actor Barry Foster. Mel was a chain smoker who dressed impeccably in his signature navy-blue blazer, and had a ruddy complexion that lent some credence to at least one of the rumors. His voice was made for broadcasting: rich, mellow, with just a pleasant touch of the Edinburgensian. He clearly fancied himself to be an accomplished Shakespearean actor (without the lines); as a character actor, the role of Iago might have suited him. He had a cruel streak a mile wide, and took the utmost delight in hearing of anyone else's troubles. He spoke ill of everyone, especially behind their backs. He was critical of every other teacher's teaching skills, but never managed to be as critical of theirs as the pupils were of his. One day he announced to the teachers and pupils, gathered informally in the kitchen before the afternoon's sessions were about to begin, that his greatest desire in life was to witness an execution. What a guy.

But to Carmen he was the Prodigal Son, and the sun shone perpetually from his posterior; she not only showered him with praise, but with all the working hours he wanted, at the expense of more competent teachers whom the pupils preferred. (I didn't have to worry about my own hours. Even though Carmen was furious with me about the union business, I was the clear favorite of most of the pupils, and business was business.) One day during a short break, when many of the teachers were in the teachers' room busily writing on the charts that Paul set up to facilitate the progress reports on the individual pupils, Mel marched in and glared at a reminder that said "Please update these charts!" Mel instantly burst out, with indignation blazing, "*What's this?! Who wrrrote this?! 'Update??' That's Ameddican! I won't have it! It's called 'brrrring up to date!'*" Paul, the Londoner, looked up at him and said calmly "*I wrote that. It's English. You're not.*" Mel was stunned and – for a moment – speechless. Then he huffed, "*Well, I still don't like it. 'Brrrring up to date' is so much more elegant,*" and he sailed from the room.

The school administration was falling apart at the seams. Carmen was raking in the money while bitterly begrudging the teachers their paltry 18 kronor an hour. She was also overbooking. One morning she arrived at the school on Exercisgatan and agitatedly announced to the teachers that she'd booked two pupils more than there were classrooms for. In order to have enough space, she told Mel and me that it would be necessary for us to take four of the pupils on an excursion to Copenhagen, leaving in the late morning, having lunch on the ferry, and making sure not to return to the school before five o'clock.

When Carmen informed the four pupils of this new arrangement, I heard some low grumbling from the pupils (Carmen didn't hear it), that they'd paid quite a lot of money to have *individual* lessons, and what the hell?! I didn't like it either, but I was determined to do all I could to smooth things over and give every pupil a worthwhile learning experience anyway. When the six of us ordered lunch in the restaurant on board the ferry, Mel thought we should all have *snaps*, several shots of it, and when the rest of us couldn't keep his pace, or simply had no interest in getting drunk before noon, he graciously permitted us to fall behind.

He disappeared for a while towards the end of the meal (and the crossing), and emerged as we were disembarking, visibly soused out of his mind. He could barely stand up (although he did stand out), ranted unintelligibly, and seemed to find himself infinitely more amusing than the unappreciative members of the human race who stared disapprovingly at him. I did my best to see to the needs of all four pupils and distract them from his unintelligible slurring. As we were leaving the ferry, Mel became entangled with one of the velvet ropes intended to guide passengers to the terminal building, and he ended up in a laughing stupor, lying flat on his back, clutching the velvet rope above him as though he had turned into a three-toed sloth trying to hide beneath a narrow vine. I eventually guided the four highly irritated pupils around Copenhagen as best as I could, then back to the ferry and Malmö. Mel Smith had simply disappeared.

When we got back to the school just after five o'clock, Carmen asked how things had gone, and wondered where Mel was. When I told her, she turned pale, but said nothing about it, only that the two extra pupils would report to her apartment on Kungsgatan the next day, where she'd hastily converted two of the rooms into classrooms. I don't remember who their teachers would be.

I later heard her on the receiving end of some vociferous complaints from the pupils. From that point forward, Mel Smith was no longer anything but a pathetic figure to me, and to most of the other teachers. My colleagues met his continued attempts to bully them with sighs and sneers. I met every snide remark he directed at me with a penetrating stare into his eyes, and he always backed down, and eventually just avoided me. He'd defanged himself. Carmen, on the other hand, miraculously still thought the sun shone out of his rectal orifice; Enid Burhe and Mrs Fredin wafted through their haze as though nothing had happened or ever would or could; history was dead. Pupils began asking me whether I could take them privately for follow-up immersion courses, by-passing the school altogether.

I was meeting all kinds of pupils from all kinds of Swedish companies, including some of the major industries: Volvo, Saab, SKF, LKAB, Sandviken, L M Ericsson, you name it. Since the more advanced pupils needed to be able to practice their English by talking about their fields, I began learning more English too: the trade jargon for a huge variety of fields. Sometimes the jargon was technical, sometimes financial, sometimes marketing. Just about everything I studied during my undergraduate years, which I thought would never have any relevance for me, was suddenly being jerked into my consciousness. It was an amazing learning experience, initially every bit as much for me as for my pupils.

One of the more difficult aspects of learning another language, I found, was mastering the correct use of those elusive little words called prepositions. There is hardly a one that can be translated into another language with a single word; context is everything, and logic is seldom a welcome guest. But while teaching English to my Swedish pupils, I discovered – quite serendipitously – that I could learn a great deal about Swedish prepositions by observing my pupils' mistakes in English. For example, when they said "*I had lunch on the restaurant*", I knew that "*on*" is usually "*på*" in Swedish, and "*på*" in other contexts is usually "*on*". Their mistakes in English thus helped me to avoid the corresponding mistakes in Swedish.

I also learned, from the relatively few pupils I had who were beginners, a surprising and painful lesson. So many times, particularly in the context of certain Olympic sports like gymnastics, those who don't begin their hard training early enough in life will never, ever reach any level above mediocre, with very few exceptions. The same generally applies to top-level musicians, mathematicians, chess players and many other areas of skill. I'd heard that there are areas of the brain that need to be activated early and kept active in order to achieve and fully develop such skills, and if those areas are left dormant too long, they might become forever inaccessible. That sounded a bit harsh to me, but then I began to consider my own experience in teaching beginners.

I'd had some beginners who couldn't say more than *yes* and *no* on the first day of a course, yet learned to carry on simple conversations in English on a wide variety of subjects within two weeks of immersion training. And then there was Mr Hindgren, a barber from Gothenburg. Nothing seemed to sink in. My questions would remain unanswered. I tried telling him jokes, and I think his training as a barber taught him to recognize when a customer was telling a joke, and to laugh at the appropriate place, whether he'd heard or understood it or not. His laugh was unlike any other I'd ever seen or ever would see. At the end of a joke, when I stopped talking and he recognized that this was the place to laugh, his body would go stiff, his head would jerk back *very* suddenly, his mouth would open extremely wide and emit a powerful burst: *hhhhhhhhhhhhhhhhh!!* Then just as abruptly, the sound would stop, his head would jerk back down to its normal position, and his forced smile would *vanish* instantly. Because I was so startled the first time it happened, I had to tell a couple more jokes to see if my eyes and ears hadn't been fooling me. They hadn't. On the Thursday of his second week, I walked into the classroom and said, slowly and clearly, "*Good morning, Mr Hindgren, how are you today?*" He stared at me for a few seconds, then grinned and said "*Tree o'cloak!*"

I've often thought of these cases later in life, when hearing people complain about immigrants who fail to learn the language of their adopted country. Maybe they simply cannot. Three of my four maternal great-grandparents, the ones who emigrated from Sweden to the US in the late 1800s, *never* learned proper English. You can't take a tone-deaf middle-aged person and command them to learn to play Chopin. Sure, it's reasonable to insist that they try to learn the language of their new country, and to help them do so. But to demand that they succeed? Perhaps critics of immigrants need to show a little humility here – to recognize that a task that may be easy for me may not be easy or even possible for you, or vice-versa.

I've also observed, with the help of people like Mel Smith and George Bernard Shaw,[7] how some people use language as a weapon of one-upmanship rather than as an amazing and unparalleled tool for communication, the one upon which consciousness and civilization are built. When native speakers – British or American or others – say things like "should of went" instead of "should have gone", their bad grammar doesn't confer upon them the status of moral bankruptcy. It may be true that the better you learn a language – its vocabulary and its grammar – the better the tool you have for communication, the more easily you will be understood, the less frequently you will be misunderstood, but it doesn't make you a better or even a more intelligent person. Even though it may grate on your language sensibilities when you find "it's" used to mean anything other than "it is" or "it has", it actually doesn't stop you from understanding what was meant. (Nor need it prevent you from correcting it, if you can do so without smugness.)

An incident in February 1971 helped me to gain further insight in this area. The sign said "*Semlor – 1:50*". The sign in question stood on a stand (rather than sat on a seat) outside the EPA supermarket at Värnhemstorget, part of the same building complex where the immigration police were located. I saw the sign as I was walking home from work to our apartment, and I recognized the name of the pastry traditionally enjoyed at this time of year, early February, from one of Elsa's lessons. I knew enough Swedish by now to get along well with anyone so inclined, and I also knew that *semlor* was the plural of *semla*. The pastry is made from a somewhat sweet bread-like bun with the top sliced off, part of the soft inside scooped out and mixed with almond paste, then filled back into the scooped-out bun, topped by a thick layer of whipped cream, then further topped by the sliced-off part of the bun, like a hat. Finally, it's sprinkled

---

7   cf. *Pygmalion*

with powdered sugar.

I'd also lived in Sweden long enough to know that *semla* could also be called *fastlagsbulle* – literally "Lent bun" (Lent in the Ash Wednesday-to-Easter sense of the word) – and that was why this particular pastry was sold only at that time of year (even though no Swedes practiced Lent any longer), back in the days when Sweden's traditional seasonal specialties were only sold during or close to the relevant special seasons and not year-round. But I hadn't lived in Sweden long enough to have actually tried *semlor* more than once (at Elsa's place when she had the whole class over), nor to have learned enough Swedish to fulfill my ambition to achieve linguistic perfection in terms of grammar, vocabulary and accent, although I was doing rather well, especially on the first two.

So I decided to interrupt my homeward journey a few hundred meters from my final destination, and reacquaint myself with a bun that I recalled might be well worth a detour. From the entrance to EPA, a row of check-out counters for the grocery store itself spread out straight ahead and to the right. But immediately to the far right, before the store itself, was the bakery department, which handled its own cash transactions. The bakery had a long row of glass cases, about shoulder height, broken by a countertop and cash register in the middle. Another floor-mounted sign was there to remind everyone of the offer of *semlor* that brought people like me – or at least people subject to the same temptations as me – in from the outside. The glass cases were full of other tempting pastries as well, accentuated by the smells of lemon, cinnamon, almonds, vanilla, chocolate and the generally witheringly delightful fragrances of freshly baked breads.

Two or three people were ahead of me in line at the counter on this particular February day. Each was greeted in turn by a somewhat plump woman whose youth had long faded and whose possibly forced smile filled out the wrinkles it created, without matching the other wrinkles of her eyes, which appeared to be more interested in sizing people up than in conveying friendliness. But her manner towards each of the people in front of me in the line was impeccably (if not exaggeratedly) and formally polite, and she greeted each with "*Goddag, vad får det lov att vara?*" (Good day, how might I help you?), whereupon she swiftly filled their orders, bagged their goods, took their money, gave them their change, and wished them a good day again, with equal doses of sincerity.

When it was my turn, I stepped up to the counter, and with a confident smile responded to her standard greeting question, taking the utmost care to enunciate properly, "*Goddag, jag skulle vilja ha två semlor, tack!*" (Good day, I would like to have two *semlor*, please!"). After about the third word of my carefully rehearsed, meticulously enunciated but heavily accented request, I noticed that her otherwise permanent smile had evaporated. By the end of my sentence, her smile had turned into a scowl. My confidence was somewhat shaken. What had I done, inadvertently yet utterly, to destroy this façade of politeness?

"*Va'?!*" (Huh?!) she hissed at me, her scowl hardening fiercely. I repeated my order with painstaking clarity. She hissed again: "*Fastlagsbullar*!! They're called *fastlagsbullar*!!" Having known the other word for the buns I wanted, I was not confused about whether or not she'd understood me, but I was very surprised that it could seem to be an issue, nearly a crime, that I incomprehensibly failed to grasp which synonym an upstanding person should use. I mumbled a confirmation that *fastlagsbullar* were indeed what I wanted, handed her a yellowish five-krona bill, got my change and a suitably sized box containing the buns from the still-scowling lady, and left the store greatly puzzled.

As I walked the block and a half home along Lundavägen to Vårgatan, I was trying to figure out why she insisted on using *fastlagsbullar* when the signs, both outside and inside, said *semlor*?! Could there be a difference between spoken Swedish and written Swedish in this particular case? Or maybe *fastlagsbullar* was a more modern term that was replacing a more old-fashioned one? Or maybe it had something to do with local dialects or accents? Or maybe it was a personal preference in terms of her own vocabulary? (Or maybe she was just a bitch? But I didn't consider that option at the time.)

But none of these questions yielded a satisfactory answer, none that made any sense to me. And nothing that could account for the total collapse of her politeness. That part was just plain *weird*, but obviously I couldn't understand what was going on, not yet having learned enough about Sweden and its many cultural nuances. I told Jeanette about it when I got home, after bounding up the four flights of stairs of the old building.

While she was putting the coffee on, I recounted the inexplicable incident at EPA while its implications and the coffee were brewing. Jeanette and I had reached about the same level in our quest to master the Swedish language at this point, but sometimes she picked up words and phrases I hadn't, and vice-versa, which often enabled us to learn a bit more from each other. This one stumped her too. By the time we gave up trying to understand what had transpired in the bakery, the coffee was ready, and we prepared to enjoy our second-ever whatever-it's-called bun.

Elsa was the one who taught us about the bun with more than one name. I salivated as soon as she mentioned the almond paste, having first learned to love the almond crescents – croissants filled with almond paste – that I got on Thursday mornings, fresh and still warm from the local bakery when I finished my weekly paper route in Oak Park as a boy. My next encounter with almond paste or marzipan was when one of my parent's Meeting friends, a Mr Fiedler visiting from Pittsburgh, came to our home (not our roof) for dinner and brought a box of deliriously delicious marzipan candies shaped and colored like various fruits. The next time I enjoyed almond paste was when I discovered it in the candy department (or actually the candy department's stock room) at The Emporium in San Francisco – little cylinders of pure almond paste, about eight centimeters long and two or three in diameter, some of them coated in dark chocolate, and individually wrapped in cellophane. I seem to remember they were imported from Austria. I couldn't get enough of them.

Elsa showed us how to eat *semlor*, by first removing the "lid", then using it to scrape off and enjoy the most excessive part of the slightly sweetened whipped cream that was on top of the almond paste. The next step was to dive into the main part of the bun, which still had enough whipped cream to leave some on your nose and chin in your eagerness to get as much into your mouth as possible. Like Sweden's traditional eating of crayfish in August, the eating of *semlor* represent a departure from the normal dignity (which borders on rigidity) that characterize most other rituals of Swedish dining etiquette.

Jeanette and I took our first bites, and looked up at each other across the plane of whipped cream still mostly beneath our noses. Our eyes oozed pleasure, and everything distasteful that happened in the bakery was evicted from my mind. Some people savor a dish by spending an hour consuming it. With our approach it took a couple of minutes at most. (It's funny how people who take a long time to savor something often seem to feel entitled to tell the quick-savorers that they can't really appreciate what they are eating, but the quick-savorers seldom say that about those who take a long time. I've even heard these judgments when a dish that is at its best when hot has grown stone cold on the plate of the slow-savorer, while the quick-savorer has captured every morsel at its intended and ideal temperature.) Once we'd finished our *semlor*, we confirmed and re-confirmed to each other how much we enjoyed them, and then our day progressed to evening and to other activities, topics and food.

The next day, my teaching was in the morning only, and when I reached

Värnhemstorget on my way home, I involuntarily thought of the *semlor* at EPA. The same lady was serving at the counter at the bakery stand. There was just one other customer; it would be my turn next. To that first customer, the fake smile and rehearsed politeness were perfectly intact. But as soon as that customer departed with his treasures and I appeared as the next customer, the smile inverted itself like an eel writhing to escape. My powers of deduction being as blindingly brilliant as they were, I realized that the lady behind the counter recognized me, even remembered me, and was not pleased. Since her polite question was not forthcoming, I offered an answer to what it would have been if she'd bothered. "*Goddag, jag skulle vilja ha två fastlagsbullar, tack*!" – placing extra emphasis on the word *fastlagsbullar*, to make certain that she understood that I was eager to learn and that I'd learned something useful from her.

But she stared at me, her scowl a deepening shade of livid, far deeper than the day before. Then she sneered and hissed, really hissed: "<u>Semlor</u>!!! They're called <u>semlor</u>!!!" as she pointed angrily at the sign, like she might have been pointing out the murderer of her family in a court of law. I was stunned. I was speechless. I felt a sickening confluence of rushing streams of anger, sadness, disappointment, outrage. I think my jaw dropped a bit. An impartial observer may have thought I'd been hit on the head with a silent bludgeon. But I had no words, no witty reply with which to cut her off at the knees, no smart remark to bring down the house. I only felt a kind of dizziness, a sense of unreality. *People aren't really like this, are they*? *Not here too!?* I managed to nod in assent to the order of *semlor*, placed my money under her glaring gaze and within reach of her claws, and hightailed it out of there, buns in tow.

As I walked home, my pulse was racing, and the sense of outrage was mounting faster than I could mount the four flights of stairs up to our apartment. Jeanette saw the box of *semlor* and my face at about the same time, and couldn't figure out what the one had to do with the other, but of course she knew that something had upset me greatly. Totally unlike her, my emotional state was almost always written in big bold letters across my face, in my voice and in my body language. I explained what happened. Once again calling on my powers of deduction, I realized that the *fucking* bakery *bitch* was dishing me the dirt because of my accent, because I was a foreigner, because despite my correct grammar and painstaking enunciation, my pronunciation wasn't up to her elevated standards of excellence, thus rendering me worthless as a human being. I felt nauseous.

Jeanette told me to forget the whole thing, not to dwell on it, that I shouldn't waste any effort at all on someone who behaved like that. I knew she was right. But I couldn't stop thinking about it. *I'll go back and spit on her*, I thought for a split second, until my more sensible and reflective me banished that thought. *I'll tell the store management*, but it would be my word against hers, and they'd probably have a hard time understanding me – or bothering to try if they could hire someone like that, even though I was well aware that most Swedes were nothing at all like that bitch. I thought of other things, back and forth, the rest of the evening, until I fell asleep.

Since I was free from work the next day, I didn't need to pass EPA. But I walked over there anyway, at about the same time of day as on my two previous visits. I entered cautiously and looked over. There she was. I got in line. When my turn was approaching, I saw that she spotted me in the line – her eyes widened momentarily, then narrowed and a scowl quickly appeared, only to be quickly fought off for the sake of the Swedish customer she was serving. But when it was my turn, her eyes met mine with full force – and I glared right back. She recognized that I recognized that she recognized me. Without waiting for the polite question I knew would probably not come anyway, I stated my demand forcefully, in my accented Swedish: "*I want <u>one</u> <u>semla</u> and <u>one</u> <u>fastlagsbulle</u>! Please!!*"

This time *her* jaw dropped. She went pale. She was totally unprepared for being linguistically outwitted by an awful foreigner. I smiled. She fulfilled my request without a word, and received payment. Not another word was said. I took my beautiful buns and my smile kept growing as I walked out the door of EPA, never to return. (I soon learned a third name for those glorious buns: fettisdagsbullar. Imagine her eyes if I'd ordered one each of all three!)

We not only enjoyed these *semlor* more than the others. I changed my plans and ambitions. Oh yes, I still wanted to learn Swedish grammar as well or better than any Swede. I still aspired to acquire a huge vocabulary. But the accent was another matter. Suppose I learned to have no accent at all? Then I could spend – *waste* – a lot of time getting to know someone before blowing their cover as a xenophobe. With an accent, maybe they'd give themselves away at once and save me a lot of bother. Besides, people who moved from Stockholm to Malmö as adults almost always retained their Stockholm accents. And vice-versa. When adult Swedes move from one part of Sweden to another, you hear where they come from. Why not hear where I'm from?

Fairly early in our stay in Sweden, I began to discern something I would eventually call "the pen effect". Nearly every time I had to phone some authority, official office, bank, or anywhere that required me to state my full name, an exchange (in Swedish) would take place along these lines. What is your last name? *Erisman.* Ersman? *No, Erisman.* Eriksson? *No, Er-is-man.* Erlichman? *No Er-is-man!* Can you spell it please? *Yes, E-R-I-S-M-A-N.* Oh, just like it sounds! *Uh, yes....* And your first name? *Stanley.* Sten? *No, Stanley – like the tools, S-T-A-N-L-E-Y.* And do you have any other first name? *Yes, Larson.* (At this point, they would audibly slam their pen down on their desk, in exasperation – hence "the pen effect".) Now look here, is your last name Larson-Erisman or Erisman-Larson?! *It's just Erisman.* And your first names? *Stanley Larson.* Well, I've never heard of anybody with Larson as a first name!! *Nor have you ever met my mother!!!*

Other aspects of learning Swedish were both fascinating and hilarious, at least to people with our sense of humor. Among the first sources of our uninhibited laughter were signs we'd see at gas stations, parking garages, etc: *infart* and *utfart*. We guessed correctly that they had to do with "in" and "out" respectively, and also that they didn't really have anything to do with farting. The "out-fart" was kind of obvious, but what was "in-fart"? Rumbling in the stomach? We laughed our heads off. We realized that they actually meant "entrance" and "exit", but then we encountered *ingång* and *utgång*, which meant the same things. Except that they only meant the same things in English, not in Swedish; Swedish had separate words for entrances and exits if they were done by means of walking or driving.

It gradually became clear that any two given languages are not merely two sets of interchangeable, directly translatable words, but are also two somewhat different ways of *thinking*, and the magnitude of the differences often depends on how closely related to each other the two languages are. I remembered having learned in my general semantics class in San Francisco that people who were bilingual in English and Japanese could display quite different perceptions and values when being interviewed, depending on the language they were thinking in at the time. Even with Swedish (a Germanic language like English), the language itself can force you to look at things in slightly different ways. There is, for instance, no Swedish word for "grandparent" – you have to specify father's father (*farfar*), mother's mother (*mormor*) etc. But in English you cannot identify a specific grandparent with a single word, which you can in Swedish. A rather simple statement like "I have 16 great-great grandparents," is almost impossible to express in Swedish, at least conversationally. You'd have to say, "*Det finns 16 människor vars barnbarns barnbarn jag är.*" (There are 16 people whose great-great-grandson I am.)

It was also fascinating to learn about Swedish traditions and customs, especially how they differed from what I'd brought with me in my often unconscious cultural baggage. On hearing about a Swedish tradition for the first time, I was seldom content to learn the *what*; I also wanted to know the *why*. Many times, the *why* part had been lost in the dust of history; people were doing things for reasons that long ago might have been valid, then continued to do them even after the reasons or validity no longer existed. I'd heard an old story about how sheep would jump over a stick to get out of a corral, and then if the stick were removed, the rest of the sheep would jump where the stick used to be, because they simply followed the sheep that went before, like sheep do. On analyzing the merits of a Swedish tradition, I became aware of the many questions that were simultaneously popping up in my mind: *It's strange that Swedes do it this way. Why? And how did we do it? And why didn't we do it their way, and why did we do it ours?? And is it any better? And are other nationalities doing things different ways, and why? And do they realize there are other ways they could do things? And is anyone not behaving like a sheep here?*

I conjectured that few people are even aware of many of the traditions they blindly follow. Society is better at conditioning us to follow than to think independently and exercise freedom. Yet what is "freedom" but one of those Big Words that tend to cause a visceral reaction long before the brain is engaged? Everyone says they want to be free. But do they? The will to *think* of oneself as free often seems to be much greater than the will to actually *be* and *act* free. The popular assumption in the West is that people all over the world want to be free, yet most of those Western people practically line up to show their subservience to regents, gods, corporations, leaders, fads, celebrities, cliques, rituals, traditions. The assumption is thus highly flawed, if not outright false. How many people in Western countries could react with total emotional indifference on discovering that the shoes they put on that morning didn't match, even if they caused no discomfort whatsoever to their feet?

Some would say freedom is the freedom to act in any way one chooses – which would be tantamount to anarchy. We would be free to murder, rape and rob each other. Fortunately, few people seem to want that. Or could true freedom be the freedom to think any way one chooses, free from thought police? That could mean being unbound by conventions and subservience, the ability to act freely provided one causes no injury or harm to others, halting the free swinging of one's arm before the nose of another begins.

Most people seem content to do what those before us have done and/or what those around us are doing. Sometimes conformity is like a warm blanket; if you follow and conform, you're secure. There's no chafing, and it certainly is easier than all that thinking work. At the same time, I realize that traditions can impart a sense of community and belonging, which can feel pretty nice. Where should you draw the line? And what if the traditions are based on ignorance or outright lies, or are used simply to manipulate people? Aren't religions the biggest tradition-makers, tradition-enforcers and manipulators of all time? I felt I needed some more time and experience to try to start figuring these things out.

As winter turned to spring, with Jeanette sailing along in her secretarial course and I plowing along at Demaret's, the frequency of our contacts with Elsa naturally diminished, although we remained in touch almost weekly. Elsa and Sven came to dinner at our place a few times, and we had very nice evenings together, but Sven seemed to find the fact that our standard of living was significantly lower than theirs somewhat disquieting, even though we were proud of our new hot water and the great boost it gave us. Or he may simply have found our four flights of stairs laborious.

Unfortunately, our contacts with Boris were now far less frequent. He was finishing high school but seemed unable or unwilling to find ways of utilizing his extraordinary language skills or to develop his considerable aptitude for electronics. The little we witnessed of his home situation led us to believe that his mother was most eager for him to remain her little boy. She seemed determined to hold the mild-mannered Boris under a kind of emotional blackmail to remain under her wing. Boris appeared to feel very awkward about our efforts to help him find ways forward.

In late March, Jeanette and I decided to buy a couple of used bicycles, not only for transportation to and from the Parador parties, but also to use for many of the short errands we had around town, including the laundromat. As long as we weren't hauling boards or furniture, the bikes were easier to get around on, easier to park and much cheaper to own and operate than the Saab. It wasn't long before we found ourselves doing nearly all our errands by bike, which meant that the only times we were using the Saab were to move it from the even-numbered side of the street to the odd-numbered side to match the even- and odd-numbered days of the calendar, in order to avoid parking tickets. And we occasionally took the car to the repair shop to satisfy its seemingly insatiable demand for replacement of parts that were individually not terribly expensive, but added up to quite a drag on the budget to which we were limited.

One day when everyone was out to lunch at Demaret's, somebody broke into the school and stole whatever they could find, including that nice leather attaché case Jeanette bought me when I started my full-time university studies back in 1965. I felt very bad about it, but Carmen told me I could buy a new one and give her the bill – she would be reimbursed by her insurance company.

To our great delight, Bob joined us for a full week at Easter, in early April, which we were looking forward to with unmitigated joy. This time, we met Bob at Bulltofta, the Malmö airport, just a short drive out Sallerupsvägen from our place. As before, he arrived in a state of considerable exhaustion, but this time his stay took place in far less of an alcoholic haze. Jeanette and I certainly had no moral issues with alcohol (our Parador parties would have disqualified us from any such inclinations), but we were very concerned about possible adverse effects on his health from the copious consumption that seemed to be a daily thing.

His misery at Roche still weighed heavily on him, and we sensed a growing desperation. (Bob described Roche as "a filthy-rich capitalist organization in which policy has almost nothing to do with anything other than financial considerations.")

On his trip to see us – he had to take a train to Zürich, then a flight to Copenhagen, then the flight to Malmö – he picked up a European edition of an American newspaper (perhaps it was the *International Herald Tribune*), in which he found an ad for a job that he intended to apply for during his stay with us, with the help of our typewriter. The position was that of Managing Director of a small pharmaceutical company in or near Switzerland. Jeanette and I were stunned and incredulous. We'd seldom met anyone who seemed less suited to running a company, making swift decisions brimming with business acumen, and oozing confidence that would reassure shareholders as well as the board of directors, the medical community, the politicians and the general public. We thought he might be joking, but he was deadly serious. Then we realized that it was a measure of his doomed desperation to get out from under Erich Theiss. Jeanette helped him formulate something approaching a business letter and typed it out in keeping with business practice, but we both knew it was destined for the wastebasket.

Perhaps Bob did too; the letter-writing exercise was accompanied by the greatest alcohol consumption he had that week.

Bob was amazed at the improvements in our apartment, and thrilled on our behalf. Our place was looking and feeling more and more like a home, like *our* home. But he was a bit disappointed that I hadn't painted any more, and in this he was fully and visibly supported by Jeanette.

Almost automatically, our daily (and nightly) conversations drifted back to our ongoing efforts to get down to the bottommost layers of the religious indoctrination to which we'd both been subjected. Although Bob began his liberation process in the early 1950s, when he was in his mid-20s, we agreed that I was the one who had a big head start: first, thanks to my never having joined the Meeting, while Bob plumbed its depths; second, thanks to my far less brooding nature; and third, thanks to my willingness more swiftly to shift the burden of proof to religion itself, rather than taking upon myself the nearly impossible task of proving negatives.

Bob kept saying how refreshing and liberating he found my approach, even though he remained largely determined not to win without a much bigger struggle. We discussed how we'd both been brought up in the Plymouth Brethren to believe that every word in the Bible – especially the King James Version – was the literal and immutable Word of the living Creator of the Universe, a God incapable of error or evil or ignorance, and that any attempt to change a single word of the Holy Scripture was a sin unto death. We recognized that by the 1950s, when Bob left the Meeting, many of those beliefs were no longer mainstream in the leading Protestant denominations. Because literal interpretation of the Bible was simply too full of obvious errors and contradictions, mainstream Christianity was retreating from literalism, cherry-picking as fast as it could, trying desperately to invoke figurative interpretations where the literal ones became untenable to any reasonably reasonable person. But how could even the most figurative interpretation of the slaughter of the firstborn in every household in Egypt, the direct order of God Himself, portray that God as anything but a psychotic sociopath?

My brothers responded to such questions from me with apologetic parries like "*I don't have the answers, but <u>He</u> has the answers, and He will reveal them to me in His own time.*" Those were no answers at all; they were utter cop-outs. Who on earth would believe such a myth if it were invented today? I take that back; there is abundant evidence that people will believe *anything*. It doesn't even seem to require the incredible force of millennia of blind tradition behind it, a force that doesn't need truth, doesn't want truth, can't handle truth, can't handle doubting or questioning. Just how pernicious does this masquerade get?

Bob and I felt that we'd broken through a barrier we hadn't seen before, one that had made us afraid to ask these totally iconoclastic questions, turning bright lights of doubt onto the shady sources of our brainwashing, and at last questioning the first premises. It was both exciting and deeply disturbing. One of the things that made it disturbing was that by overthrowing of all the religious traditions of Western civilization, we were placing ourselves in a tiny minority. Insisting on validity and evidence as criteria for believing can be a lonely road.

Jeanette and I were fortunate to have unwittingly (almost) chosen one of the world's most secular countries as our place of refuge, but although most Swedes had abandoned their age-old religious beliefs as such, they still clung to many of the traditions that arose from them. And yet Swedes turned out to be one of the most "Christian" countries of all – not in the religious sense of believing in superstitions – but in the context of American Christians' use of the expression *"the Christian thing to do"*, by which they generally mean showing kindness to others, helping the poor, sick and elderly – the very things that Jesus kept going on about.

This was something that the majority of Americans definitely did *not* do, and many became absolutely livid at the thought of their government assuring a minimum level of decency for all – something the Swedish government did. Americans called it *"socialism!"* spoken with great emphasis, greater sneering and greatest dread, despite the fact that the Bible and Jesus himself not only commanded but nagged about doing everything possible to help the sick, poor, and elderly, and despite the fact that few Americans could distinguish between *Socialism* and *Communism* (upper-case C, not to mention lower-case c).

There was clearly a strong case, based solely on the Bible itself, to be made for a premise that Jesus was a revolutionary socialist. *"From each according to his ability, to each according to his need"* (attributed to the political theorist Karl Marx) fits right in with the dozens of biblical injunctions to help the poor, the sick and the elderly. In my view, the fact that Swedes accomplished such help through taxes rather than charities only showed how much more Swedes believed in their own democracy: that the government was the creation and instrument of the people. I couldn't understand how any American could call him- or herself a Christian and deny anyone else medical care, food, clothing, shelter, as well as an equal opportunity for education, the only means to avoid ultimately condemning people to inherited poverty. Bob told me that many, if not most European countries in fact offered free medical care and education; it was our homeland that was the most "un-Christian" of them all, despite its drooling and hypocritical lip-service to Jesus.

Nor could I understand how any American purporting to defend the US Constitution, with its *"We, the people"* preamble, could rant about how Government itself was *"them"* and had to leave *us*, the people, alone. *How can we leave ourselves alone if we are the people?* I felt that if a democracy is to remain healthy, the people must do their best to see that they remain informed *and* willing to challenge the actions of their elected officials and remind them that they should be serving the people, not vice-versa.

By the time Bob left to go back to Binningen, we had many more questions than answers, but we were determined to find out, or more accurately, to develop viable working hypotheses, but keep doubting them. We did *not* see that living on autopilot – just following what everyone else does or has done for ages – could be a defensible option. In the light of our discussions, the fact that my parents were coming to Sweden – and to Basel – less than a month later was titillating.

Mom and Dad announced that they intended to fly to Amsterdam on April 30th, rent a car, drive to Basel to see Bob, then drive up to Sweden to see us as well as the places my mom's paternal grandparents came from, add a visit to Halmstad to see their Mr Gullens and take him to dinner, then the four of us (including Jeanette, not Mr Gullens) would drive back down to Amsterdam with them, from where we would all fly back to our respective homes on May 13th. It would have meant seven nearly full days on the road for a 14-day trip, plus the fact that both Jeanette and Bob had very limited time off from their respective course and work obligations. Bob had pretty mixed feelings about a visit from his aunt, who occasionally (all too often) sent him preachy letters, but since he was also very curious about family gossip dating back farther than I could provide answers about, he agreed to take two days off work.

I tried to suggest some major modifications in my parents' itinerary, but since they'd already booked their flights to and from Amsterdam before asking us whether it fit our plans, there was nothing to do about their flights. After several exchanges of letters, with Bob as well, I managed to persuade them to drive up to Malmö directly, arriving on May 1st, then spend a week with us and visit the ancestral homes. Then I would join them on the leg to Basel, arriving there on May 10th, before we left for Amsterdam on May 12th and flew home to our respective destinations the next day. There was no Mr Gullens in the revised itinerary. My parents had never met him, but had apparently heard through their special network that he was a "true Christian" with whom they thought I should have "fellowship" – and he had the additional distinguished merit of having written a gospel tract of which they approved enough to send him unannounced to visit our home and inspect it thoroughly! Apparently I and the events of the past eight years or so had not yet made it clear to them that "Christian fellowship" – particularly their version – was not my thing!

Perhaps Mom and Dad realized from my letters something of the extent of my departure from the path they chose for me, but it seemed to me that they were too frightened to do any kind of real probing. Or maybe Dad warned Mom not to begin castigating me, fearing that I was likely to castigate right back. I loved them deeply, but I was beyond their command, and they knew it.

From the moment they arrived, however, Mom clearly had no intention of showing restraint. She was constantly talking about the Lord, spouting clichés like a broken record, fixing her bun at every turn, occasionally criticizing our home and lifestyle openly, in a manner that in normal human social practice would be characterized as extremely rude (in spite of our having made the effort to hide our alcohol and suppress our "uncouth" vocabulary). She wept histrionically at my having turned from Him, never showed a sign of approval or enjoyment, made an abundance of condemnations, sometimes subtle, sometimes blatant, made Jeanette feel like the world's worst hostess, and thus largely wasted their time and ours.

Dad watched her with a look bordering on horror, but he was not about to rebuke her. Instead, he sought balance by sticking to the non-controversial, practical aspects of our acclimatization in Sweden: food and language. Despite a standard of living well below what they were accustomed to, they'd seen me living in worse conditions in Daly City. And fortunately for all of us, I'm sure, they spent their post-dinner evenings and nights at a small hotel on Sallerupsvägen, a couple of blocks away. Had they spent their nights in our apartment, all hell might have broken loose.

During their visit, however, I had more of a chat – almost a conversation, a discussion, a talk – with Dad than I'd ever had before. The starting point was the word *"you"*. He was fascinated to hear from me that modern Swedish had both formal (*Ni, Er*) and informal (*du, dig*) second-person-singular pronouns. Even more astonishing to him was the fact that the *in*formal forms were used to address the deity, as they were in King James English; he'd always assumed otherwise. It was as though I'd told him that his prayers were the equivalent of "*Hey God, what's up?*" And yet I wasn't being facetious or sarcastic, just factual. To find out, after all this time, that *Thee* and *Thou* were the ordinary *in*formal forms of *you* (not words quivering with holiness and quaking with reverence) seemed rather difficult for him to take in. I think his acceptance of this fact was on the intellectual level only; his faith employed emotional criteria. This was probably only the fourth or fifth time Jeanette ever met my dad, but each time she liked him more. She saw my best sides in him, she said, but I think Dad had more good sides than I ever did.

Why would I think that? I was beginning to understand a few things about myself and how I interacted with others, i.e. how I came across. I didn't like it much. When stating or explaining my position, views or hypotheses about practically *any*thing, I tended to state them forcefully to the point of belligerence (like the police using excessive force), thereby putting people off (or on the defensive) and achieving the opposite of my intended effect. In my own mind, I was simply presenting a case and stating why I took the position I did, expecting, hoping to be challenged so that I could discover the weaknesses of my positions, so I could modify them accordingly. But to others I was charging with a sledgehammer, insisting on being *right*. Dad, on the other hand, stated his views softly, if at all. I seldom agreed with him where matters of belief were concerned, but he didn't put people off – including me. He was always likeable; I far too often became strident and shrill without knowing it or wishing it. Many would agree with me that I've never really figured that out. My sincere apologies!

But neither have I been able to figure out why religious people (as well as other ideologues) of nearly all stripes feel entitled not only to be respected for who they are as human beings, but for whatever they believe. Surely it is possible to love a person but repudiate their beliefs/faith/religion?! That's what I always did for my parents once I'd broken free. I think Dad got that; it took Mom an awfully long time, but I think she eventually got it, much later in her long life.

Looking at the world and its plethora of religion- and ideology-based conflicts, however, there don't seem to be many who get the difference, a difference that seems crucial to resolving conflicts just about everywhere.

The first stop on our ancestral outing, starting on Monday, May 3rd, was Stengårdshult, the birthplace of my mom's paternal grandmother. It consisted of a church and a few surrounding houses – no shops, nothing else – deep in the forests of the province of Småland, the part of Sweden most traditionally associated with Sweden's most religious people. Mom claimed to recognize a few names on some of the tombstones in the churchyard. Then we drove on about 45 km to the town of Jönköping, somewhat sarcastically referred to by many Swedes as "Little Jerusalem", the headquarters of several of Sweden's small fundamentalist Christian movements (a.k.a. sects).

This was where we would spend the night. At first we only saw one hotel, in the center of town, but Mom and Dad rejected it the instant we entered the lobby, on observing that alcoholic beverages were served on the premises, and that the restaurant featured a dance band on Wednesday evenings and weekends (even though this was a Monday!). Instead we found a very small and very plain hotel a few blocks away, but since that hotel had no dining facilities, we were obliged to head back to the town center for our evening meal. The main hotel's restaurant was already crossed off the list, but we managed to find a small, nearly empty diner with cozy fluorescent lighting and charming Formica tables. They offered a selection of one type of sausage and mashed potatoes served with ketchup and/or mustard. Apart from one other somewhat disheveled man in his 30s, sitting alone, we were the only customers. But we'd no sooner begun eating (after Dad's brief chat with the Invisible Guy in the Sky, of course) than an acquaintance of the other customer entered the diner, and the two of them began shouting angrily at each other. Punches were thrown and missed. A chair was overturned, and the new arrival stormed out. Years later, Mom would solemnly declare to me that Jönköping (remember, "Sweden's Jerusalem") was the most sinful, wicked place she'd ever visited. She was totally convinced of this assessment – a prime example of the power of first impressions, or rushing to judgment, or prejudice?

The next day we made a brief stop at an old abbey (originally for both priests and nuns) in Vadstena, on our way up to Motala. The abbey dated back to the mid-14th century (Sweden remained Catholic until the end of the 16th century), and its history included horrifying 15th-century scandals involving priests and nuns bumping their bodies against each other, perhaps to be expected from a co-ed convent. From Motala, we headed east into the countryside, to the picturesque old Vinnerstad Church. Mom's paternal grandfather grew up on one of the farms belonging to that parish.

We returned to Malmö on the Thursday evening and had two more long days together, briefly relieved by short local outings. On Sunday morning, Mom, Dad, and I began our southbound journey to Basel, and Jeanette sat down to write me a beautiful love letter, "*...as you set off on the boat with your judges,*" to assure that it would reach me while I was at Bob's place. Mom and Dad seemed determined at first to take advantage of having me in the confined space of the car for a day and a half, that they might preach at me. (Time to wake up, Stan! I keep saying "they", which is grossly unfair to Dad; Mom did *all* the preaching; Dad limited himself to the pre-meal one-way conversations with the invisible guy in the sky, a role that would have been most unseemly for Mom to assume while an adult male Meeting person was present.) I was every bit as determined that our time together would not be wasted on her telling me over and over what I'd already heard over and over and over and over for the first nearly 19 years of my life.

She started preaching. I pointed out something in the landscape, in German history, or asked about their impressions of their first visit to Sweden. We repeated this procedure countless times. I simply refrained from responding to her preaching, much as I would have liked to respond. But I was convinced that she would exercise her "right" to take great umbrage, to the point of profound grief, if I exposed her to rebuttals of the beliefs she was shoving in my face. In deference to both of them, I held my tongue. I was aware of the risk that they might choose to interpret my refusal to refute them to mean that I found no way to refute what they said. I took that risk, but only because I could find no *polite* way to refute what she said.

Eventually she realized that her efforts were in vain, and she largely desisted. They probably also realized that they would soon be meeting similar resistance from Bob if she tried out such arguments on him or in his presence. I'm sure she told herself that our hearts were "hardened", without for a moment considering that Bob and I were almost infinitely more inclined to compassion towards the human race than the god of their Bible, and by extension, that she was herself. In any case, Bob, in his hard-heartedness, booked and paid for a comfortable room for them at the Drachen hotel in central Basel. I would be staying on the floor of his living room in Binningen.

We made it as far as Göttingen on May 9th, then got up very early the next morning and made it to Switzerland, driving straight to Bob's place, by mid-afternoon. Mom and Dad took a brief look around. Bob had made no effort to conceal his liquor bottles or his pipes, but Mom must have realized there were no takers for any histrionics this time. Both of my parents seemed nervous about being there (perhaps Dad only for Mom's sake?), and highly uncomfortable at how obviously close Bob and I already were. After not too many minutes, Bob and I accompanied them to their hotel. We agreed to pick them up for dinner a few hours later, and Bob and I took the tram home to get a drink and have a stimulating talk between two adults.

I was a little disappointed at the reappearance of the clutter – the numerous stacks of papers everywhere, although there was less laundry on the floor. The dates of the newspapers at the bottom of several of the new stacks corresponded to the date of Jeanette's and my departure in October. I made a trip to the bathroom the moment we arrived to make sure it was decent if my parents needed to use it. It was a good thing I did. But the lapses in Bob's maintenance of a semblance of tidiness or cleanliness were far outweighed for me by the noticeable reduction in his "mental clutter"; his depression now seemed merely serious, no longer alarming. (Not that I was an expert yet!)

Anyway, once Bob and I were back at his place alone, we had a couple of whiskies each (possibly three…), knowing that we would certainly be having a prohibitionist meal with my parents that evening, again out of deference to *their* values. (I might have asked why their flimsy, unsupported, arrogantly unquestionable values should always be permitted to set the bar, but it would take a few more years for that question to occur to me.)

When it was getting to be time for Bob and me to leave to go meet them, it suddenly occurred to me that I probably reeked of alcohol, and even though I didn't even feel high (or guilty), I felt I ought to do something about my breath. (My parents almost certainly never knew what highly deferential efforts I was making!) I hurried down to the Migros next door and bought some chlorophyll chewing gum and began chewing two or three pieces at once. Bob didn't bother. As we were about to leave his apartment, Bob said something that made me grin, and my grin made Bob laugh harder than I'd ever seen him laugh before. My teeth and my tongue were bright green from the chlorophyll. Amid our sobs of laughter, I brushed my teeth vigorously for quite a while to get the color down to a pale greenish white, and my breath to the level of a slightly fermented rose. (I realize I've already related this anecdote in *Natural Shocks* [Part One of *Hindsights*]. I relate it again here just to check that you've been paying attention.)

Dad insisted on picking up the tab for our meal, but hard-hearted Bob was not to be outdone. He'd already prepared a special treat for the following day: first a walking and shopping tour of Basel's winding streets, medieval neighborhoods, majestic cathedral, and superb vistas of the Rhine, before we took the car across the Rhine to a country inn in the Black Forest, a fairly short drive across the border into Germany. Bob had booked a table for us, and had pre-ordered a fabulous meal of roast pheasant, a dish Dad said was more scrumptious than any dish he'd ever tasted before. I'm sure Mom also liked it very much, but since Bob decided that such a meal could not be fully enjoyed with water, he ordered a large glass of wine for himself (still fettered, I discreetly declined), which made Mom squirm with disapproval, undoubtedly numbed her taste buds, and made her forget her manners to thank Bob for generously treating us all to such an exquisite meal. Bob felt it best not to mention to my parents that the delicious pheasant was cooked in *Sekt* (German sparkling wine) before roasting.

My parents dropped us off at Bob's place late that afternoon. Mom said they needed the evening on their own to do some Bible study. I thought it sounded like a good idea; I also thought that if they really studied what the Bible said, they would surely see that they'd been worshipping a pretty nasty god. But Jesus said a lot of good stuff, didn't He? All right, He was still OK, and yet He commanded people to worship His evil father – who was in some weird way Himself. How did that fit with anything? Maybe I should study it some more.

A letter for me from Jeanette was waiting for us on our return to Bob's apartment, and I was thrilled. I'd written her a strikingly similar love letter from Göttingen, and I missed her greatly too; her letter made it clear that our feelings were completely mutual. It's usually harder for the one left behind, in familiar surroundings minus the loved one, than for the one who has left, in new surroundings where so much is unfamiliar anyway. But we were both keenly aware that we didn't much like being apart.

The next morning, Dad and Mom picked me up and we headed for Amsterdam, arriving there in the late afternoon. Our flights weren't until the next day, and since their travel package included a night at a nice hotel in the center of town, already paid for, the plan was for us to spend the evening looking around the city. But even before they checked in, Mom declared that Amsterdam was far too wicked a place to be exposed to (more than Jönköping?!), so Dad acquiesced (as usual) to her demands and found us a "safe" hotel by the airport instead.

The next day, Mom wanted to check in several hours before our flights were scheduled for departure. That was no surprise to Dad or me. Their flight was at around noon; we got to Schiphol right after a rather early breakfast. Their gate wasn't even posted yet; and my flight wasn't until mid-afternoon. We walked around looking at all the shops, and I found a nice leather attaché case to replace the one that was stolen from Demaret's. Shortly afterwards, their gate was posted, and I went to it with them at once (it was still hours before the departure time). I got the impression that Mom began to panic about having failed in her Mission to lead me back to the Lord. She had, in fact, failed utterly. But I knew that Mom and Dad both loved me in spite of my wicked ways, and that I loved them. It was enough for me; I couldn't help that Mom wanted me to understand that it wasn't enough for her. Dad and I gave each other a long, heartfelt bear hug, little knowing that it would be for the very last time.

My heart aches when I think of how unfair I'd been to Dad for his prodigious efforts to keep Mom's "spiritual side" from making her foam at the mouth. And when I look – with hindsight! – at my missed opportunities to ask Dad about his childhood, his upbringing, how his parents really treated him, what his aspirations had been, how he dealt with puberty, what traumatized him, whether he ever wondered if everything he was being told was true, how he got to be such a kind person when his father was such an asshole, all of which I knew nothing about, I could weep and kick myself.

The departure of my flight turned out to be delayed a couple of hours, for no apparent reason – the aircraft had been at the gate for some time. When we were finally allowed to board the plane, we were informed that somebody had phoned in a bomb threat. They had to conduct an extra-thorough search of the aircraft, baggage, catering cargo, and all boarding passengers. Sitting on the plane as it at last began taxiing out to the runway, I found myself thinking, *What if there is a bomb that they haven't found?* It made me very ill at ease, the only time I've ever felt that way about flying, but then I also thought, *The pilot does not by any means seem to be a kamikaze; he wants to get home too*, and *There is absolutely nothing I can do about it, so worrying is futile*. I still worried, but not for my own sake. I'd already found the notion of an afterlife to be nonsense; my worry was about how hard it would be for Jeanette. The emotions we both poured forth in our letters (in rather good Swedish, I now realize!) to each other made the reciprocity clear. Our reunion a few hours later was of the profoundest joy, but I wondered whether it included a hint of desperation....

Not long after my return, we felt that the financial burden of having our maintenance-intensive car was not outweighed by the benefits of holding on to it; there were none. Consequently, we sold it, and suddenly all the money we'd been pouring into repairs, gas, vehicle tax, insurance, vehicle inspection, parking etc could go into savings instead. We were living very simple lives, with no expensive tastes, and no particular unfulfilled materialistic desires. We wanted to travel in Europe, and the availability of cheap charter flights to places like London and Paris would now be easily affordable and still allow us to save, in spite of the fact that my work was less than full-time and Jeanette had no income at all.

Then, on April 30th, I (and all the other employees at Demaret's Language School) received a letter from Carmen in which she announced that she was closing down the school, going out of business, as soon as the contractual minimum notice period elapsed. She claimed that the contracts she'd been forced into were too ruinous for her to manage – which seemed highly unlikely to us teachers. In spite of her mismanagement, overbooking fiascos, and embarrassments like Mel Smith, the school was running at full steam. But we were well aware that she absolutely *hated* to lose a fight, that the contracts were thorns in her side, and that she might well be willing to cut off her nose to spite our faces.

The sudden uncertainty came as a shock. A teacher named Hamadi Klilib began talking about starting up his own school. Hamadi, a short guy around 30 years of age, came from Tunisia, and was a teacher in both French and Arabic. He was livid about Carmen's behavior, as was Arno (so was I). Several of the teachers who'd come over from England with no intention of settling in Sweden, found that this would be as good a time as any to simply pack up and leave. I'd had several inquiries from pupils who wanted to come back and study with me directly, as my own private pupils. I hadn't considered it seriously before Carmen made her announcement, but now that I'd been given notice, it was a different matter.

The first shock wave was not even over when Carmen began going around to her favorite teachers (including me), one by one, telling us that she would "soon" be reopening another school, in the Demaret family's vast apartment on Kungsgatan, so not to worry, there'd be plenty of work – selected teachers would be re-hired, but there would be no more of that contract stuff. Her actions turned out to be technically legal, thanks to some small loopholes she'd found, but there was little doubt about her union-busting motives and feudal mentality.

On June 11th, the Indians who'd taken over Alcatraz in 1969 in accordance with the old Federal treaty entitling them to take over unused Federal lands (the Federal prison that constituted the island was abandoned in 1963), were forced off the island. Like so many times in the past, the US Government only felt obliged to honor its treaties with the Indians until their White rulers could find some reason not to.

But at least the US invasion of Laos in February fanned the already roaring flames of protest, extending them beyond America's campuses and streets, and on June 13th, first the *New York Times* and then the *Washington Post* began publishing "the Pentagon Papers" – secret documents revealing the military's true assessment of the dirty and hopelessly unwinnable Vietnam War, as well as the Pentagon's bold-faced lies to the American public, and the treachery towards the troops. This resulted in two polarized outcries in the US: one was from the anti-war movement, about what was really going on; the other from the "my country right or wrong" contingent, about the allegedly treasonous act of *revealing* what was really going on.

I could not understand the blind-follower contingent. Think about it: Lying to the American people was OK; getting young American men killed by the tens of thousands in a worthless cause was OK; killing Vietnamese by the hundreds of thousands was OK. But revealing it is *not* OK??

CHAPTER 8

The feeling of freedom

In early June 1971, with my future at Demaret's looking bleak, I decided this might be a good time for me to follow Jeanette's lead and get out of the language school racket once and for all. My thought was to resume my graduate studies, this time at Lund University, possibly lecturing in English literature there part-time while pursuing my thesis work. I went to the office of the Faculty of English, and in keeping with the nature of my business, started speaking English with the staff. They replied in Swedish, thus not very subtly indicating that Swedish would remain the language of our conversation, even in the office of the University's Faculty of English.

I had my school records in tow, as well as a glowing letter of reference from Carmen (not that they would be impressed by anything as blatantly non-academic as a private language school). A couple of staff members scrutinized my documents, then asked what I had in mind. When I told them, they looked at each other, mumbled something, and without going to great pains to hide, disguise or mollify their haughtiness, informed me that my academic studies in English in the US and Canada were of little or no value here; I would first have to meet the English standards of Swedish academe (*I dare say!*). But it would not be sufficient for me to prove my knowledge in some form of test, they kindly informed me; I would have to go all the way back to *high school* level and get a proper Swedish high school diploma before I could be considered for admission to their auspicious University, at least for any courses for which I might aspire to receive academic credits! They would, however, deign to admit me for the purpose of allowing me to *audit* certain English courses, but these courses would not be considered part of any work towards an advanced degree. *Academe!* As far as I was concerned, these condescending offspring of unwed parents ought to go engage in coitus with or among themselves. I walked out before the steam building up in me exploded.

One of Demaret's new and potentially biggest customers (if the school managed to stay afloat) was the Volvo plant in Olofström, a small town of around 17,000 inhabitants at the time, to the northeast of Malmö, not too far from Tingsryd. Their education manager, Bo, who'd been a pupil of mine, was planning to enroll

40-some pupils in English classes, but he wanted to have them come to the school in pairs or even threes, instead of individually, in order to save money. I told him I thought the benefits to Volvo could be written as a fraction, with a numerator of one and a denominator equal to the number of pupils being taught at the same time. I told him that learning a language quickly was not only about aptitude but also motivation, and that the benefits would go proportionally to the most extroverted and aggressive of the pupils, given how important it is to speak and not just listen when learning a language. There would be little left over for the shy, much in the way that some individual salmon spawned at the same time in the same fish tank grow many times faster than others in the same tank over the same period of time. But he was determined to go ahead with it his way.

In order to create these groups, the potential pupils would first have to be assessed to determine their existing levels of proficiency, so they could be paired or grouped accordingly. I was asked to devise a test and to spend the week before *Midsommar* in Olofström, first giving a 30-60-minute lecture in the morning about what it means to learn a new language and how to get the most out of it. I would then conduct the tests, the written parts to the group as a whole and the spoken parts individually, of course.

I foolishly felt that although I had no experience in conducting lectures (I had already conveniently forgotten the panic I felt on standing in front of my pupils at ABF the first time), I knew my subject well. Thus all I would need were a few note cards, and then I could speak mostly extemporaneously from them. I entered the large conference room with the 40-some prospective pupils sitting at tables moved together to form a single huge rectangular table with me at the head. I instantly knew I'd committed a grave error. Bo introduced me to the strange staring faces. I stood there in front of them while my every thought and capability to ad lib jumped out the nearest window and fell to its untimely death.

I pulled out the few cards on which I'd written my notes and basically read from them. To my gut it felt like it took hours, but my mind (and everyone else in the room) knew that it took about five minutes – at most. My face must have been 50 shades of red. Bo recognized my predicament and graciously came to my rescue, talking to the group while he and I were still standing in front of them. Then he more or less interviewed me to draw out the information he knew I had in me but couldn't find due to my stage fright. He was brilliant; he took his time, and he was as relaxed as I wished I could be. He managed to keep pumping me for the full hour, as well as during the ensuing coffee break, until I actually ended up conveying a lot of information to the group while becoming more relaxed and sociable in the process.

After the break, the group returned to the conference room to devote the rest of the day to my written test, while Bo and I sat chatting softly in a corner. I guessed that at least two-thirds of the group consisted of engineers, with a few secretaries, finance people, marketing people and others thrown in. About two-thirds of them were male. Since I was to be in Olofström until Friday afternoon, I would be having a lot of time on my hands, so Bo thought it might be fun if I brought along my American football and offered to teach anyone interested in finding out about the game in the local park that evening. (Mom and Dad had brought me the football at my request.)

About 10 of the guys showed up to check out this novelty called American football, which most Swedes at that time equated with rugby and knew no more about than most Americans know about rugby, or cricket, or bandy, or soccer (at that time). A few of the younger women from the group also came to watch. Nobody knew how to hold the ball, throw it or catch it, and I had only the one ball for 10 guys to practice with. It was bizarre. Bo had contacted the local Olofström newspaper, and they sent a reporter out to cover this major news event in a corner of a park in a corner of Sweden where news was particularly hard to come by.

Bo was grinning when he brought the paper to show me the next day. Just about the only thing they managed to get right was the spelling of my name. According to their intrepid reporter – or perhaps the editor decided that the story needed spicing up – I was a *professional* American football player of the highest order (they probably would have called me an NFL Pro Bowler if they'd known the term). I'd allegedly come to Olofström for the express purpose of teaching the locals this weird new sport. I realized that any sport one doesn't understand is regarded as weird, but the sport described in the article was particularly peculiar, and was allegedly played by even more peculiar rules than I'd never heard of. This was not, however, the first time I'd seen examples of journalistic disregard for fact; the latest time involved political asylum – a situation slightly more serious.

The end result of my testing efforts in Olofström assured a steady stream of new customers for Demaret's from Volvo, as well as a continued source of a lot of the income for my colleagues and myself. It would also turn out to be a precedent for Carmen to turn to me for another, ultimately far more important week-long assignment.

Perstorp AB, a chemical company founded in 1881 in an eponymous village in the north of Skåne, was largely based on formaldehyde chemistry and many of its derivatives. It was a family-owned business until 1970, when the family stepped aside and Gunnar Wessman became the first president not part of the founding Wendt family. In addition to taking the company public, Wessman diversified into new fields of plastics and launched a business development company, Pernovo, as part of his expansive and innovative efforts to breathe new life into a rather staid and tradition-bound business. He was also determined to make the company truly international, and started up business ventures outside Sweden, increased focus on exports and, as a result, strongly encouraged company-sponsored language training for all those who would be needing more than Swedish to cope on the international business scene. In doing so, he tried a few somewhat bizarre approaches that were generally viewed with considerable suspicion and even overt disdain by the more fastidious members of the staff.

One of these approaches was to invite Dr Edward de Bono, author of books on lateral thinking, to come to Perstorp (the village) and meet with young people (15-16 years old) from the 8th and 9th grades at the local school, and together with them try to solve or at least look with new and fresh eyes upon a number of hard-to-resolve problems submitted in simplified terms by various divisions within the company. But before the kids spent their week with de Bono, Perstorp's education manager Stig Troell arranged for the kids to spend a week with me.

Although most of the kids had fairly good passive knowledge of English – it had been part of their standard curriculum since the middle grades of elementary school, their daily TV viewing, and their constant popular music for years – their ability to *speak* English was rather limited. I was to give them a crash course, get them to speak as much as possible, and oil their linguistic jaws to get their English engines warm by the time they met Dr de Bono. I spent five days and five long nights in Perstorp. It was the kind of town where practically every single person (as well as every married person) had a family member or neighbor who worked at the company, where your colleagues were your neighbors were your friends, and where senior company management frowned on any manager who failed to make the village his or her home.

Stig did his best to keep me entertained in the late summer evenings, first as his caddy on the mosquito-infested golf course, later at his home. He was a rather avuncular man even though he was only in his mid-40s, determined yet lethargic, friendly yet withdrawn. He liked to project more authority than he had; as education manager, he headed a department of one, and his favorite position was behind the desk he kept his feet on, smoking his pipe and looking studious.

The course with the kids went rather well, although it involved a lot of dentistry work on my part – pulling words out of the kids' mouths felt as hard as pulling teeth. But by the end of the week I think we all realized we'd had some fun and they said they felt much less intimidated about meeting the lateral-thinking expert the following week. I never met him, but Gunnar Wessman sent me a nice plate in black thermoset plastic with an artistic silver-inlaid deer on it. And when the Swedish filmmaker Jan Troell (Stig's younger brother) released his fabulous new film *The Emigrants*[8] in the fall, Stig sent me two tickets to the premiere in Malmö.

Jeanette continued her full-time secretarial course in the autumn and was doing very well. She was a good student and had a sharp mind. She was also reading more than ever, ranging into all kinds of new topics, but she found some of the philosophy books that Bob and I were reading a bit abstruse, or perhaps simply boring.

Henry Carlsson was now a regular private pupil of mine – not Demaret's – at our home, but sometimes we had our lesson in the top-floor Översten restaurant in Kronprinsen after having played an hour of tennis together on one of the two fine courts in the basement of that building. It was the first time I'd ever played tennis indoors. Henry was concerned as much about our having a good time and developing our friendship as he was about learning English, but he seemed to be embarrassed about the rather slow speed of his linguistic progress. Since most of his lessons were just an hour at a time, however, he couldn't really immerse himself in it, and no real speed could be expected.

Jeanette and I noticed, for the first few months after we started speaking only Swedish with each other, how frustrating it could be and how irritated we could become. Sometimes we just wanted to say *Screw it!* and speak English, just to be able to express something important. But it was the very frustration and irritation that drove our learning – we *had* to learn, in order to relieve the pressure of not being able to express ourselves. That alone enabled us to learn more, and faster. After a while, words that used to be hard to find became easier

---

8   Recipient of numerous international awards and accolades

to find the second or third or fifteenth time. And when we could find the words readily, the frustration disappeared.

I also had some hours with a few other pupils who chose to study with me instead of at Demaret's. I didn't see any need to explain myself to anyone; I'd been given notice from Demaret's, my contract had expired, and no new contract was forthcoming. Carmen found her loophole to beat the union; I had mine to beat her. Moreover, my private pupils made it clear that they would not have gone back to Demaret's if I turned them down. But even with my freelance work, my total hours didn't amount to more than part-time work, which suited me fine. We still had renovation projects to undertake in our apartment.

We now had a bathroom, the best one we'd had since Pueblo Street in San Francisco. Our kitchen was highly satisfactory and certainly better than it had ever been since the building was built in around 1900. But the wall-to-wall carpets in all three rooms – part of the excuse for our 5200-kronor outlay for the contract – were worn, filthy and definitely beyond redemption. And the walls all featured rather dirty wallpaper that was peeling and bubbly in places. We'd seen a relatively inexpensive floor covering called needle-loom carpeting that was available in some attractive muted single colors. For the walls we found a burlap material intended for use as wall coverings, in the manner of wallpaper, and we thought it would go well with and make a good backdrop for my paintings. Henry was able to get us super-cheap prices on both, making the whole project affordable. In effect, we were using the medieval system of bartering: I traded him lessons for building materials, and he was very generous about the terms of the trade.

I was also going to cover one entire big bedroom wall with closets and cabinets, with our bed partly recessed into them, and reading lights in the recess. The closets would block one half of the door to the entrance hall. But since it was a door we seldom used anyway, I decided to build a bookshelf into the other half, a bookshelf facing the bedroom that could still be opened as a "secret" door into the hallway. I'd seen such things in movies and thought it would be great fun to have one, and even more fun to build one. But since it would be very heavy when loaded with real books, and not just false spines, there had to be a wheel under the free corner to keep the weight of the books from pulling the whole contraption off its hinges.

I had plans for the living room too. The cheap sofa we'd bought just prior to Bob's arrival was a little narrow for use as a bed, yet unnecessarily deep for a sofa.

It occupied a lot of floor space, and made the room as a whole quite narrow. We therefore decided on a built-in sofa with storage cabinets (which could also serve as end tables) at either end to take up the diagonal part of the living room wall as well, making a straight line instead. The sofa was narrower that the old one we'd bought, but could be folded out to twice its width, thus making a wider bed than before. And we found a place to get thick foam rubber cut to any size – perfect for the mattress/cushions. Jeanette sewed the covers.

These were complicated projects, especially the closets, with interlocking joints for the wood frames, and I owned very few tools: a crosscut saw, a hammer, a few screwdrivers, a hand drill, a rasp and a box cutter. No power tools, and no chisels. When making notches for interlocking pieces of lumber for the closet frame, I sawed two cuts down to the desired depth of the notch. Then I took a hammer, and using a screwdriver as a chisel, I tried to remove the block between the two cuts, but I rarely got an even break. If it broke off *almost* clean, I could finish it with the rasp. But if there was a knot in the wood or for any other reason it failed to break away clean, I had to use the box cutter.

There is hardly an air traveler who hasn't heard the safety instructions on planes numerous times, and yet when the members of the cabin crew go up and down the aisles before takeoff, there's always somebody who's forgotten to buckle his or her seat belt. I *knew* that one should never, ever cut *towards* oneself, especially when using a very sharp knife. But one day, probably in late October or early November, when Jeanette was out shopping and I was constructing our new bedroom closets and making a deep notch in a particularly knotty piece of wood, I just had one little corner to rip loose with the sharp blade of the box cutter. I pulled it hard – towards me – with my left hand while clutching the piece of wood in my right (I'm left-handed, of course). The blade slipped and went straight through the base of my right thumb. I felt an intense icy shock, looked down and saw my *bone* for a split-second – until the blood began *gushing* out. I rushed into the kitchen to get some towels to press around it, then picked up the phone to call the hospital and was told that an ambulance would be there in a couple of minutes. I looked around frantically for a paper on which to scribble a note to Jeanette. I managed *"Gone to the hospital! Love you!"* on the blood-stained paper which I left on the blood-stained kitchen counter. There seemed to be blood everywhere. I didn't know whether to go down the four flights of stairs to wait for the ambulance or not, but decided that since I was feeling dizzy and cold with shock, it might be wiser to wait for them to come up and escort me down, which they did. I think I remembered to lock the door behind me.

At the hospital they gave me four big stitches and a tetanus shot and told me I was lucky it hadn't gone a millimeter deeper or I might have lost my thumb, or at least all feeling in it, forever. I didn't feel terribly lucky, and thought about all the people I'd heard about in similar situations praising their "guardian angels" for not allowing the very worst to happen, as though any such angel couldn't have prevented the entire very bad thing, or prevented it from afflicting everyone else. It's awfully strange how people think – or is it awfully strange how people *don't* think?

I phoned home as soon as I was all bandaged up; Jeanette was understandably frantic. My note hadn't been very well thought out; I could have been stabbed in the heart for all she knew, and I told her how sorry I was to have caused her such alarm, but her relief that I was going to be all right far outweighed any other feelings. I had no way of knowing whether any seeds of profound fear might have been planted then; nor, I suppose, did she. [*This is me still searching for answers as I write* Hindsights.]

Back in early September, when we were looking ahead towards our anniversary on October 8th, we decided to try to continue our private tradition of spending our anniversary in a different country every year. There were ferries once a day from Ystad, a town on the south coast of Sweden, to Świnoujście, across the Baltic in Poland. (The closest approximation to the Polish pronunciation I can come up with is to say "*svee-no*" and then sneeze explosively.) It sounded kind of exotic or dramatic – our first-ever time behind the Iron Curtain and all that. We'd also heard that everything in Poland was dirt cheap, including hotels and meals at restaurants. I don't remember who we heard it from. But since travel to Poland required a visa, we went to the Polish consulate in the NK department store building in downtown Malmö, and filled out some forms, lots of forms, and they certainly weren't free.

We also found that we were required to purchase a certain number of zlotys – at the official exchange rate – for each day of our planned three-day extended weekend in Poland. Since we held American passports, we had to exchange more than Swedish passport-holders did, for some untold reason. We booked what the travel agent assured us was the best hotel in Świnoujście, and we got the names of the best restaurants in town. Our visas came through, and the day before our anniversary, we took the train to Ystad and the boat across in the late evening.

The feeling of freedom

The crossing took about seven hours, with a bit too much rocking and rolling for our taste, but fortunately the effects didn't continue beyond the early signs of cold sweating.

When we arrived early the next morning, not really having a clue what to expect, we instantly realized we could never have expected what we saw, and we suddenly understood the growing gloom among those passengers on the *Stefan Batóry* who were continuing their voyages after Copenhagen. The gray, chilly weather was, of course, no fault of the Polish government, but we felt certain that nearly everything else was. Every building was a further declension of "drab". No effort seemed to have been made anywhere to keep anything tidy, much less to make anything attractive or cheerful or welcoming. There was not a smile in sight.

We were told – first at the Polish consulate in Malmö, then on board the ship, and once or twice again at customs – that it was illegal to exchange money on the black market. We wondered to ourselves why on earth we would want to seek out any black marketeers. But some fellow passengers not making their first trip said that the black market exchange rates gave you 10 times more zlotys for your krona than the official rate. The moment we left the drab, gloomy, unwelcoming, even hostile customs building, which reminded me of the Oak Park Meeting Room, we began to understand what those people were talking about. Within the first hundred meters, we were approached individually by half a dozen young Polish men speaking in subdued tones, wanting to buy dollars or Swedish kronor or Deutsche marks for *lots* of zlotys (*I give you very good rate, sir!*). We didn't dare, but we saw many others doing it openly. We thought that we should first see how much we'd want to buy with the zlotys we'd already been obliged to exchange.

We hailed a taxi. We were picked up by a driver we'd seen hanging out and talking to one of the guys who'd been offering to buy foreign currency. On our way to our hotel, he waved at several rather scantily clad and heavily made up girls along the otherwise fairly deserted streets. They waved back. He also waved at a couple of police officers who were conversing casually with a couple of the girls, and they also waved back. Our luxury hotel had a nice enough (definitely not luxurious) lobby, but after we'd checked in and surrendered our passports as required, every step beyond the lobby felt like a journey backwards into gloom. Our room was rather dark. It was very chilly. Every surface – walls, desktops, bathroom fixtures, bedspread – felt a bit greasy, clammy and damp, almost wet.

We sat on the bed, and immediately thought we'd just sat on a hammock, due to the tremendous sag. *Was this was the <u>best</u> hotel?! What were the others like?!*

We decided that at least we'd go to the best restaurant and have a fabulous anniversary dinner. The place was a few blocks from our hotel; we decided to walk. The only people we saw out and about seemed to come from the four categories we'd already encountered: *C*abbies (taxi drivers), *C*hangers (black-market money exchangers) *C*ops (policemen) and *P*rostitutes.[9] They all seemed to know each other and to have carved up their world among themselves. Were we getting the real picture? Were we suffering from imaginations run wild, or paranoia? We had no way of knowing.

At the restaurant we saw a couple of groups of people we thought were Russians, due to the red Soviet flags on their tables, whereas the other tables had the red-and-white flags of Poland. The Russians, if that was who they were, were eating dinner-plate-size steaks with some sort of sparkling wine, as well as mounds of black Russian caviar and tumblers of vodka, and were getting frequent visits to their tables from some of the girls we'd seen earlier. The "Russians" were very loud. We'd never tasted caviar before, and since it was on the menu, we ordered some. *"No, sir, is finished,"* our unfriendly waiter informed us curtly. (It turned out that not all Polish waiters were kind little old men eager to help us in any way they could.) But since the Russians' steaks looked good, we ordered steaks and sparkling wine. What we got were greasy hamburger patties with some greasy potatoes and a bottle of sweet white wine with no more sparkle than our waiter's eyes. After nibbling just enough to chase away our hunger, we tried to spend our zlotys to pay the bill, and were informed that this restaurant accepted Western currency only. But what about those Russians, whose caviar supplies were replenished *after* we were told there was no more?! We returned to our hotel and tried to find warmth between the greasy, clammy sheets, and to try to find the least uncomfortable positions at the deep sagging bottom of the hammock-style mattress.

The first thing we both thought on waking up on Saturday morning, freezing and aching all over, was *Why the hell aren't we going home today?!* But maybe we'd missed something, like a nice part of town, where the friendly people lived. What might have seemed to us like a simple matter for our friend Krzysztof in Poznań to take a train up to see us was out of the question. These were the days of

---

9   What abbreviation do those four words give you?!

the Iron Curtain, with the severe and oppressive restrictions their "democracy" placed on its own people. But we could at least phone him?! It would, after all, be a *domestic* phone call.

After a tasteless breakfast, we asked at the reception desk if we could make such a phone call. We had Krzysztof's phone number with us and we'd already agreed by letter that we'd try to phone him from Świnoujście that Saturday. The desk clerk said he'd be unable to place such a call, and he summoned the hotel manager, who asked suspiciously why we wanted to phone someone in Poznań. We said we had a friend there, someone we'd met on the boat from Canada, the *Stefan Batóry*. He asked for the number, then dialed another one than the one we said, spoke for a while in Polish, to someone, then waited quite a while, and somehow the call was eventually put through to Krzysztof. The receptionist said something to him before handing us the receiver. He made no move to leave our side while we spoke. We realized that we'd better keep it brief for Krzysztof's sake. It was thus a very short, very superficial conversation, not much more than *how are you, so you're in Poland, hope everything's OK, how's your schoolwork going, hope we can meet again sometime, well, gotta go now, bye-bye, take care*. It was clear that Krzysztof didn't dare to speak freely, that he knew that his every word was being monitored (and recorded?), and ours as well. And we were of course equally uneasy about asking him anything that could get him into trouble. The whole thing made us very sad.

We left the hotel to head into town to find something – anything – to spend our zlotys on. One of the gloomy shops offered a few little trinkets that we'd never have looked twice at if we'd had any other goal than to get rid of zlotys. Then we found an attractive shop window full of stuff we wanted to buy. It was all was very cheap: Polish and Russian vodka, Scotch whisky, French Cognac, as well as tins of Russian caviar (which we'd still never tried). There were some nice-looking cigars, probably Cuban, there were leather goods and French perfumes. All with very low prices, but indicated in *dollars* only. Yet even at the official exchange rate, some of the stuff still seemed like a bargain. We wondered how much they cost in zlotys? It turned out that zlotys were not accepted at that shop, not at all, nor at any other shop that had nice-looking products on display. Western currency only. Poles couldn't use their own currency to buy goods in nice shops in their own country. No wonder the black-marketeers were so eager to get their hands on dollars! And we'd come ill-prepared to spend anything but those useless, worthless zlotys.

We went out to the beach and strolled along it for a couple of hours, looking out over the Baltic and wondering how and why life could be so vastly different on the other side. Wherever we went, there were hardly any people out and about. Yet we were never quite alone. Somebody was always lurking around somewhere. We began to notice two men in hats and raincoats, in the distance, pretending not to see us. If we turned and left the beach, they would be there, off the beach too, a block behind us. If we returned to the beach after a couple of blocks, that's where we'd spot them again. Or were we just being paranoid?

The ferries from Ystad had a rather long turn-around time; they arrived early in the morning, but didn't leave again until early afternoon. We went straight to the terminal after breakfast on Sunday, in the hope of being able to board early and get out of the nightmare that was Świnoujście. Or did that apply to all of Poland? There were many countries in the world that called themselves democratic and wouldn't let the people decide anything. There were also many calling themselves republics, but had dictators demanding royal subservience. And there were many calling themselves socialist without having the slightest intention of helping each other to achieve a decent life for everyone. Words became meaningless, mere buzzwords that made people salivate and jump through hoops. And far too many people never looked beyond the labels, never questioned, just accepted what they were told, don't rock the boat, just make it through – to what? To the void at the end of their miserable existences without having really ever lived? Our Polish weekend hadn't been the experience of a relatively luxurious weekend we were aiming for. It was a far more important experience than that.

Bob's divorce went through in early November, to Bob's great relief and ours. Unfortunately, the concessions he'd made to Sigrid in terms of alimony gave him less financial relief than he'd hoped for (and that his own lawyer urged him to fight for) and deserved. It would take years before Bob's adoption of Erich and Sigrid's daughter Karin was annulled (Erich eventually re-adopted his own daughter). As a result, Bob also had substantial child support payments to make (Erich had none). Sigrid's filthy-rich relatives remained content to let Bob continue to pay her a huge chunk out of every paycheck, but Bob was not about to fight it, nor to question the great Tante Lore's implied wishes. And of course Sigrid's lawyer was out to get as big a slice of Bob as possible. At least Bob was coming to stay with us for a couple of weeks at Christmas.

Also in early November, I taught my first course under the auspices of Hamadi Klilib's new school, which lacked premises of its own. He rented rooms at a hotel on Drottninggatan, near us, when he had any pupils. He also he gave the school an odd name: "Sprint". I'd worked with him now and then during the summer, before his language school was officially launched. Hamadi came from Tunisia to study in Lund and had lived in Sweden quite a few years before we arrived. He spoke fluent Swedish and English, as well as his native French and Arabic. He was determined to make his new language school work, and said he wanted me to be the head teacher in the English department, which initially consisted of me. Unfortunately, I was in for a shock when my work for him involved his new official role as "managing director". It went to his head, sometimes causing him to shout "*I'm the boss here, I give the orders!*" He clearly didn't know me very well.

But I had to take work from wherever I could get it: from Demaret's, from the few pupils of my own I already had, and now from Hamadi. He didn't yet have much to offer anyway. I was getting by on the part-time sum of my job sources, while continuing to work on the apartment.

At the end of November, Jeanette and I were able to apply for our PUT (the Swedish acronym for permanent residence permits). In practical terms, if we received them (and by now we were confident that we would), it would mean that we would no longer have to apply for any more extensions of residence and work permits; we could even start a company if we wanted to. Basically, we would have almost the same rights, privileges and responsibilities as Swedish citizens, except voting. Citizenship would be the only remaining step. Thus PUT was also a powerful symbol of freedom – we'd won our struggle to build a new base for our lives and future together in our adopted country – and our anxiety levels plunged.

In early December, my parents wrote that they were buying a piece of land near Knoxville, Illinois, with a view to building a home for themselves there when Dad retired. I wrote and congratulated them on the prospect of leaving Oak Park, thinking that they could at last escape the horrendous (as I saw it) influence of Aunt Maxine, as well as their entrenched conservative environment. Then they replied that Ralph and Maxine were also buying the property there, next door, to build a home for their own retirement. A great sinking feeling swept over me when I read that news. I sighed deeply.

On December 11th, Hamadi threw a party at his new 6th-storey apartment at Limhamnsvägen 6C, one of the more prestigious eight-storey high-rises in the western part of Malmö, with only a beautiful park and beach between them and the sea. Hamadi's place had three bedrooms (two of them tiny), a very large open living and dining room, a small galley kitchen, a bathroom and a separate lavatory. The apartment not only served as Hamadi's residence, but would now also be the premises for the new school, fortunately renamed "Interspråk". (For any non-Swedish-speaking readers who haven't already figured it out, *språk* means language/s. "Interspråk" thus suggested "international languages"). Jeanette and I hardly knew anybody there except Hamadi himself, and Klaus Franke, from Berlin, who'd also become fed up with Carmen's antics. He was going to be the German teacher at the new school. The party was pleasant enough, and Hamadi seemed to have come down off his high horse. I supposed that anyone sitting on a high horse couldn't, by definition, have his or her feet on the ground, and perhaps he felt uncomfortable up there, particularly in view of my scant interest in his attempts to flaunt authority.

For the school business, Hamadi's plan was to use all three bedrooms as classrooms, with the option to use one corner of the living room as a fourth classroom. At night, the sofa-bed in the living room became Hamadi's bed – business always came first. For lunches, pupils and teachers went to Per's Krog, an excellent restaurant also along Limhamnsvägen, just a two-minute walk away. The school paid for the lunches; Hamadi cut a deal with Per himself. And Hamadi paid me 25 kronor per hour.

When Bob arrived on December 20th – only his third visit to Malmö – we could see a vast improvement in his mental stability compared to Easter, just as major an improvement as his second visit was over his first. He was much more open, positive, alert and witty. In fact, he could be downright hilarious. When he told a joke or made a risqué quip, which he was doing frequently now, he would stare piercingly at you, then his complexion would become slightly ruddy as a powerful, broad, but firmly suppressed smile would appear, and then one of his thick eyebrows would shoot up in a wicked, twitching arc across one side of his forehead, until he was certain that you comprehended the subtle point of his humorous remark. It was one of the most endearing and comical expressions I'd ever seen on a human face, and he would freeze it until you couldn't contain your laughter, whereupon he would break out into one of the biggest and heartiest grins you'd ever seen.

Unfortunately, shortly before Bob arrived, Jeanette and I were asked to undertake our first-ever professional translation job during the Christmas holidays. It was a user's manual for a kitchen stove, a small pamphlet that didn't look difficult, and the pay (by the word) was good, provided we could do it as quickly and easily as we presumed. We hadn't learned how to look. We didn't know that when you have no experience in translating, things happen to words when you are about to translate them in writing. Suddenly you are overwhelmed by doubt and insecurity; you almost have to look up words like "and". Technical terminology became a nightmare, self-doubt wrestled us to the ground. The number of hours we put in on that damn pamphlet probably worked out to be our lowest hourly wage ever, and we were almost prepared to pay someone else to take it off our hands. We eventually persevered, but it was a long time before we would accept any translation work again.

Bob was amazed at the outcome of the renovation work in the living room, and the still ongoing work in the rest of our apartment. He found the simple, basic style with muted colors very much to his liking. I suggested to him that his apartment in Binningen had much more potential than ours would ever have. When we were walking around in town one day just before Christmas, battling the crowds, we ducked into Silverberg's, a fairly exclusive store specialized in furniture, home furnishings, and other items of exquisite Scandinavian design that went straight to Bob's heart, almost literally making him drool.

He found a pottery vase and matching ashtray that he insisted on buying for us for Christmas, and he got himself a sleek rawhide briefcase, completely without frills, that he said would be perfect for taking his important papers with him when he went on errands to the bank, post office, etc. But Bob's near-drooling reaction to the Scandinavian furniture suggested that a seed must have been planted for his future home decorating plans.

He asked me if I was doing any painting. I had to say no, but I explained that once I had the work on the apartment behind me, I would definitely get back to it. He again raved about *Sanctuary*, and Jeanette and I were glad we hadn't wrapped it yet; it was to be his Christmas present from us. The moment he understood that, he was overwhelmed; he was lost for words for quite a few minutes. Gratitude poured from him in buckets. He protested that we'd already done so much for him, Jeanette with her marvelous cooking, and both of us with all the work we'd already done on his apartment and on his mind and well-being. Jeanette and I were both focused on how much more we'd like to do; it didn't really feel like we'd started, but Bob just sat there looking at the painting, shaking his head and trying to control his emotions. To facilitate his return journey, I removed the painting from its stretchers and rolled it up in the tube we'd used for bringing my paintings to Europe so he could bring it safely back to Switzerland.

Bob got his revenge. On the 27th, he announced in the morning that he was taking us into town, right into the after-Christmas-sale crowds, to find us a really good stereo, and there was to be no discussion about it. He wouldn't accept anything second-rate, and if he approved our choices, he would insist on paying the bill. The only upgrade we'd made from the cheap radio we'd bought with Mike was a small audio cassette player, but we had very little music, and almost no classical music, even though we'd always enjoyed what we'd heard. Bob knew what he wanted to do. He not only bought us an impressive stereo – a receiver, a turntable, a cassette deck and speakers – he also threw in nearly a dozen LPs with carefully selected forays into selected areas (and a few arias) of classical music.

By the time Bob had to fly back on January 2nd, 1972, we'd spent hours and hours listening to the amazing music. A couple of the albums were collections, potpourris of the most famous composers. Each time a new piece would come on, Bob would nod and smile in recognition, and say, "Ah, that's the second movement" of this or that piano concerto by Mozart or Beethoven or Liszt or Grieg or whomever. He knew them all. He knew when they lived, how they lived, what was happening in their worlds and in other parts of the world at that time, how far along medical science had come by then, what things had been invented or were about to be, what was happening in China at that time, when this or that treaty was signed and what impact it had on the contemporary composers and still had on us today.

In one of our endlessly unfolding crossword-puzzle conversations on all manner of topics, I told Bob how I first noticed, then suspected, then discerned a pattern in my mom's correspondence to us, that when she referred to him in her normal mode, he was always "Bob", but as soon as her "spiritual longings" took over her personality, he invariably became "Robert" or even "dear Robert". We howled.

January 1972 primarily occupied me with work for Demaret's and redoubled efforts to move forward on the apartment renovations. February was much more eventful. On the 1st, we got called to the police station to have our PUTs stamped into our passports and to receive them as separate certificates (valid even if our passports expired) – a great cause for celebration. On the 2nd, the celebration continued, since Jeanette got her first proper job, a secretarial position at a small Swedish company in central Malmö, with the freedom to take time off pretty much as she wished.

Her job was actually for two small companies with the same owner and boss: an engineering company called Sveremo and an offshoot called Smetco (Swedish Middle East Trading Company). Apparently the engineering side of the business was for dabbling in a lot of things, including the development of industrial dryers that were ideal for drying dates to make them non-sticky without drying them out. Smetco was thus founded as a date business. They bought dates, mostly from southern Iran, shipped them to Sweden, dried, packaged, and sold them in Sweden and wherever else they could find buyers. Jeanette worked for the boss and found it very thrilling to be employed again. It was also challenging to be doing it in Swedish, but her considerable secretarial experience from the US quickly kicked in, and she soon got high praise.

In mid-February I had my first private pupil for a full-week course. His name was Bengt Valdemarsson. He had his own direct-mail advertising agency in Vällingby, an affluent Stockholm suburb. The course went really well; he was an eager learner and made great progress. He was also a very nice guy, and wanted Jeanette and me to come up and see Stockholm for the first time and stay at his big house. We arranged to make the trip for the May Day holiday weekend.

Another February event that would turn out to have a somewhat more significant impact on global politics than our planned trip to Stockholm was the February 21st trip Richard Nixon made to China. I remember feeling outraged – not because a US president visited China (that part was absolutely great and wonderful and *about time* for the cause of world peace), but because China fulfilled the same criteria the US otherwise used for *penalizing* other countries: China was a Communist dictatorship. So what now was the reason for continuing the unfair embargo on Cuba? It seemed like a humungous case of hypocrisy to me. I realized that issues like that could really wind me up. My brothers would shrug and say "Well, I don't know...." My parents would look at the ceiling and say "It's all in His hands!" How is a democracy supposed to function if people don't react?

In early March, I got a rather unusual teaching assignment. Bosse Parnevik (a famous Swedish comedian and imitator of politicians, celebrities and other public figures) somehow got hold of my name and contacted me for private lessons that were a bit special: he needed to polish his American accent for imitating Nixon for his upcoming show. He also needed a script in English; it doesn't really help to get the accent just right if the grammar is all wrong. He reminded me a lot of my brother John – he seemed more eager to be *perceived* as having fun than actually having it – but, like John, he was a nice guy and we got along well. He even gave us tickets to see his show on March 10th at the nightclub in Kronprinsen.

It turned out that Henry and Elsa Carlsson also had tickets for the same performance, and we went together. Bosse called me again the week after the show. It had been a great success, which emboldened him to expand into other English-speaking celebrities, for which he wanted my help again. We spent three afternoons working together, while I spent the mornings on the last touches of the work of renovating our living room. When I heard that Bosse had brought his wife and kids along to Malmö (they were from Stockholm), I invited the family over for dinner. Jeanette cooked a fantastic meal, as usual, with *escargots* as the first course (and something else for the kids, of course).

We finally finished the last of the renovation work in the whole apartment the weekend before Bob's arrival. Jeanette undertook most of the painting, and we worked on the carpeting and burlap wall coverings together. I did the carpentry. We were mighty pleased with the results and couldn't wait to show Bob, who would be arriving on March 30th for a 10-day stay over Easter. As soon as the work was done, I went out and bought some canvas and stretchers and began preparing a couple. I had no idea about the volcanic eruption that was about to take place.

Bob was not flying beyond Kastrup (the Copenhagen airport) this time; the extra expense and poor connections for that last 15-minute flight to Malmö ruled it out. I had to work that day, but Jeanette took off early to take the ferry and bus over to Kastrup to meet him. He was unfamiliar with that airport, and we felt he might find it daunting to figure out where to go on leaving customs, find his way to the bus that would take him to the harbor, aboard the ferry, and to the central station in Malmö. We observed that battles like that exhausted him thoroughly. He was most grateful to have Jeanette as his guide.

He was also eager for us to start prowling the music stores for more serious and systematic purchasing of classical music. We'd responded so well to the

The feeling of freedom

"appetizers" he picked for us at Christmas that he now felt it was time for a proper introduction to music, with complete works instead of selected movements: things like Handel's *Messiah*, Bach's cantatas, Schubert's impromptus and song cycles, Mozart's woodwind concertos and sonatas for violin and piano, Chopin's études, Beethoven's piano concertos and all nine symphonies. Bob's shopping list was long and seemed to grow until the bags of LPs he'd bought for us began to weigh heavily upon us – almost too strenuous to carry (and there were the 89 steps to consider).

The three of us hurried home, opened a bottle of wine, sat on the sofa (the one we'd bought to double as a bed for Bob's first visit, which we moved into the studio when I built the sofa-bed in the living room), and asked Bob to pick the playing order. We'd just brought home the likely equivalent of a full week of non-stop listening; there was no time to waste.

The music was so beautiful it hurt. We recognized occasional snippets from things we'd heard on the radio or from movies or in restaurants, but much of it was entirely new to Jeanette and nearly all of it was brand new to me. It welled over us and through us, like when you open black-out curtains in an unknown room, to discover that you are standing alone in a garden of unparalleled beauty. Hours passed, and the music continued to flow, sometimes like a rich, dark chocolate syrup pouring over our shoulders; sometimes like the stunning rush of a waterfall where you're standing so close you get drenched and nearly knocked over; sometimes like your very lifeblood.

It was difficult to take breaks for the toilet or to eat or to say goodnight. Jeanette and I were enraptured; Bob was thrilled beyond words that we responded in this way, far beyond his hopes for us, he would later say. It was hard to sleep; the music was becoming visible in my head in the darkness, painting unseen images in my mind's eye. Once I finished a sketch in my mind – my inner vision captured and held it safely – it was just a matter of painting it.

The first thing I did in the morning, after throwing on some clothes, was grab a 70-by-70-centimeter canvas I'd prepared. I propped it up on one of our four trunks that served as coffee tables, end tables and storage. Then I got out my box of paints and began spreading them out on another trunk, took a piece of charcoal from the box, and quickly began sketching the painting I'd already painted in my head during the night. Tears of joy were streaming down Jeanette's cheeks, she was so overwhelmed. She looked at me, then at the stereo, and I nodded. She put on more of that mind-blowing music. Bob came in from the living room to watch, enthralled, mystified.

Using the same type of randomly sized and shaped geometric planes I used in a number of my earlier works, I created a central figure, along the lines of the figure of Mike in *Sanctuary*, but even more abstract and symbolic. I already knew the colors as well – I'd seen them in my mind – not the color of each individual plane exactly, but the overall chromatic effect.

The planes that form the body are blues and greens. The table/chin and cheeks are brown and more of a flesh color, respectively. The lamp shaft is light, rather neutral, while the lampshade/brain is pale yellow, lit up – enlightened. The empty parts of the head (where the eyes and ears would be) are black – the void – being filled by streams of brilliant reds, yellows and oranges, with smaller streams coming in from above to complete the colors of the rainbow. The background strips are also the colors of the rainbow, but in very muted, grayed shades. I call it *Introduction to Music*.[10] This was it; the volcano was erupting, the floodgates were opening.

All the while I was painting, I was listening to the music, almost in a trance-like state. Jeanette sat ready to change the records quickly as we listened to all five Beethoven piano concertos, played by the remarkably talented Emil Gilels, a Russian pianist whose interpretations Bob said we should be very pleased to have acquired. Then it was Handel's complete *Messiah*. On and on it went; on and on I worked. Jeanette was listening too, but also watching, and sometimes scurrying around to set a coffee cup discreetly beside me, or a sandwich or a glass of wine. Bob was also watching and listening, wide-eyed. The work on this logjam-breaker of a painting was incredibly intense; when I was finished, I nearly collapsed. Jeanette couldn't stop hugging me. I loved her support more than anything on earth, except her. And I was glad I'd already prepared a couple more canvases.

I thought of what Professor Walsh said, back in San Francisco in 1964, about the interrelatedness of the arts. I hadn't expected as arcane a word as *interrelatedness* to pack such a punch when music interrelated with painting. And I realized I was terribly hungry. That initial blast, that triggering explosion, completely altered my priorities. *I was no longer an English teacher who did a painting; I was a painter who taught some English to pay the rent.*

Bob hadn't been expecting to witness a creative explosion during his 10 days

---

10 Painting #14 (see Appendix 2)

with us. He said he merely felt strongly about certain music and wanted to share it with us, and to thank us for all our help on his apartment so far, and even more for helping to haul him out of the deep black hole he'd spent several years in before we came along. He'd changed, drastically, for the better. And life felt very wonderful to me right now, better than it had ever felt. I hoped Jeanette and Bob felt the same.

Jeanette and I boldly ordered an inexpensive but comfortable black leather sofa and easy chair from Domus Interiör on Östra Farmvägen. They arrived just a week or two after Bob left, and the studio was now complete except for a special cabinet I wanted to build because I couldn't find one close to what I needed: a worktop big enough to spread out some tubes of paint and my palette; two drawers beneath it (one for my many tubes of paint, the other for my many brushes); ample storage space below for bottles of turpentine, rags, spare tubes of paint and whatever else came to mind; and the whole thing on wheels to enable me to move it to any part of the room where I wanted to paint, according to the light, instead of feeling chained to it.

It never felt like Jeanette and I were particularly or intentionally reclusive, but compared to most others we encountered we probably were. Perhaps the forced isolation of my youth nurtured my ability to deal with and appreciate solitude; I never felt any compulsion to surround myself with other people, but I didn't avoid the company of others either. Jeanette seemed to feel exactly the same way.

I began to observe and reflect upon certain patterns I could perceive in my own behavior in social contexts. In groups of up to five or six people, I was very outgoing, gregarious, interested in others, totally uninhibited. In larger groups, I tended to keep in the background – the bigger the group, the deeper in the background – getting to know people first by observing them at a distance, then gradually entering the fray. In all of this, Jeanette seemed to work in the same way. But after entering the fray, I (unlike Jeanette) would tend to try to meet and speak with as many as possible, to get to know them individually if possible, and ultimately to become completely at ease and enjoy myself.

Jeanette had none of the restrictions I had growing up, but she nevertheless had only a few friends, and almost no social contacts with mere acquaintances. It wasn't that she couldn't manage social situations; she did that very well, almost professionally. But she didn't enjoy them. Her tolerance of superficiality was much lower than mine (and mine was low). Compared to me, she was very withdrawn. (Compared to her brother, however, she was very outgoing.)

The only kinds of parties we ever went to were the "Parador parties" among the few teachers at the school, a bit similar in nature to the small spontaneous parties we occasionally went to from the Precarious Vision in San Francisco, where we met in October 1964. At the small school parties we went to, there were generally around 10 people and never more than 20. Jeanette would begin in the background and remain there most of the time, observing, seldom speaking except when spoken to. Yet she was a very gracious and outgoing hostess, a role she seemed to enjoy thoroughly, but she withdrew from small talk, only plunging in wholeheartedly when the discussion got deeper.

I *had* to get along with my pupils, of course, but it was seldom a problem. I liked many of them very much. There were only a few that I really couldn't stand: those who were snobby or greedy. I felt comfortable discussing any topic except celebrities' private lives and other gossip, but I didn't *enjoy* discussions that were limited (or restricted!) to superficialities, such as the comings and goings of royalty.

Royalty – Swedish or otherwise – was a topic I loved to hate. (I'm referring to the *principle* of royalty; gossip about royal family members and their public and/or private lives was and is excruciatingly boring to me.) In Sweden, of all places, with its progressive society and very real democratic values in all other respects, having a monarchy remains a strangely stubborn vestige of bygone days of non-democratic repression and subservience that has taken forward-thinking people centuries to overthrow.

Many Swedes who otherwise cherished the principles of human rights – increasingly *equal* rights – couldn't seem to see the utter contradiction in having a monarch. *"But a president would be not better,"* they said. *"Look at Nixon!"* I tried to explain that in a parliamentary system (which the US is *not*) a president or head of state need not have any power at all, nor cost taxpayers anything, as in Switzerland, Germany, Italy, and many other democracies. But for many Swedes, the monarchy is an *emotional* thing, a traditional thing. I'd learned only too well from my battles with my brothers over religion, that emotional dependency has precious little to do with rationality, and was ultimately immune to rational arguments.

Towards the end of April, we received word from Jeanette's mom that Rosanne and Maureen (Rosanne's equal-age cousin, thus also Jeanette's cousin), would be spending two and a half weeks with us in or around July. Jeanette had very mixed feelings about hosting them for that long, since she and her kid sister never had much in common, and Jeanette regarded her as spoiled due to various things in their childhood that I hadn't witnessed and that Jeanette preferred not to talk about. But the behavior of Mike (the elder) towards his "baby", Rosanne, made it clear who his favorite was, an assessment that Jeanette's other siblings seemed to share.

On Friday evening, April 28th, Jeanette and I took the night train to Stockholm, where we were met by Bengt Valdemarsson and his darling little boy (about five years old) early in the morning. Bengt was eager to show us the sights of Sweden's capital during the rather chilly First of May holiday weekend. It was indeed a beautiful city, particularly the Old Town. Water asserted itself everywhere, dividing the central city into islands and promontories in a wild, unpredictable sort of way, unlike the ordered and orderly canals of Amsterdam. The big palace was a pompous and rather majestic building, yet dull, a fitting reminder of the pompous nature of roles of the majesties whose inherited titles and positions of privilege stood in sharp contradiction (so much more than "contrast") to the otherwise democratic state of which they were the titular heads.

Bengt also drove us out to see Drottningholm Castle, a 200-room second residence of the royal family, perhaps in case the 600-room palace got a bit too boring. The grounds of the castle comprised a beautiful park, which their majesties graciously deigned to open to lowly commoners. (Were they also "proud to reign over us"?)

Bengt had a big Mercedes and a beautiful home, but was divorced and only got to see his boy on weekends. He ran a successful, high-powered advertising business in the direct-mail sector. He designed and printed the kinds of ads that were sent to households all over Sweden to give Swedes a bit more paper to add to their weekly trash accumulation. But he made a good living.

A week after we got back from Stockholm, I had a private pupil named Åke Strömberg. He owned Weinerbagaren, a successful commercial bakery in Loftahammar, a small town along the east coast of Sweden, a bit more than half the distance up to Stockholm from Skåne. He was hoping to learn enough English from me in a week to be able to manage a study visit to a US bakery convention in the beginning of June. The day before he left, he wondered whether he could leave his car – a new, top-of-the-line Volvo – with us while he was gone. We would be free to use it as much as we wanted, he said, even take trips if we felt like it. It felt incredibly luxurious driving around in a car like that, especially after our old two-stroke Saab, but we didn't really feel comfortable driving someone else's car – like we would somehow be taking advantage of his generosity – and we felt a bit nervous about leaving it parked on the streets as well. On his return, I think he was surprised to find we'd put so little mileage on it, but we understood that his trip went as well as could be expected after a one-week crash course; he'd started from scratch, or close to it. And we neither crashed nor scratched his car.

Late Friday evening, May 20th, Jeanette and I took a night train to Berlin, for the three-day Whitsun holiday weekend. Prior to coming to Sweden, I'd never heard of Whitsun – White Sunday, Pentecost Sunday – and yet here it was, another national religious holiday in secular Sweden. In the US, as far as I knew, Whitsun was only observed by Catholics, and I'd been well trained to know what *that* meant! But what Whitsun actually meant was something I had to look up, and found that it was supposed to mark the arrival of the Holy Ghost 50 days after Easter Sunday (except that they're both on Sundays, and I'd always thought 7x7=49...), when the earliest Christians were supposedly able to speak in tongues (but did worse on their math?). I wondered if they managed English and Swedish among their tongues, neither of which had been invented yet.

Anyway, Jeanette and I were very curious about the divided city of Berlin and wanted to see it for ourselves. The night train first took us from Copenhagen to Gedser, in southern Denmark, where the train was driven in the middle of the night onto a ferry across to Wärnemünde, in East Germany – the grossly misnamed German Democratic Republic – on the Baltic coast, roughly halfway between Lübeck and Świnoujście. On arrival in Wärnemünde, in the very wee hours of the morning, two hostile-looking soldiers or policemen (or both) entered our train compartment and switched on the brightest lights they could find. One of them stiffly snapped out a gloved hand while barking *Passe!* and sternly awaited the immediate submission of our passports. Each of our American passports was minutely scrutinized. The officer had a look on his face as if every word he saw was a major personal insult. When he came to the pages with the photos, he studied them as if we'd committed a capital offense. He jerked his gaze back and forth between each detail of the photos and the corresponding details of our physiognomies, then just as abruptly closed the passports and thrust them back at us before making an instantaneous about-face and leaving the compartment. I had to bite my tongue to keep from barking *Heil Ulbricht!* or saying something about this officer's behavior suggesting the darkest period in

German history shortly before my birth.

We were glad that was over. Except that it wasn't. Before we could get back to our much-needed sleep, a new officer stomped in, demanded our passports again, then stamped them with transit visas, then stomped out. Then came the customs officer, who looked through our bags with great suspicion, asked strange and stupid and invasive questions, then *stürmed* out. It wasn't over yet. Another officer entered, demanding to see all of our currency. We had some Swedish kronor, a few Danish kronor, and a few dollars we received from our parents for birthdays, which we thought we might as well bring along, and a few Deutsche marks we'd exchanged for use in West Berlin, our destination. Each amount of each currency was duly noted in a book before he too retreated. There were four controls in all, by at least four different gruff and unfriendly officers, with nary a smile among them, lots of lights going on and off, and precious little sleep.

The train ride through East Germany in the early morning was gloomy. Everything outside the windows managed to look brownish gray, despite the glorious late-May time of year. There was no improvement when the train pulled into the penultimate station, East Berlin. And there was no question of anyone getting out to stretch their legs during the half-hour stop before the final short run into West Berlin. We weren't even allowed to open the windows. But our eyes weren't confined, and through the glass we could see the uniforms carefully checking *under* the train with flashlights and huge mirrors mounted on long poles, like gigantic dental mirrors searching for human-size cavities; they were looking for stowaways trying to escape to West Berlin. *Why would anyone want to leave that East German paradise?!* During our lengthy stop in East Berlin, there were the same four controls again, this time conducted in even fouler moods by different sets of surly officers. East Berlin was drab and brownish-gray as well, with few people out and about.

It wasn't a very long way from the East Berlin train station to the border, at least as the crow flies, but people aren't crows, and the government of the Democratic Republic seemed to be somewhat reluctant to allow them to behave that way. We'd heard about "the Wall that Ulbricht built" in the summer of '61, just before I started my junior year at Oak Park High. They called it a "wall of protection" from the West, but nobody was trying to get in. It was the best idea Walter Ulbricht & Co. could come up with to prevent a brain drain to the West, and damn the consequences – or shoot them. How exactly did they stop the brain drain by shooting dead the people with the brains (and courage) that were trying to leave?

As the train at last rolled slowly towards the Wall, from the inside (although it was the inside that was outside, considering the donut hole, the oasis, that West Berlin was), we could see that all buildings within some 100 meters of it on the East side had been torn down, and in the nearest buildings that remained – the front line – all windows facing the Wall were bricked or boarded up. About 20-30 meters from the wall, there were big concrete tank barriers, a.k.a. Czech hedgehogs, like giants' kids had been playing jacks and abandoned them in a strip parallel with the wall. Beyond them was a very high chain link fence, presumably electrified, tastefully topped with plenty of lovely barbed wire. Beyond this fence was an empty strip about 10 meters wide, patrolled by attack dogs. The whole glorious no-man's-land was supervised from strategically placed guard towers manned by soldiers with machine guns ready to fire lethal salutes at any and all trespassers. It was shocking to read about; it was far shockinger[11] to see.

And then, beyond the Wall itself, spring blossomed and bloomed. It was crowded, smiles were liberally sprinkled among the people, there were smells of Currywurst and Schnitzel, the sidewalk cafés were packed with beer drinkers, traffic was raucous, people weren't hiding their faces or watching their tongues. We managed to get tickets to the Berlin Philharmonic for a beautiful Mozart concert one evening, visited the Brandenburger Tor, the English Garden, walked up and down Kurfürstendamm, explored the vast department stores, spent half a day at the fabulous zoo, and had a wonderful couple of days. For the trip home through East Berlin, it was like playing the tape of a bad movie backwards: four more controls on entering, and another four on leaving, all performed with the same special friendliness.

"Freedom's just another word for nothin' left to lose," begins the chorus of a Kris Kristofferson song from 1969, a song that a romantic like me found hauntingly beautiful. Berlin – East Berlin, the two Berlins – knocked me over the head about this thing called "freedom". Does anybody know what it is? Does anybody *really* want it? Many East Germans risked or gave their lives to flee the East (where it definitely seemed not to be) and find it in the West (where they hoped and believed it would be).

But I grew up in the West, in the country that loved to proclaim itself "the

---

11 I hold a license, number CX2433190-B, which entitles me to make 34 such declensions annually.

land of the free", yet Black people and Indians had nothing like the freedom of *White* people, or at least White *rich* people. And I'd had nothing but restrictions (a polite word for chains) in my parents' home, and religion, despite the ranting about "*If the Son therefore shall make you free, ye shall be free indeed*" (John 8:36). It was certainly no "freedom" to live in constant, never-ending fear of having your every action – even your every *thought* – monitored, recorded and ready to doom you to eternal punishment! Yet people everywhere were *choosing* such enslavement, sticking their heads into the noose of religious faith because generations before them did so, following the ancient writings and creeds of frightened, superstitious nomads trying to explain the world to themselves and getting most of it wrong.

Why couldn't people try wiping the slate clean and find the courage to be iconoclastic, to find new ways (even new traditions!), things that actually make sense and can serve as a moral code worthy of the name? And above all, to retain the right – the *freedom* – to go on questioning, doubting, challenging?

Dishearteningly many people – especially Americans, because they are especially religious – are fond of claiming that without the Bible there can be no morality. It doesn't seem to me that it takes much research or a terribly high IQ to figure out that the great majority of wars in the world have always been based on religion. It isn't enough to *open* the Bible to discover that God/Jehovah *Himself* condoned and *commanded* wars and wholesale slaughter, even of women and children, not to mention endorsing slavery, treachery, theft and all manner of barbarism. To discover that, you have to actually *read* that Bible with at least a modicum of mindfulness. The Ten Commandments as the basis of morality? In the context of the Bible, they serve only to command how God's Chosen People should behave towards each other and towards their god. Others, outsiders, are lawful prey – what a great recipe for morality!

Is the New Testament any better? Jesus – at least the figure about whom almost nothing is mentioned in his alleged contemporary historical record from any other source than the Bible itself, which was compiled hundreds of years after the alleged events allegedly took place – seemed to have said a lot of good things, sensible things, revolutionary things. But also a lot of crap. He still commanded worship of his odious father. He promised eternal torture for failure to believe in the supernatural powers he claimed to possess, thereby making the New Testament even worse than the Old in terms of the duration of violence and cruelty to which outsiders would be subjected.

When I've asked a few religious people how anyone purporting to be good, to be the very foundation and author of morality, could subject *anyone* (especially anyone he claimed to have created in the first place) to eternal torture, I often get the same pathetic answer: *free will* – if we fail to choose freely to adore their god, he is not only entitled, but somehow *compelled* (by himself only – *he made all the rules!*) to torture us forever. Couldn't the mythmakers have come up with something better and far more moral than that?

And is this "free will" thing real or an illusion? Or some of each? You're free to play the hand you're dealt any way you like, but you're not free to choose the cards you're dealt.

Look long and hard at my "free" country, my fatherland, the one that forced me to choose between an unjust war, prison and exile. This was the free country that virtually enslaved whatever Indians they didn't massacre, that wrote the slavery of Blacks into the Constitution, and that denied women the most basic civil rights for well over a century. It's the country where *legal* racial discrimination has persisted into my old age, where sexual behavior usually was and sometimes still is defined by cruelly puritanical laws, where women remain on an unequal footing with men, where "freedom" in practice often seems to mean the freedom to exploit, where people are free to starve and go to early graves because others are free *not* to help them.

So am I free now, in Sweden? The most common argument I've heard against that proposition is Sweden's high taxes, as if taking some of one's earnings is the equivalent of taking most of one's freedom. I admire a quote from 1927 attributed to US Supreme Court Justice Oliver Wendell Holmes Jr, to the effect that taxes are the price we pay to live in a civilized society. If a wealthy person has to pay so much tax that he can't afford a third luxury car to go with his second luxury yacht, is he losing more freedom than the freedom gained by an indigent person who gets to eat or go to school thanks to taxes? That was the reasoning behind the relatively minor imbalance in wealth distribution that existed in Sweden in the 1970s, at least as practiced by the Swedish government under the Social Democrat Olof Palme, whose high-profile opposition to the Vietnam War strongly influenced Jeanette's and my decision to move to Sweden. (Palme was, however, savagely hated by many Swedish conservatives as well as some on the radical left.)

One of the difficulties with a word like *freedom* is that it means nothing and everything and whatever is in between – unless or until you define the context.

You can only have the freedom to choose the kind of car you want to drive if you have the money to pay for it. You clearly have more freedom *in this context* if you have more money. In the context of the material world, freedom is pretty much synonymous with purchasing power. But who has more freedom to become a star athlete or a star entertainer? Despite the wealth of Florence Foster Jenkins, money doesn't buy talent. But lack of money can prevent people with talent from developing it. The same applies to intelligence.

And then there's freedom of the mind, freedom to think without indoctrination or coercion. In Sweden, I've felt that I enjoy freedom *from* faith; nobody's pushing any religion on me, few seem to view religion as anything but a personal matter, most view it as little more than harmless tradition.

Believe whatever you want, but don't call it Truth if you can't prove it. That approach seems much freer to me than latching on to somebody else's historical, unproven creeds, then going through life holding on tighter and tighter to something you should never have believed in the first place, and probably wouldn't have believed if you'd been old enough or free enough to use your brain to think with before you decided to believe it. But by the time many people are old enough to think, they're already holding on too tight to let go.

In early June, Sixten Bagge, a friend of Henry's, asked him if he knew anybody who could serve as an interpreter at a business meeting with an American visitor. Henry suggested me. The meeting was to be held on June 16th over lunch at the Översten restaurant, which made me salivate; I said yes with no further thought of the consequences. It would be a three-way meeting (not counting me), with two Swedes from a Malmö-based company, one of whom (Sixten) spoke and understood a fair amount of English; the other (let's call him Lars) spoke little English and understood less. The third person (let's call him Tom) was a youngish American businessman. The business, the agenda, was to discuss valves. I knew that "valve" is *ventil* in Swedish (etymologically related to "ventilation"), but I had to find a book with illustrations and a glossary of the names of the all parts and functions a valve might have, some of which were totally new and thus very foreign to me, even in English.

We sat down at a table in a *chambre separée*, and the personal introductions went smoothly. They were just heading into the technical side of things when the first course of our lunch arrived. Tom asked both Swedes a question using some terms I had to think hard to remember, and before I could interpret it for the

Swedes, Sixten replied, in English, and Tom commented on his reply. I had to put up my hand, go back and recapitulate a few things for Lars: Tom's question, Sixten's reply, then Tom's reply to Sixten. Then Lars commented, and while Sixten waited patiently, I interpreted Lars' comment for Tom, then they were all at it again, and again, and again. When the waitress came to take our plates after the first course, I hadn't yet touched mine. Sixten kindly suggested they all shut up for a minute so I could get a bite in. I wolfed it down far too quickly to get any enjoyment out of it – even for a fast eater like me. The meeting lasted three hours, and it went on like that the whole time. At the rate my head was spinning, if I'd been a helicopter I'd have taken off sometime during the main course.

With (and thanks to) Jeanette's highly active encouragement, I at last felt free to paint. Since my *Introduction to Music* explosion in the first days of April, I completed four other paintings before the arrival of our summer guests. My inspiration for the first of these four came from observing discussions between the very academic Bob and the very down-to-earth Jeanette. Bob spoke English in a very bookish way, with very little resembling normal conversational language, probably the result of his rather extreme isolation from human contact, particularly in the most recent six or seven years. (I would later figure out that he spoke German in much the same way.) It was almost as though Jeanette and Bob were holding a discussion in two different languages, the way Swedes and Danes can each speak to each other in their own languages and usually understand each other enough to get away with it. I call this painting *Discussion*.[12] Are they communicating at all? Certainly, but how well? *When you say something, can I assume that you mean what I would have meant if I said the same thing?*

Many of my paintings deal with isolation and loneliness, but my next painting – *Human Contact*[13] – is about twosomeness. Although the word *twosomeness* (Swedish *tvåsamhet*) exists in English, it is unusual and fails to convey the contrast or counterpole to "loneliness" or "lonesomeness" (Swedish *ensamhet*), and the notion that where there is love, two are never lonely. That was how I perceived Jeanette and myself together, an island of love.

My next painting is based on a poem by Wallace Stevens, about a guitar player whose audience complains that he fails to "play things as they are". They

---

12 Painting #15 (see Appendix 2)
13 Painting #16 (see Appendix 2)

miss the point: *"Things as they are / Are changed upon the blue guitar."* Since the development of photography, art no longer necessarily has the task of depicting reality as it is; art transforms reality and chaos into a new order. I call the painting *The Man with the Blue Guitar*.[14]

The final painting that I completed before the end of June depicts a man who has been felled by warring and warmongering religions. He is impaled by their symbols and prevented from interceding. I call it *A Fallen Man*.[15]

The late summer of 1972 meant that a full three years had gone by since we stepped off the *Absolon* and set foot in Sweden for the first time. Now we had jobs, a home, we both spoke Swedish fluently (and could even think in Swedish). We'd found some Swedish friends – and a deep and unexpected friendship with Bob. How was all of this possible? It seemed far-fetched, and yet it was very real. Sweden had become part of us, much more than we had become part of Sweden. We'd been looking for freedom from the harassment of the American military. We found it. Freedom to find our own way, without the pressure of families, American society, convention. We found it. Freedom to breathe, to find harmony in simplicity, to be in Europe, to work only to live, not vice-versa. We found all that too.

Our lives were simple and sweet. With cheap rent, no car, no kids, no regard for status symbols, we lived an uncomplicated and comfortable life, largely free from external anxieties and practical problems. I could now paint – whenever I wanted to – with Jeanette as my muse, my energy, my driving force, my life. We were living below the radar, close to each other, at home in Malmö, a place we'd never even heard of before that one afternoon in Vancouver when we decided where to move.

END OF BOOK THREE

---

14 Painting #17 (see Appendix 2)
15 Painting #18 (see Appendix 2)

No Traveller Returns

APPENDIX 1 – Apartment in Malmö

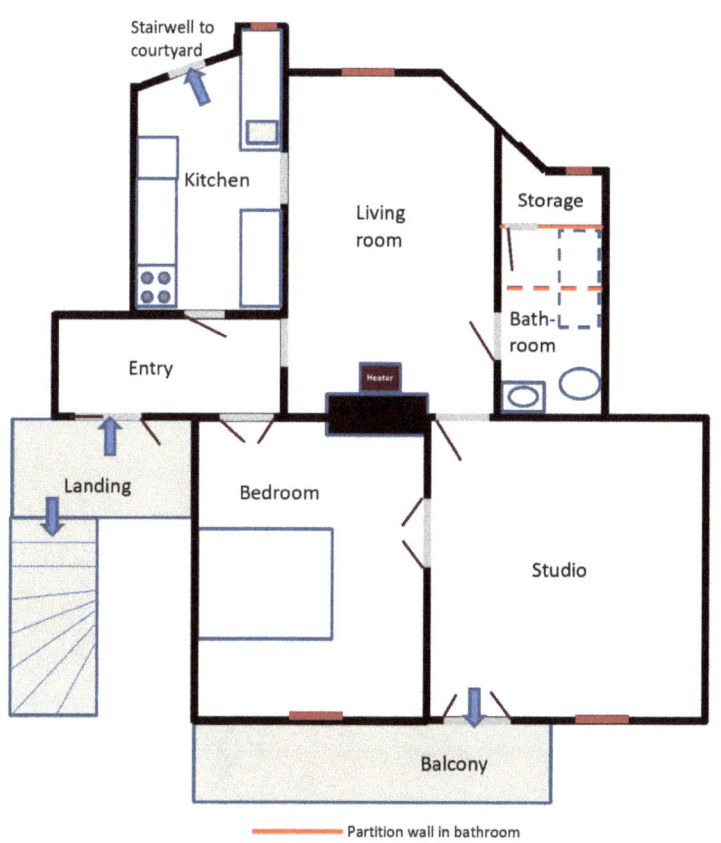

APPENDIX 2 – Paintings 13-18

Paintings 13-18 were painted in Malmö, at our apartment on Vårgatan.

#13 Sanctuary

#14 Introduction to Music

Appendix 2

#15 Discussion

#15 Human Contact

#17 The Man with the Blue Guitar

#18 A Fallen Man

Hindsights
the six-part autobiography of an unknown artist

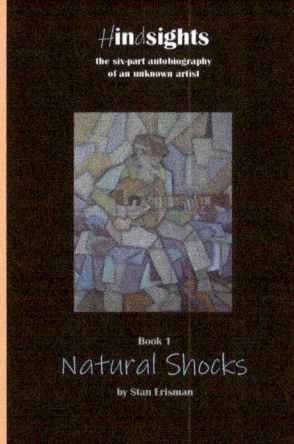

Book 1
Natural Shocks
by Stan Erisman

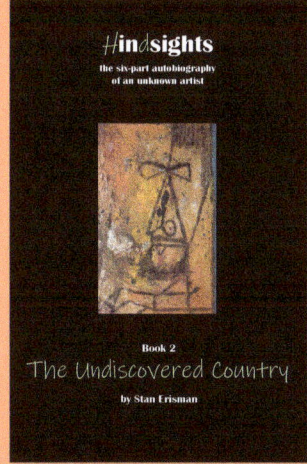

Book 2
The Undiscovered Country
by Stan Erisman

Book 3
No Traveller Returns
by Stan Erisman

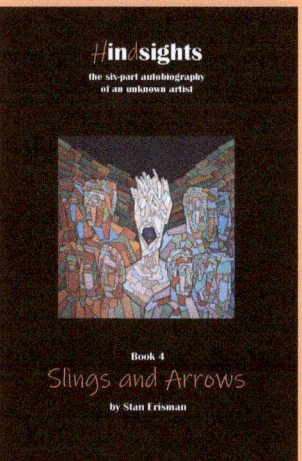

Book 4
Slings and Arrows
by Stan Erisman

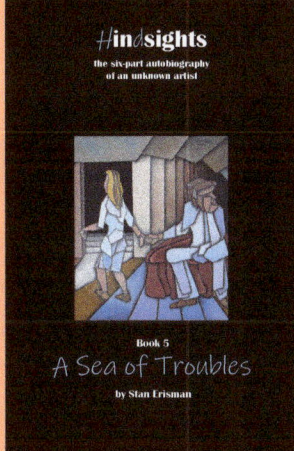

Book 5
A Sea of Troubles
by Stan Erisman

Book 6
Perchance to Dream
by Stan Erisman

www.ingramcontent.com/pod-product-compliance
Lightning Source LLC
Chambersburg PA
CBHW040252170426
43191CB00019B/2388